CW01391106

Advance Praise for *Ring of Salt*

"A searingly painful yet stunning and hopeful piece of work. I am in awe of Cornwell's determination and courage and her ability to draw meaning from the darkest times. She has created a profound and beautiful piece of art from these experiences."

—Sophie White, Shirley Jackson Award–winning author of *Where I End*

"A stunning memoir, intimate and vast at once . . . Cornwell refuses to simplify or polarize her experience. Instead, she wrangles with the messiness of human connection, of the twin pull of an abusive relationship, the exhilaration and exhaustion of parenting, the power and abjection of motherhood. Braver still, is her insistence on looking, face-on, at our material reliance, debunking the myth of the American Dream to remind us of our dependency on one another, our interconnectedness. This is a very special book."

—Elske Rahill, author of *Between Dog and Wolf*

"*Ring of Salt* is the best memoir I've read in years. Think *Practical Magic* set on the Irish coast. As transportive as a fairy tale but as real as the Connemara wind on your face, every page pulses with the wild spirit of Ireland. This memoir is for anyone ready to believe in the power of resilience, reinvention, and the communities that catch us when we fall."

—Marian Schembari, author of *A Little Less Broken*

"A beautiful and deeply moving memoir. I could not put it down. Cornwell explores with honesty, humor, and courage what it takes to start over and chronicles how she drew strength from female friendship, motherhood, community, and Ireland itself. A must-read."

—J. Courtney Sullivan, *New York Times* bestselling author of *The Cliffs*

"*Ring of Salt* is so vast and tender and urgent, it's almost like reading a novel. I couldn't put it down. I haven't cheered for a heroine like Betsy in ages."

—Jen Hatmaker, author of *Awake*

"Betsy Cornwell has written a wondrous book. Free of the pitfalls of sentimental and saccharine prose one often sees in memoir, it is a book of resilience and fortitude and a testament to the power of determined women. This book renewed something in my own heart. A beautiful tale of love, survival, and community."

—Rachel Louise Snyder, author of *No Visible Bruises*

"When I grow up, I want to write like Betsy Cornwell! She's poetic and gritty and funny and heartbreaking . . . often in the same paragraph. *Ring of Salt* captures what it's like to rebuild from the ruins, to mother while mourning, and to find a safe home inside yourself when the world hasn't offered one. Cornwell doesn't mistake escape for freedom, and she writes beautifully about what comes after survival—the long, brave, often invisible work of building a new life. It's honest, lyrical, and quietly revolutionary."

—Lara Love Hardin, *New York Times* bestselling author of
The Many Lives of Mama Love

"*Ring of Salt* is a beautifully written story of resilience, hope, and hard-earned triumph. In sentences that shimmer like the incandescent Irish coastline, Cornwell enriches our definitions of survivorship and shows us how she found magic in everyday life. Readers will cheer for her as she weaves together a community—both near and far—that rallies around her as she leaves the dark chapters of her past behind and builds an abundant life."

—Christie Tate, *New York Times* bestselling author of *Group*

"Book clubs will pull Betsy Cornwell from these pages and into their circles in triumphant solidarity, rallying around her bravery, heralding her riveting story as one of their all-time favorites. I was rapt in anticipation through every turn, every moment of grit and grace in her journey. *Ring of Salt* is a lyrical, intimate account of self-empowerment, survival, and the intricate assembling of courage necessary to take your child by the hand and know that where you're going is more powerful than where you came from."

—Carine McCandless, *New York Times* bestselling
author of *The Wild Truth*

"*Ring of Salt* is clear-eyed, openhearted, and brimming with hope. As an artist, an ex-pat fleeing family violence, and an immigrant searching for a home in the world, Betsy Cornwell writes with urgency and candor, pulling readers along on her wild roller coaster into love and heartbreak and out again … There are echoes here of ancient creation myths, of the timeless need for harmony with the natural world, and Cornwell's deep kinship with all the women, past and present, who have muscled a better life into existence for their children."

—Anonymous, author of *Becoming Duchess Goldblatt*

"A powerful and deeply empowering book, *Ring of Salt* is a hymn to the strength of community, a rallying cry against systemic injustice, and a testimony to the resilience of one woman's spirit. Beautifully written, this is an immersive exploration into the joy of finding home in unconventional places."

—Roisín O'Donnell, author of *Nesting*

ALSO BY BETSY CORNWELL

Tides

Mechanica

Venturess

The Forest Queen

The Circus Rose

Reader, I Murdered Him

Ring of Salt

A Memoir *of* Finding Home *and* Hope
on the Wild Coast *of* Ireland

Betsy Cornwell

**ЯENE
GADE**

RENEGADE BOOKS

First published in 2025 by Avid Reader Press
An imprint of Simon & Schuster, LLC
First published in Great Britain in 2025 by Renegade Books
An imprint of John Murray Press

1

Copyright © Betsy Cornwell 2025

The right of Betsy Cornwell to be identified as the Author of the Work has been
asserted by her in accordance with the Copyright, Designs and Patents Act 1988.

Scripture taken from the New King James Version®. Copyright © 1982 by
Thomas Nelson. Used by permission. All rights reserved.

Interior design by Ruth Lee-Mui

All rights reserved. No part of this publication may be reproduced, stored
in a retrieval system, or transmitted, in any form or by any means without
the prior written permission of the publisher, nor be otherwise circulated
in any form of binding or cover other than that in which it is published and
without a similar condition being imposed on the subsequent purchaser.

A CIP catalogue record for this title is available from the British Library

Hardback ISBN 978 1 408 74897 8
Trade Paperback ISBN 978 1 408 74896 1
ebook ISBN 978 1 408 74894 7

Typeset in Garamond Premier Pro

Printed and bound in Great Britain by Clays Ltd, Elcograf S.p.A.

John Murray policy is to use papers that are natural, renewable and
recyclable products and made from wood grown in sustainable forests.
The logging and manufacturing processes are expected to conform
to the environmental regulations of the country of origin.

Carmelite House
50 Victoria Embankment
London EC4Y 0DZ

www.dialoguebooks.co.uk

John Murray Press, part of Hodder & Stoughton Limited
An Hachette UK company

The authorised representative in the EEA is Hachette Ireland,
8 Castlecourt Centre, Dublin 15, D15 XTP3, Ireland (email: info@hbgi.ie)

from one mother to another

Author's Note

In recounting the events in this memoir, chronologies have been compressed or altered and details have been changed. Where dialogue appears, including texts and online communications, the intention was to re-create the essence of conversations rather than verbatim quotes. Names and identifying characteristics of some individuals have been changed.

This book discusses domestic violence and child abuse. My goal in writing it was not to shame anyone else involved, but to share my experience in a way that might help someone else in a similar situation.

Others who were present might recall things differently. But this is my story.

Cupla fócail

a few Irish words used in this book, for reference

Bóithrín: small country road
Céad míle: a hundred thousand
Damhán alla: spiders
Fáilte: welcome
Féileacán: butterfly
Féilire: calendar
Gaeltacht: an Irish-speaking region
Gardaí: police
Go raibh maith agat: thank you
Inis: island
Lá Fhéile Padraig Shona Duit: Happy St. Patrick's Day
Le do thoil: please
Lough: lake
Mhuillin: mill
Mna: women
Mór: big
Naíonra: preschool
Saoirse: freedom
Sláinte: health
Slán: be safe / goodbye*
Sliabh: mountain
Spríocdhata: deadline
Suth talún: strawberries
Trá: beach

*Short for slán abháile: safe journey home

Prologue

We left home on my baby's first birthday.

I hadn't known when I packed his diaper bag that morning that it would never feel safe to go back. I baked a loaf of soda bread and left it cooling on the counter. I put in a load of laundry. I packed a spare outfit for my baby, but not for myself.

That evening found us in a hotel an hour away, booked in under a false name so that my husband wouldn't find us. My trunk was full of store-brand baby food, diapers, and a cardboard box of ill-fitting donated clothes from the domestic violence center.

I set my baby down in the hotel's folding cot, planning to take a shower, but as soon as I stood up, I knew that if I let him out of my sight for a second, I was going to throw up.

I got down on the floor with him instead. I helped him stack the soft fabric blocks that the shelter had also given me, their bright sides decorated with fruit and flowers, numbers and houses. His chubby baby hands reached out to pat my knees, my face, my recently buzzed-off hair. My body would not stop shaking.

I pulled him onto my lap and felt his warmth and weight. He was here with me. He was safe. No one had taken him away.

But I did not know how long that would be true.

In this unfamiliar hotel room, in this small town, in this country that was not my own, we were completely alone.

There, on the floor with my baby, I thought of water. The receptionist had told me the hotel had a pool, and I was suddenly overcome with longing for a swim: for the antiseptic smell of chlorine, the cool blue lights, the relief of buoyancy. I wanted so badly to feel held.

Spending any of the little money I had—money I knew we'd need to stretch as far as possible into an unknowable, frightening future—felt shameful. But I paid a couple of precious euros for an individually wrapped swim diaper in the lobby. I wore a black tank top and underwear and hoped it looked like a one-piece suit. I took the towels from our room and brought us down, down, into the belly of the hotel, to the small round pool.

I descended the wet tiled stairs with Robin in my arms and let the water gradually take his weight and mine.

He had never been in a pool before, or any body of water big enough to hold him. My husband and I had dipped his fingers in the sea once, months ago, but that was all.

He loved the pool at once, smiled and cooed and laughed, and I tried to laugh with him, our voices echoing in that little shell-like space.

He snuggled closer into my arms, and I realized a body of water had held him once before. The body had been my own.

An older woman was swimming laps at the other end of the pool, encased in a bathing suit with long sleeves and a high-zipped neck. She moved steadily and methodically through the water, back and forth, back and forth. Watching her, I thought of the Selkie Bride.

Hers was the story that first brought me to Ireland, the story I retold in my first novel: a seal maiden captured by a fisherman, forced to marry him and bear his children until she could find the sealskin he'd stolen from her and escape back to the sea.

What I had just done, running from home with my baby, didn't feel like an escape. I didn't feel safe and free, the way I imagined the selkie must have, reunited with her own long-lost skin, diving through the depths of her native ocean.

I hugged Robin close, never letting his impossibly soft and slippery body leave my hands. Slowly, holding him all the time, I let my feet leave the bottom.

One

The Selkie Bride

AUTUMN 2012

for the Aran Islands girls

I arrived on Inis Mór in selkie weather: the ocean, sky, and shoreline all shone silver with the gentle mist the Irish call "a grand soft day." Foam plumed out behind the Aran Island Ferry, seaweed trailing like handwriting on the waves. As we pulled into Kilronan harbor, with its pale crescent-shaped beach and scattering of B&Bs, I could already see the hostel where I'd be doing work exchange for the next month. I was so eager to get there I nearly leapt off the boat.

I hurried up the pier and around the beach, shaking my head shyly at the lineup of men in flat caps offering tours of the island by bus, bike, or trap—the local word for a horse and cart. I climbed the steep cement steps up to the harborside hostel and stepped through the door.

A group of radiantly beautiful women were sitting at the long table just inside. The smallest of them looked up at me, grinned, and said something to the girl next to her in quick-fire German. After a pause, she asked me in English, "You are the new one?"

I smiled back at her nervously. "I'm the new one. Betsy." I set my backpack down and hoped my face was hot from climbing the stairs, and not from blushing. Pretty girls have always made me shy, and the world is full of pretty girls. Now they seemed to be having some kind of global summit at this oilcloth-covered table, holding their mismatched hostel mugs.

"I am Eva," she said. "And they are Sjonelle, Kelsey, Shirong, Christina..."

The goddesses waved and offered their hellos in different accents.

Eva got up from her chair and opened her arms for a hug. "We are glad you are here," she said. I recognized her accent from Johanna, a German exchange student who had once lived with my family and who had become my quasi-sister.

I hugged her back, hoping I wasn't too sweaty: she was far shorter than my six feet, so she'd know it if I smelled.

But Eva is one of those people who immediately make everyone feel loved. Her embrace soothed some of my always-present awkwardness, and I felt my spine relax. She hoisted my huge backpack, almost as big as she was, onto her shoulders and gestured toward the stairs. "I will bring you to your room, and then you can be free. There is no more work to do today."

I flinched a little. I knew I was there to work in exchange for my bed, and I'd been taught all my life that you don't get anything for free. I'd expected to start scrubbing toilets as soon as I arrived. The idea of sleeping here before I'd earned it made me wary. "Are you sure?"

"Oh, ja, it does not matter."

Sjonelle added in laughing Australian tones, "We'll work you hard tomorrow, no worries."

"Sure," I said, "no worries." In all my life, I didn't think there was a single day I hadn't worried. I couldn't imagine my time here would be any different.

Three months before I arrived in Ireland, I finished a creative writing master's program. I'd wanted to be a writer all my life—I remember being six years old and looking at books and thinking I wanted to write them one day—and in my senior year at Smith College I'd gotten up at five every morning to work on my first novel and my graduate school applications before class. I'd gotten a place in a fully funded MFA, and then sold that novel, a modern retelling of the Selkie Bride story for young adults called *Tides*, in my second year there, along with a proposal for a second novel, a Cinderella retelling. I was going to be paid $12,500 for each book, which felt like a jaw-dropping sum. The most I'd ever made from my writing before was a $100 prize in a high school poetry contest.

I'd chased down the dream of *being a real writer* with every scrap of energy and will I had, the way I'd been taught to go after anything I wanted even an outside chance of deserving. A book deal was evidence, finally, that I really could make a living from my books—at least if I combined it with teaching.

But then I found, for what felt like the first time, that I'd used all that scrappy energy and willpower right up. At twenty-three years old I was starting to feel broken-down and burned-out, spent twigs for a spent fire. I did everything quickly, heart in my mouth, because I felt sure that if I took any extra time I would collapse into ash. I was teaching twice the prescribed student limit, tutoring, writing, finishing my thesis and my classes, and editing my first novel for publication the following year—all jobs that filled me with whiplash joy and panic and soul-crushing insecurity. I'd fallen for someone who kept showing me such grinding ambivalence that I'd had to let him go, and I spent far too much time imagining our never-to-be future together. There was a cushion-laden corner of the floor in my little apartment that was alternately a nook for grading papers and a nest to curl up in and cry until I fell asleep. I ate whatever I thought would make me feel better, mostly cheese and Vernors ginger ale. My heart was broken and my belly ached.

I come from a wealthy, WASPy family: I was not the first in mine to go to Smith, where my grandparents paid my tuition. My friends didn't always understand why I was working so hard, especially after my books sold for about what each of us made from a whole year's worth of adjunct teaching. I knew my family's wealth had given me freedoms and opportunities most people didn't have—including the freedom, and the opportunity, to leave them behind.

There were two things, really, that I'd dreamed of all my life. The one most people knew about was being an author. The other—the one I'd only told a few trusted friends—was leaving my family. Now that I was finally managing the first, I kept asking myself why I hadn't yet been brave enough to do the second, too.

A third and more recent dream was to go to Ireland. *Tides* was about Irish folklore, and I had just come in second for a Fulbright arts grant to do further research about selkies in Dublin. The near miss had left me determined to get there on my own. But when graduation loomed and I looked at my finances, I realized that even with my book advance, I'd have to choose between Ireland and more earthly concerns like healthcare and rent.

That same day, my father called and said he wanted to know my schedule for next summer because he was taking the family to Africa. It was for his and my mother's twenty-fifth wedding anniversary, a big trip of the kind the family did every few years. I'd declined to come along since I started college, offering to stay behind and house-sit in New Hampshire instead.

I loved to travel. But feeling safe was better.

My dad beat me to the house-sitting excuse this time, though, and said they'd found someone else, so there was no reason I couldn't come along. I'd have just graduated, too, he pointed out, so even if I managed to get a job offer, it wouldn't start until the fall semester. Come with us this time, he said. We'll go on safari and sleep in tents together.

I stood up from where I was sitting at my desk while I spoke to him on speakerphone. My father's voice was something I needed to be able to walk away from, even when he was calling from a thousand miles east.

I have spent much of my life figuring out how to avoid being in the same place as my father, especially at night, and that day, for the first time, I told him so. One advantage of being so very tired, on the threshold of adulthood, is that your childhood nightmares start getting tired, too, and it is harder for them to frighten you.

"I can't go," I said in a voice that shook but was still my own. At least, I knew it was coming from my own body. "I can't sleep in the same room as you."

The other end of the line was silent. After a few seconds he said, "All right. That doesn't make me happy, but I understand." We hung up soon afterward.

I stood still in my little apartment for a few minutes, not quite able to move. I hadn't spelled out to my father what I remembered, why I couldn't fall asleep in his presence—but I also hadn't said I had another commitment, hadn't made any excuses. Before, there had always been some pretext. This time, for the first time, I let my sentence end with plain refusal.

A shudder of relief ran through me.

A few days later my father called again and offered to buy me a ticket to Ireland instead. He said he would give me enough money to get by there for a few months.

It felt like hush money: If I was brave enough to tell him I remembered, whom else might I tell?

I felt sure I should say no, but the dream of Ireland was a hard one to give up. I said I would have to think about it.

That afternoon, I went into town to have coffee with Maeve, a fellow MFA student who was more than twice my age, yet somehow felt like someone I grew up with—a friend I often called my spiritual guide.

As soon as she sat down I started crying—big, gasping sobs from a shy girl who could rarely even manage to raise her voice in anger. I don't think I'd ever shown that much emotion in public before.

Maeve stroked my arm. I wept into my giant bowl of latte.

When I finally quieted, she laughed and said, "Honey, I wouldn't go through my twenties again for anything."

I snorted tears and coffee and started laughing, too.

I told her what my father had offered, how it felt like a bargain I didn't want to make, because I never wanted to owe him anything ever again.

She scoffed. "He could give you money until the end of the world and you'd owe him nothing."

I blinked. I had been shaming myself for taking my family's money for years, but Maeve said that as if it was obvious.

She shook her head. "Go to Ireland. It's where the world keeps its magic. And don't go to Dublin. In fact . . . " She pulled out her tablet and did a quick image search. "You need to go here."

She showed me a screen thick with pictures of green cliffs, dark waves, and small stone-bound fields. A girl's feet dangled over the edge of one cliff, her legs mid-swing and relaxed.

"The Aran Islands?" I laughed. "It's mostly sweaters there, right?"

"The Aran Islands," she said. "See? You're happier already. Go there." She thought for a moment. "For at least a month. It will heal your soul."

Journal: September 14, 2012

I had my first day of work at Kilronan & it really wasn't bad at all. The first room we cleaned smelled terrible, & some of the sheets were bundled up on the floor in an ominous pile, but hopefully I ingratiated myself with the other staff by putting on cleaning gloves & throwing the sheets away. We were done by half eleven (I have finally learned that half means half past, not half 'til) & now I have the rest of the day to myself even though I'm staying for free.

& oh, the island is gorgeous. As soon as you walk outside you're on tiny roads bordered with waist-high, gray stone walls & little grazing areas too small & steep really to be called fields, filled with donkeys or cows or the occasional odd & lovely horse. & the ocean, too—the beaches are not brown at all but pale & mottled silver-gray, & sometimes just ripple patterns barely covering black rock, with lots of big flat scallop shells & smooth small white shells & sometimes crab claws or broken razor clams. Wild blackberries grow all along the stone walls, & the sky is gray & the sea is blue & green, & it rains a little every day. It's all both absurdly wholesome & incredibly romantic.

I'd started filling journals cover-to-cover when I was thirteen, at a rate of three or four per year, so I had a solid collection hidden in a cardboard box under and behind boxes of textbooks in my childhood bedroom by the time I left for Ireland. When I was home and had to go to sleep at night, I'd slide those boxes of books against the inside of my closed door to help me sleep more soundly. After two years of graduate school, I'd accumulated so many boxes of books that I felt pretty confident my journals wouldn't be found and read while I was away.

I spent a lot of time, in my journals, wondering when I was going to make the police report about my father that I'd always known I needed to make someday. So many pages' worth of anger at myself for not being ready.

In college, I had started to tell a few people the truth about my father and my childhood. By the time I arrived on Inis Mór, I'd told three childhood friends, a couple from graduate school, and my fellow trainees at the rape crisis center where I'd volunteered in college. I was working my way up.

But I could always tell my journals. In their pages, I dealt with it, over and over again. I dealt with everything by writing or reading; I always have.

And I had started to notice, as my journals stacked up over the years, a theme: their covers seemed to predict their contents. Turquoise flowers on one cover looked like the hydrangea bushes at the summer camp I'd written about so adoringly inside. A cover that looked like a *Pride and Prejudice* first edition turned out to contain a whole lot of social and romantic foibles— not unusual for a twenty-two-year-old, maybe, but I started to see a pattern. The cover of the journal where I first really confronted how I felt about my childhood showed an illustration of someone drowning, and on the back cover the words "I Will Find You."

By the time I was in grad school, I'd started choosing covers based on what I hoped would happen while I wrote in them. Shortly before I left for Ireland, I chose one with a woodcut print of a boat, cresting over the word "Shipped," and I felt shipped away. What I wrote about was the relief I felt on the other side of a whole ocean, finally far away enough from my parents that I didn't feel like they could see me. The Atlantic was the boxes of books shoved against my bedroom door. Inis Mór was an island off an island off an island, off a whole different continent from the worst parts of my life. It wasn't just the Aran Islands girls, or the hostel work, that let me feel so light and free.

I filled up that ship journal quickly, writing about every beautiful day on Inis Mór. When I finished it and went looking for my next journal, I settled quickly on one covered with pictures of horses. *Bring me that feeling*, I told it, seeing how they ran.

The joke among the work-exchange girls was that everyone came to the island thinking they'd lose weight. All that scrubbing and bed-making, plus hours on end spent hiking around the cliffs and swimming in the cold, cold Irish ocean—not to mention the hostel's rotating cast of attractive prospects for nighttime exercise—it should have been a premium diet program.

We all gained weight instead. Maybe it was all the nights at the pub, drinking pints of cider we never had to pay for. Maybe it was the endless comfort meals we lovingly cooked for each other and ate in front of *Father Ted* reruns—I particularly remember a giant casserole dish of mac and cheese I made that could have easily fed a dozen, but which four of us polished off in an hour, along with a whole ice cream cake. Another day I spent hours picking blackberries from the endless brambles tangling over the stone walls down by the beach and made a beautiful crumble, only for it to turn out salty because the berries had bathed in, or drank up, so much of the sea air.

We still ate it. That sea air really works up your appetite, too.

But I think it was mostly that we were happy. Our time at the hostel felt wrapped in a haze of blessing. We woke up in our bunk beds every day, laid out breakfast for the hostellers, and sat together drinking hot milk mixed with Nutella, eating toast dripping with incomparable Irish butter, as the guests drifted in and out, watched over by a huge, vaguely threatening mural of a chicken. Then we changed bedsheets, wiped clean bathrooms, took out trash, vacuumed and mopped floors, cleaned the kitchen, and did laundry. It's amazing how much you can get done when the people around you are friendly and happy, and when you don't mind too much about getting it absolutely perfect. We took turns blasting music from phones tucked into our back pockets, Cher and Cœur de pirate and Shirley Ellis. We talked the whole time, about lovers we'd left behind and ones we'd found on the island, about where we'd come from and where we were going. Between us we almost always had the work done in less than an hour.

And then we really were free, free to roam the nine-mile expanse of Inis Mór, which might as well for us have been the world. Each day we wandered the island, hopping over the thousand-year-old stone walls that we'd learned had been built mostly by women while their husbands prepared the ground for planting. We got to know the buck-toothed donkeys and gentle cows who lined the roads, watching us from their tiny postcard fields. We got to know each other, from our different corners of the world, with our different heartaches and dreams. We laughed and screamed and edged each other closer to the sheer drop from the cliffs at Dun Aengus, the island's famous Celtic fort, and we called out across the wide-open sea and sky, knowing the next piece of land past the horizon was America.

And we felt beautiful. For our months on Inis Mór, we felt the beauty of our youth and freedom, those qualities that can be so hard for the young to value until they're much older. We thought each other were the most beautiful, wonderful girls in the world. I began to feel some of the sparkle that I'd seen on them that first day rub off on me too: confidence and contentment that lit me up with a faith that was both gentle and sure.

We grew rounder, softer, and stronger, too, with every passing day. Many of us had spent our whole lives dieting, and our bodies took in the sudden liberal nourishment we offered them with grateful relief.

I had told myself I was in Ireland to write, but I quickly took up the work of reveling in this happiness for all it was worth instead. I'd been pushing myself to burnout all my life, swimming in an endless sea of perfectionism, anxiety, and fear. Academic and literary ambition had been safer places for me to seat my love and energy than home, but I'd never managed to feel like I was touching bottom with them, either—there was always more to do, more to achieve, and nothing I did ever came with the feeling of being done or being good enough.

And then, in the middle of that sea, washed here by those very ambitions and fears, I'd found an island.

The ease I found on Inis Mór was so delicious I couldn't bear to sit torturing myself over my writing every day. I felt like I was playing hooky—and it was in fact the first autumn in twenty-one years, out of my total twenty-four, that I wasn't a student, which only intensified the feeling—but I started trying to embrace a gift I'd never been able to offer myself before: a real holiday. There was a value to my days that had nothing to do with intellect or achievement. I didn't have to pile any books in front of the door. I had been starving for that as much as for Irish butter.

The night I met my husband, I almost didn't go out. Kelsey and I were both tired from the extra beds we'd made and toilets we'd scrubbed for the forty-strong school group that had stayed in the hostel the night before. We'd spent hours yanking faded, pale-blue sheets off duvets and thin bunk mattresses, scrubbing down the twenty cramped hostel shower stalls and toilets, and cracking open the bedroom windows to air out the traces of last night's occupants and let in the breath of the Atlantic. From almost every window of the hostel, you could see the sea.

But the other girls were eager to go out, and after three weeks on the island, I would have done anything for them. Kelsey and I shared a smiling look of agreement. We joined our friends, without putting on makeup or even brushing our hair, wearing our oversized souvenir Aran sweaters and feeling, unusually for our time there, pretty unsexy.

"No boys for me tonight, I guess," I said on the way out, wrinkling my nose at myself in the mirror.

Kelsey laughed. "Don't say that—you'll jinx yourself and fall in love!"

The evening air was so fresh and clear it felt like we could have floated down the worn stone steps by the silvered bay to the pub next door. Eva and Shirong went in first; Kelsey and I clung to each other a little as we passed the threshold, momentarily shyer than we'd learned Americans are expected to feel.

But old Irish pubs are preternaturally designed to put people at ease. Once inside, we tucked ourselves into a cushioned bench in the corner by the back door, and I felt her breathing slow down in time with mine. The turf fire was nearby, gleaming with ruddy coals, scenting the air with peat's whisky richness. My version of heaven will always smell like a turf fire.

Kelsey pointed out a man across the bar. "Look at him," she murmured admiringly, and he was worth looking at: dark hair and eyes and brows, strong arms obviously muscled even under his pushed-up sweater sleeves, shoulders broad and steady as cornerstones. The kind of person Americans call Black Irish, who might be read as Spanish or Italian at first glance. He'd clearly graduated with flying colors from the Colin Farrell School of Irish Smolder.

He reminded me of an Angela Carter wolf: hunter and woodcutter and beast, savior and snarl, all in one.

Even with the glow the other girls had bestowed on me, I was sure he was out of my league. I let one of the less extraordinary men who'd joined our table buy me a drink.

But I couldn't stop thinking about the wolf.

I came to Ireland to tell a story. Here are some more beginnings:

I was ten years old, attending a cultural heritage talent show organized by the Girl Scouts. For one act, an Irish American mother and daughter walked onto the stage, the girl nervous in her green Juniors vest, the mother likely a troop leader like mine. The girl's hair was in smooth brown braids, the mother's permed in a style she must have had since the eighties.

They told us they were going to sing a ballad about an old Irish story called "The Selkie Bride."

It was the story I would retell in my first novel, *Tides*, ten years later— the story that would eventually bring me to Ireland:

One night, a young fisherman catches sight of a beautiful maiden singing on the shore. He starts to approach her, but trips over something on the rocky beach.

When he reaches down and touches soft folds, he knows what's in his hands: a sealskin, but larger and darker and finer than any the fishermen had seen before. A selkie skin. He puts it quickly into his bag.

The maiden follows him—or, more accurately, follows the piece of
herself he's taken—becomes his wife and bears him a child. She misses her
home and her family, but she is in thrall to her skin's keeper.
     One day, her daughter comes to her.
     "Mother," says the girl, "I found an old leather coat in the rafters.
May I have it?"

I found a book with a selkie in it in my grandparents' house, in among the
bookshelves of an aunt my parents didn't approve of: she used to be a strip-
per and was still an artist, jobs the family spoke of with almost equal embar-
rassment. Brian Froud's *Faeries* was secreted between steamy romance and
adventure novels with feathery brown thumbed-through pages. I lay in my
aunt's bed with its sixties-floral duvet and read them all, floating on them
somewhere far away.

     But the selkie in *Faeries* wasn't far away at all. As soon as I saw her I
knew she was somewhere inside me. I had a sealskin, too. It was already lost.

You shouldn't use the word "fairy" in Ireland, really, especially in front of
a child. Most of the old people I've met here call them *the good neighbors*.

     If you do say the word "fairy" when a child is around (a man in a pub
once told me, so it must be true), you have to say "bless you" afterward, as if
someone has sneezed. Saying their name calls them to you, and fairies love
to steal children. If you want to keep your child, you bless them and hope
your words are enough to keep them close.

The mother and daughter at that Girl Scouts conference sang most of their
song in English, but in the middle of their act, they stopped. The mother
explained that the next verse, in which the selkie tells her child she's returning to the sea, she had to sing in Irish, because when she sang it in English it
always made her cry.

     That was the moment from the show that my mom and I talked about
most on the drive home. "I wish she'd sung that verse in English," my mom

said, "because I can't fathom what a mother would say to tell her child she's leaving forever."

I wished I knew the words, too, but for a different reason. The selkie was kidnapped, I thought. She'd been a prisoner for years. Why wouldn't she want to escape?

I didn't have a child then, of course. I was a child then.

I don't know what my mother would say about the selkie now.

What neither of us knew in the car that day, and what I think neither my mother nor I could yet imagine, is that in some tellings of the selkie story, the child leaves, too: mother and child swim into the freedom of the sea together, leaving the fisherman alone.

That is the version of the tale that I would tell in *Tides* now, if I could. The child gives the mother her ability to leave, and the mother takes it in her hands and frees them both.

That is the story I am telling now.

Two

Sympathy for the Minotaur

AUTUMN 2012

for Surnaí

When Kelsey and I emerged from our rooms the next morning, the beautiful wolfman was still there, smoking on the hostel patio. Ever so casually, we happened to sit outside, too. He looked at us, but mostly watched the morning bay with an intensity in his gaze that I could feel in my belly. He was a cigarette burn in the fabric of the clear sky, an ember in all the sweet blue air and water around us. I felt so washed clean from those weeks of doing the cleaning myself, of wandering the beaches and fields of Inis Mór. I was ready to get burned up.

We managed to glean his name and occupation—Tommy, a horse trainer—and over the course of the day Kelsey and I started referring to him as Horse Man. This was part of a grand tradition of talking in code that my friends and I have kept up all my life, starting with Comb Guy, a summer-camp crush who fancied himself a 1950s greaser. Group chats still refer to Yoga Guy, IT Man, Hot Neighbor. After a while they become less real people than archetypes for us to analyze. (Maybe that's my favorite thing for a man to be: an idea I can discuss with other women.)

I spent the morning carrying laundry in and out of the rooms to the shed out back, holding the basket on a hip I jutted out farther than I needed to whenever I walked past Horse Man. He stayed on the patio most of the day, reading sometimes or talking quietly with whoever else was there, mostly just looking out at the sea. He seemed to have a stillness about him, an intensity and calmness, that was like salt on my tongue after too much of my own frantic, too-sweet energy all my life. I felt his gaze on me like a touch on my skin, and even though I was too shy to gaze back, I ate it all up. It was delicious to me.

Kelsey played wingman for me, asked to bum a smoke that evening so we could all start a conversation. It was a deep blue-purple evening, not long after the autumn equinox, the sky an October plum dusted with stars and painted with glimmering streaks of cloud. The patio smelled like the sea, like the exhaust from the departed ferries, horse dung, everyone's new Aran wool sweaters and spices from the dinner that some of the hostellers were making inside. The flimsy folding metal chairs were cold and hard and small to sit on, so everyone had to perch.

Somehow a conversation about consent came up. I mentioned that I had trained as a rape crisis counselor in college. Horse Man raised his eyebrows and nodded in respect. "That's important work," he said. "I admire that, now."

I had taken to mentioning the rape crisis work early on when I met a guy I liked. I thought I could measure something useful by their reaction to it. Most often it made them nervous and flustered; occasionally it would make them want to play devil's advocate. I considered both responses red flags.

But Tommy just turned his intense gaze on me, with genuine interest, and asked me what it had involved. He told me how he'd spent the last couple of years going back to school for social work, how he wanted to work with ex-convicts to help them move away from toxic masculinity. He'd grown up in an abusive home, and he'd seen what it did to his family, and he wanted to help other men change those behaviors. He wanted to take in foster sons someday for the same reason. He said all of that while looking thoughtfully into my eyes and leaning back in his chair with the casual ease of the very strong, his arms and shoulders thick and hard even at rest. He said how important it was for men to listen to women about these things.

I swooned.

I even forgot my plan to rely on Kelsey's conversational wingmanning: it turned out, impossibly, that he was easy to talk to. When Horse Man said he fancied walking down to the nearest pub for a drink, and did I want to come, I didn't even think to be nervous. We sat on low yellow velvet stools at that same turf fire I'd first seen him across the night before. He bought me a cider and we talked about books (he quoted verbatim long passages from *Ulysses* and bell hooks) and living in Germany (he had worked as a stagehand for a German theater group when he was nineteen, and he told me stories of having an affair with a much older actress and being the muse for the director's next script, about a naïve farm boy who falls in with a group of gay men—to me at twenty-four, all that seemed impossibly cosmopolitan). He spoke reverently of his mother and his ex-girlfriends, of how much he had done to try to protect them from the other men in their lives. "When I was young, I was jealous of women," he said. "I thought they had it easier because they didn't have to work. Now I only see how much pain they have to bear."

I got a text from Kelsey that the group had moved on to Kilronan's other bar. We walked there together, ten minutes under October starlight, listening to the accented music of each other's voices. In the bar we talked some more, and I felt his gaze on my mouth, but he didn't touch me or lean in toward me: in fact, he leaned back most of the time, on those strong shoulders, and let me come to him.

Then he said, "I'm going out for a smoke, but I'd like to kiss you first."

I said, "Yes, please."

His hands, rough with calluses, came gently to the small of my back. For the first time, I liked the taste of smoke.

A few hours later, we were all back in the hostel kitchen: Tommy and me, Kelsey, Eva, Shirong, Sjonelle, and some guys they'd gathered from the second pub. Everyone was a few drinks deep, laughing in a way that was starting to get sleepy. Tommy picked me up by the hips and placed me on the countertop—all six feet of me, that had never been *placed* any-where before, and he did it without a thought. I felt small with a man for the first time in all my life, the dainty sweet thing I'd always known I was failing to be.

He kissed me again, slowly, and then he said: "I'm going out for a smoke, and if you're not here when I get back, I'll understand."

"I'm sorry, what?" I said, thinking *what part of my wrapping my legs around you while you kiss me on this kitchen counter makes you think I want to be anywhere else but where you are?*

"I just don't want you to feel any pressure," he said. He touched my nose gently, like I was something precious, and then he turned and walked away.

Wild horses couldn't have torn me from that spot.

I was sitting in the exact same place on the counter when he came back. He stood in front of me, smiling a little shyly, until I slid down and kissed him. "See? I'm still here," I said, his shyness making me bold.

"Aye, you are."

That night happened to be my turn in Room 11, the tiny private room on the hostel's top floor. I took his hand and led him up, and there I spent the longest and sweetest night my twenty-four years had yet shown me. This beautiful, hard man held me with a reverence that made me shiver. He growled low in my ear about how gorgeous I was while he touched me in ways that felt better than anything I'd known, better than I knew how to touch myself. I had never experienced desire like this before—at least not desire for someone who was openly desiring me back. The way I wanted him made me drunker than the sweet cider ever could. It was like every romance novel I'd dismissed as hyperbolic but still devoured: waves, fireworks, worlds changed. It was so good I still can't write about it well.

The next day he said he'd call me. I said no, you won't. I was grateful that the universe had gifted me a weekend with an actual real-life romance novel hero, a salt-of-the-earth Irish horse trainer who was somehow also an avid reader, fluent French and German speaker, and bestower of multiple orgasms. I could comprehend that I might deserve one night as good as fiction, because I thought most women did: if for nothing more than to warm us up in memory when we are old.

But that guy, romance-hero, memory-fodder guy, he doesn't call you back. At least not when you're me. You might get a dreamy moment, if you're lucky, but then he vanishes. I knew I didn't deserve more.

I kissed him goodbye as he waited in line for the ferry that afternoon. "You won't call me back," I told him. "It's okay."

But later that night, he did.

He called me in between training horses, walking his sister's dog, helping his mother shop for groceries. (He always just happened to mention, at the beginning of every conversation, how much he was doing for them.) He told me how much he missed my body, how perfect it was—the body I'd been taught from infancy was shamefully big and awkward, but that he told me looked like every painting in the Louvre. We talked more about books and our bad parents and our time in Germany and France (I'd lived with a host family for a summer in high school).

He came back a week later and booked a room at the island's real hotel, and I took a day off from hostel-cleaning to stay with him there. We walked down a twilit road again, just as we had the last weekend, from the hostel to the much more adult-feeling and fancy hotel, with flags flying in front of its doors. There was going to be live traditional music in half an hour, and Tommy suggested we get drinks and wait for it to start.

I'll be honest: as much as I enjoyed his conversation, I just wanted to get back to the room. I'd gotten hooked on what we'd done last time and I needed my fix. I also felt nervous about doing anything else—I felt confident about sex in a way I never had about conversation. I was still freshly out of a lifetime in school among my fellow nerds, and I was sure that soon this more experienced person (I wasn't sure of his age, but thought he must be pushing thirty) would realize how naïve and silly I was.

But it seemed like he actually wanted to talk to me. He remembered what I'd said about my first book when we'd last met, that it was about selkies, and he asked when I had started writing it.

"In college. I took a class with a professor I really loved—her name is Betsey, too, Betsey Harries, she made me like my own name for the first time in my life because I liked her so much. The class was called 'Fairy Tales and Gender,' and it really set me on the path I'm still on now. I'd always loved reading fairy tale retellings, loved Robin McKinley and Gail Carson Levine and Jane Yolen growing up, but her class was the first time I saw that there was a life I could make inside those kinds of stories, reading them and writing them. In that class I read Angela Carter for the first time—she's still my favorite writer, she wrote this collection of retellings called *The Bloody Chamber* that's just everything to me—and Anne Sexton and Emma Donoghue—"

"She's Irish, you know," Tommy said.

I nodded eagerly. "All those writers helped me see the kind of writer I wanted to be. I'd always wanted to be a writer, always. My mom taught me to read really early, she was a literacy coach before she got married, and by the time I was six I knew I wanted to spend my life writing books. But Betsey Harries helped me see what kind. At the end of her class, we wrote our own retellings, and she told us to choose a source tale that we didn't just love, but one that bothered us, one we wanted to tussle with in some way."

He laughed at that. "And you wanted to fight a selkie?"

I blushed. "I retold a story called 'Thousandfurs' for her class," I said. "I think I wasn't quite ready for the selkies yet, but I was already thinking about them. When I wrote *Tides* as part of a special project my senior year, Betsey was my advisor. And when I teach now, my students almost always have a favorite story, one that bothers them, too." I was yammering, I realized. I was full of anxiety, and he was all stillness, watching me thoughtfully. I wanted to take that calm and patience inside me again.

I smiled at him. "What's yours?"

He took a moment to think, his gaze never leaving mine. "Theseus," he said. "I always liked the story of Theseus and the Minotaur. The idea of having to find your way through an impossible maze. No one to help, no one you can trust, because everyone has betrayed you. Having to fight that monster in the middle of the maze, all alone."

"Did you never have any sympathy for the minotaur?" I asked.

He raised his dark brows, and for a moment he did look away. He took a huge breath, and then he laughed. "Sympathy for the minotaur," he murmured. "By god, I never did. And I should have. Sympathy for the minotaur. Jaysus." He laughed. "D'you know, this is the best date I ever had."

Something scared inside me warmed and melted, and I smiled the wide and hapless smile of a young American back at him. "Me too."

The music was starting. We stayed another hour, listening, before we went back to our room, and I didn't wish a minute of it away.

"So, what did you do last night?" Eva asked with an ironic snort when I came back flushed and glowing the next day.

"Oh, we talked, then we had sex, then we talked, then we had sex, then we talked, then—"

"Ach, I know! You don't need to make the rest of us more jealous!"

In those in-between talking sessions, I learned that he was actually about to turn thirty-four. He was properly horrified when I told him I was twenty-four, saying he had been sure I was nearly thirty, or had at least had my twenty-fifth birthday, which made me feel deliciously sophisticated.

He told me he'd grown up on a farm in Clare, that he'd spent time in both France and Germany "breaking heartses."

"Breaking hearts?" I asked, startled.

"Heartses," he said again, I was sure—but by the third time I realized he meant horses. He'd paid his way through his life with horse training, a gift he said he'd inherited from his grandfather—"I hate when they call me a horse whisperer, y'know, it's insulting to the horses"—or working on building sites, which was how he'd put his little sister through college and helped his mother pay her bills. He was living with her at the moment, he said, just to help her out. She'd always been fragile. He felt responsible for her, he said.

When I told him how my dad had hurt me—every time I spoke about it I felt I was drawing lines, at last, around something that had once felt like it could consume and destroy my whole life—he said it had happened to someone he loved, too, and he knew the lasting pain it caused.

"I'd like to break your father's jaw," he murmured into my hair, and I lay in his strong arms and knew he could.

And I swear: in the morning, I stood up from the bed and felt sure there were children outside waiting for us. Our children, waiting to be born. I felt it as a sure and swift premonition, real on an almost sensory level, the way you can feel the barometric pressure change before a storm.

After my month on the island, I sublet a room in a small flat from a grad school friend who was studying abroad in Dublin. I spent November in a freezing shoebox with a hole in the floor that I paid €800 for. I finished revisions for *Tides*, which would be published the following June, and I hacked determinedly away at my second book, the retelling of Cinderella I was now calling *Mechanica* that my publisher had scheduled for release the year after. Guilt at the brief respite from hard work I'd found on the island ate at me. I also had head colds in perpetuity, one of the least glamorous aspects of relocating to a different country.

Tommy offered to take a weekend off from his horses and visit me in Dublin. I was recovering from a particularly horrible cold the day he came, and I decided to will myself to health, because I could not bear to lose out on any of the time we had together. My roommates would be gone for the weekend, so we were going to have the whole apartment to ourselves, and I was not. Going. To be sick.

So, of course, when he had me topless on the couch that evening, I started shivering with fever like a consumptive novel heroine. He wrapped me up in his jumpers and every duvet he could find and held me all night, waiting for the fever to break. He lit a real fire in the hearth that my roommates had never gotten to take a light.

"I feel too hot," I told him, my teeth chattering. "Please let me take off a blanket."

"It's false warmth," he said. "You're cold to the touch. You need to sweat out this fever. It's dangerous. I've never seen a girl so sick. Shh, just listen to me." He spoke with the same gentle-but-will-brook-no-disobedience tone I knew he'd use on a horse.

I'd thought I was in love with someone else when I got to Ireland; have I mentioned that? He'd never been able to decide if he wanted to be with me or not. I told Tommy about him, and he said he'd have to write him a thank-you note for leaving me free. I thought of what I'd felt from that boy. False warmth. And this was real.

"I love you," I told Tommy, addled with fever. And I meant it.

"Now I know you're ill," he said with a laugh. He held me closer, and quietly he began to sing Robert Burns's poem "Now Westlin Winds, or Song Composed in August." He would sing it often in the coming years, and every word is still pressed on my heart.

> We'll gently walk and sweetly talk
> Till the silent moon shines clearly
> I'll grasp thy waist and, fondly pressed
> Swear how I love thee dearly
> Not vernal showers to budding flowers
> Not autumn to the farmer
> So dear can be as thou to me
> My fair, my lovely charmer

The real fire crackled in the grate. My fever broke.

Tommy invited me to visit him in east Galway, and we rode horses through the mountains, the green-golden coins of gorse petals and changing leaves sparkling all around us, the air clean and wet as holy water. He rode ahead of me on a horse he was still training, arguing it over every stream and fallen log we passed, the corded muscles in his forearms straining with the reins. I rode a mellow mare he had pronounced "bomb-proof." (I had some riding experience but knew my limits.)

It was a warm day, but dark clouds hugged the edges of the sky, looking cold even from a distance. "Winter's coming," Tommy said. "I've always loved the winter."

I snorted. "Ugh. Dark and cold." At twenty-four, a student all my life, to me winter meant exams, all-nighters that lasted through the longest nights of the year, or at best, holidays with my frightening family, where my mom wept in the kitchen but still demanded everyone smile for the Christmas-card photo. Any smile I'd seen in winter was a lie.

"Farmers can't work long days in winter," he said. "The light won't let us. We go home at half four, and we have the fire, and the dinner, and the tea." (In Ireland, everything has a definite article.) "Nature knows that winter is a time for rest." He looked away, and his face became more vulnerable for a moment. "It's the only time I get to read much, like, when it's too dark to work outside. I read a lot more in the winter."

My heart reached out in love and longing for him. It occurred to me that I might seem as deliciously exotic to him, with my nerdy glasses and grad school stories, as he did to me with his horses and rough hands.

Tommy trained a few horses here and there for cash, or in exchange for room and board. It seemed he never had money, but he was free from the grinding trap of overwork I'd been getting crushed in all my life. On the mountains, riding his horses through the heather as slowly as we needed to for me to feel safe, I felt him showing me a life of peace and quiet and rest that let me long for nothing more than the sweet darkness of winter in a small room with him, reading by the fire.

Tommy found wild damsons, and we ate handfuls of the little black-skinned plums with their tart gold flesh. Nearby we saw a huge hazel tree, dismounted and knelt on the ground for nuts, cracked them open with stones—fresh hazelnuts are as sweet and rich as vanilla ice cream—and then we knelt for each other, too. I felt so beautifully full and surrounded, taking everything sweet and wild and lush about the landscape and bringing it into myself. The life falling away behind me in America felt dim and small. How could I want anything but this?

Three

Happily Ever After

WINTER 2012–AUTUMN 2013

for Jackie

After three months in Ireland and the UK, my tourist visa expired, and I needed to go to another part of Europe if I didn't want to go home.

And I wasn't going home.

I'd booked a round-trip flight originally, but the plane back left without me while I slept in an Edinburgh hostel—or tried to sleep. I'd fought with Tommy that day, our first fight, because I hadn't been texting him back quickly enough and he thought I must have met someone else in Scotland.

I went to bed frustrated, but I woke up terrified. The thought of that plane with my name on a seat going home, even the ghost of the idea of me being back on the same continent as my father, had thrust me into a recurring nightmare, the one I've had all my life where he's holding me down and I can't move. I get sleep paralysis sometimes, and being frozen is part of the terror, but even worse was always that I couldn't speak. I would try to scream for help and not even be able to whisper.

For almost a decade, when I woke from those nightmares, I'd calmed myself down with promises that my future self would report him to the police someday. But now here I was, a full-blown adult, still unable to use my words to make him stop, even in dreams. I wondered if I'd ever do it when I was awake.

I had a few thousand euros left from my book advance that I'd been saving for my planned move to New York, but instead I bought myself time, more time with that wide, deep barrier of salt water between me and my parents. When my expired visa meant I had to leave Ireland, I went to Germany to stay with my old host-sister, Johanna. During the year she lived with my family when I was eight and she was sixteen, she epitomized teenage cool to me, with her extra-wide cargo pants and hair a different color every month. The next time I'd seen her I had been sixteen, on a school trip to Paris, and she had swanned in at twenty-four, now a blond and business-glam adult in a tailored blazer, and signed me out of my teacher's supervision to buy me white wine at a café overlooking the Seine. She had always been a portal to adulthood, a symbol of womanhood, for me: the cool older sister I never had.

Johanna's family lived in a storybook German village not far from the French border. It was wine country, with little twisting vineyards of gnarled grapevines in between verdant hills and miniature forests—not big or dark like the forests of the Brothers Grimm, but just enough for all the wholesome hiking and skiing that Johanna and her family and, it seemed to me, all Germans loved to do. Johanna's family had always seemed straight out of a picture book, too: sporty and willowy, varying shades of blond, laughing heartily at anything that was even a little bit funny.

Their house was tall and yellow, surrounded by a beautiful postcard garden and a trellis hung with real grapevines, from which her father made grappa every year at a local distillery. "The Grappa from the Papa," he announced whenever he poured it after dinner, and everyone would laugh as if they'd never heard it before.

Every time I met Johanna again, I was the age she'd been the last time she'd met me: eight and sixteen, sixteen and twenty-four, and now twenty-four and thirty-two. This was the first time we were both adults, and I carried my new adulthood like a precious talisman. I wanted it to have the power to shield me from the things that had happened when I was a child—some of them things that had happened while Johanna was living with us.

So far, aside from one aunt I told when I was in college who hadn't believed me, I had only told people who didn't know my family about my dad. I'd told the girls from the hostel over drinks in the pub one night, and they held it for me more easily than I'd hoped. I'd told Tommy, and he had held me, and held it for me.

Now, with Johanna, in her childhood home instead of mine, I knew it was time to tell her, too.

(If you don't want to hear more about this now, if it will hurt you to read about it—I get it. You can skip to the end of the chapter now.)

Journal: February 11, 2013

I don't want to write this down. I don't want it to have happened. I have to just write it.

Johanna saw my dad's sexual abuse when she lived with us. She walked in on it, on my father naked, rocking—I still can't bear to write it all. She confronted my mom, and they yelled at each other and screamed and cried, and in the end my parents convinced her she'd been wrong. They told her they thought she must be taking drugs.

On Saturday night she and I ended up staying up past 4 in the morning, talking about it. I'd been gearing up to tell her all day—really since I got here—that Dad molested and otherwise abused me, but I was afraid, as I am with everyone, that she wouldn't believe me. She always seemed to like my parents so much, and it takes me a while to work myself up to be brave enough to do most things. Anyway, I finally told her, and as soon as I did, she started nodding and said, "I know." She's been telling herself all these years she was wrong, but as soon as I started, she knew she wasn't. She told me exactly what she saw, and it was very clear, there's nothing else that it could be. (I still think oh god, please, what else could it be?) She was so sure of what she saw, even during the fight with my mother, but somehow my dad convinced her she was wrong. He convinces everybody.

*But I am right, and she is right, and I am right. It's hard to sleep
again, and I can't bear to write any more quite yet, but I am not crazy or
evil or a bad daughter.*

I am right.

A few days later, my Gaga died. My father's father. There are lots of things
that don't happen in the order I would put them in a novel. It didn't make
sense that both those things happened at the same time. This revelation,
and this vanishing.

The week before I left for Ireland, I went to visit my grandparents, and
they took me out to the kind of expensively gloomy restaurant where the men
have to wear jackets. During dinner, a man in probably the exact same navy
blazer that my Gaga was wearing came up to our table and shook his hand and
said: this man has been my hero all my life. He made me see what kind of man
I wanted to be. You should be so proud that he's your grandfather.

I was. And I am.

My grandfather was an excellent teacher. He loved technology and had
an iPod long before any of my friends did, loaded with James Taylor and Cat
Stevens and early Beatles. He was an active bicyclist until shortly before his
death. I remember him as intelligent and jovial; I remember him as almost
always laughing.

And also: one of my clearest childhood memories is of him and my father holding me down while I screamed and sobbed so that he could force
his hand into my unwilling mouth and pull a tooth that wasn't ready to
come out, because he was interested in seeing the shape of the root.

Johanna's mother was with us when I got the email that Gaga had
died, and that my parents were buying me a ticket home. I was not ready
to go, not so soon after that sleepless night when I had learned that Johanna had seen what I remembered, that I was not alone in remembering.
The evil that had haunted me all my life was not something that came
from inside me, as part of me had always wanted to believe—as any child
will believe themselves evil to spare their parents. It was all true, and now I

would have to go back to it. Because my Gaga, whom I loved and admired, had died.

I stood up, thinking I had to start packing right away, then realized I didn't and felt dizzy. I looked down at my computer resting on Johanna's old trunk from her year with us, still printed with my childhood address in New Hampshire.

"My grandfather died," I said. I felt too tall again. I started to cry.

Johanna's mother stood up, too, and gathered me into an embrace. I hunched down to lay my head on her shoulder. My tears matted her beautiful mohair sweater, and I breathed in her glamorous perfume.

"Oh, mein kind," she murmured, rubbing my back gently, in the same soft tone she'd have used to soothe a wakeful baby. *Oh, my child.* "Oh, kind."

Journal: February 12, 2013

What will it be like to see my mom and dad again?

It will be the same as it ever was. Just now I know for sure.

Tommy says I should make sure to be gentle to myself, too. Of course he is right.

He is not perfect, I know things could go wrong with him, sometimes he gets angry over such little things—but those are little things, and this . . . he can handle all of this. It has not scared him away. I know he wants to take care of me in the ways that he can. He says he'll come back to America with me for a few weeks in the summer, to be with me when I leave my parents, when I tell people what happened. I really want him to come, especially if we get married.

The thing is, he's on my side. He's helping me carry these awful things. He wants to.

On the other hand, I want to protect myself from having another family that hurts me. I have to tell him that, too.

As the flight descended into Logan and I saw the pale shores of New England rise under my window again, none of it felt real. Coming back to

America felt like trying to get back into my body after death. In fact, the whole week I was there I felt as if only my body, a dead and numb physical form, was in America, while my senses and my soul were safely stored in the cool mists of Ireland with Tommy. Tommy, who knew and understood, who held me with tenderness and strength, who had said he would hurt my father to protect me. I texted with him a lot.

There were plenty of things in America that reinforced my sense of unreality, of a mismatch to the things that I remembered. I wasn't the tallest cousin anymore, didn't tower over the rest of the family in the photograph my mother made us all take, reminding us to smile, before the funeral.

Each of the grandchildren did something for the service. I'd been asked to read in church as long as I could remember. I wrote down the reading in my journal, so I could carry it with me the whole time, so I would remember what was real, so the voice I'd found when I was far away from America would still be with me.

Journal: February 17, 2013

Romans 8:35–45

Who shall separate us from the love of Christ? Shall tribulation, or distress, or persecution, or famine, or nakedness, or peril, or sword? As it is written, for thy sake we are killed all the day long; we are accounted as sheep for the slaughter.

Nay, in all these things we are more than conquerors through him that loved us.

For I am persuaded that neither death, nor life, nor angels, nor principalities, nor powers, nor things present, nor things to come, nor height, nor depth, nor any other creature, shall be able to separate us from the love of God, which is in Christ Jesus our Lord.

My parents had those verses framed in red calligraphy above their bed through my whole childhood.

I interleaved the pages of my journal with my fingers as I stood at the podium reading to the congregation, bookmarking earlier pages about days and nights with Tommy, my hands holding on tight to better moments, like Tommy's beloved Theseus and the ball of string he used to find his way out of the labyrinth. Every time I closed my eyes, I was back in Ireland, and free.

My parents volunteered me to stay with my Nana for a few days after the service, and I was glad. We watched *Downton Abbey* together or read on the same couch. She still fed the chipmunk outside her porch the way she'd been doing as long as I could remember.

Nana was tiny and never ate or cooked very much. I cooked for her, and it made both of us happy. Over breakfast the first full day I told her about Tommy, and she asked if we were going to get married. I admitted that I thought we were. I told her about the dreams we'd started sharing, how he said he just wanted to train a horse or two and spend the rest of his time taking care of a wife and children, and how I couldn't bear the thought of that lucky cared-for wife being anyone but me.

"Yes," I told Nana. "We are going to get married."

She nodded. "Sometimes you just know," she said.

She and Gaga had only dated briefly before their engagement, too, when she was twenty, and their marriage had lasted fifty happy years. She held my gaze a moment longer, and I knew it was a blessing.

Journal: February 20, 2013

What I can't get over, what I keep thinking about ever since I talked with Johanna, is that I know for sure now that Mom had to have known. The whole time. Of course I was delusional to think she didn't.

She could have saved us.

Dad is—what he is—but Mom, as Johanna said, she chose her husband and her reputation over her children. She's been lying and pretending for at least twenty years now.

All the things I used to get so mad at her about—that I still do—how hypocritical and weak-minded she is, how she makes a performance of herself as a martyr—of course she is that way. She has to be that way to still live with my dad. And to live with herself, too, I guess.

I hate them both.

But I had this moment of clarity at Nana's house. That's what I came to this journal to write. I realized how glad I am to be myself and to have a life and to be in all the joy in the world, and I was grateful to my parents for having me. I am not grateful for what they did to me, but I am grateful that I exist, and that I can choose the life I have now.

I had nightmares about my parents almost every night while I was in the US. In them I still couldn't speak, and though I tried to scream, only a strangled almost-silence left my mouth, but there was a difference. This time, I could move. With a great effort, I could get to a window or door, and outside—every time—I would see a wolf. I knew that wolf was Tommy, and he was waiting for me.

When I told him about these dreams, he was always annoyed that his dream-self didn't come inside the house to rescue me. But my dreams have always been too on-the-nose, I told him. It means I'm figuring out how to rescue myself, how to get myself out. And my brain knows you will be there when I do.

I flew back to Ireland as soon as I could, using up most of my savings. Tommy had just moved to a crumbling little trailer on his friend's stud farm, and he was living there in exchange for training horses. When he brought me back to that little home, I curled into it like a hermit crab into a shell—it was small and safe and far away from New Hampshire and my father, and inside it, at last, so was I.

Let me tell you about my first Irish home, that trailer on the stud farm, dark-speckled with mold, the ceiling sagging with rotting leaves, ivy and slugs pushing their way through the cracked windows, the soft furnishings infested with mites we had to spray for every week with a chemical that made me cough. Every night we slept on a bed we made of couch cushions on the living room floor because the trailer's two tiny bedrooms were too damp, and too piled with decades of cluttered storage, to use. It was so cold it didn't matter that we didn't have a fridge: milk stayed fresh on the countertop.

Tommy brought me there in the dark, in his clanking, ancient, unregistered VW Polo. He'd joked (or at least said while laughing) when he picked me up that he carried his house on his back: the trunk, the boot as he called it, was full of horsehair-dusted blankets and clothes and an old leather saddle and scuffed riding boots and god knows what else. He didn't turn on the lights in the trailer, just pushed a path through the piles of things the couple who owned the farm had stored there, and lowered me onto the couch cushion and gave me, as it always was in those days, the best sex of my life. At least until the next time.

In the morning I saw the piles of hoarded things, the speckled mold and the ivy pushing through the windows, the slug trails sparkling on the walls. I tried to take a shower, only to scream and jump away when the spray hit my skin. That water was so cold I get goose bumps now, twelve years later, just thinking about it.

The farm was a lake of mud. In my memory the ivy-eaten caravan was the greenest part of it. It was a stud farm, which meant other farmers brought their mares there to be "serviced" for €100 a pop. It was a horse brothel, basically.

The caravan had been used as storage for years by a couple who were hoarders even in their own house, but when I moved there it felt, to my twenty-four-year-old, far-from-home-at-last eyes, like a cold Irish cave of wonders. I found a ten-year-old espresso machine still sealed in its box my first day there, so we always had good coffee, made with that countertop-fresh milk—and Irish milk was the best, the sweetest and richest, I'd ever tasted. I found a miniature sewing machine and started mending the holes in Tommy's ancient jeans and shirts and riding breeches.

He came home just after dark one day to me listening to Leonard Cohen as I mended a shirt, and laughed and said, "I never thought I'd be this lucky." He took my hand and pulled me up from sewing, lit candles, and slow danced with me to "Suzanne" in the radiant gloom. Close against his broad chest, one of his strong arms around me and his other hand holding mine, I thought that no one could ever feel so loved, so held, so happy and safe and sexy and adoring and adored, as I did in that moment. I remembered a time when I was eleven and listening to an NPR segment about the nature of memory in my mom's car, and I heard that your most-revisited memories are your least accurate, because every time you take them out of your mind's filing system to look at them you change them a little bit, just by the handling. It had snowed the day before, and outside the car it was a brilliantly bright, New England deep winter day, the kind where the white almost blinds you. I looked around at it hard, as hard as I could, and vowed that I would remember it, exactly as it was, forever. That it would be one of the memories I'd have on my deathbed.

I was an intense kid.

That moment with Tommy, slow dancing to Leonard Cohen, I vowed to remember even better than my snowy New Hampshire sunlight. They're tucked together in my mind now, always linked, and I would swear they're two of the clearest memories I have.

But I know my fingerprints are all over them. I take them out to look at all the time.

In many ways I hated the trailer, cold and moldy and leaky as it was, when I was there—but when I look back on it now, I feel sure I loved it for its smallness and anonymity, for how it felt like a shell that could seal around me and my lover and leave us in a blissful private space, where there might not be enough heat to soften butter but we heated each other enough to hardly miss it.

I went for long walks every day through the drenched springtime countryside and rarely saw another human soul. I found a book about foraging and learned the names of the plants I saw—sorrel, primrose, wild garlic, elderflower, meadowsweet, gorse—and their uses. Elders, I read, had been one of the most sacred trees in Celtic times. There was still a folk tradition of asking the tree for permission before you picked its fruit or flowers. I always made sure to ask, and to wait and listen. Once in a while, I thought I heard the tree say no, and I walked away. What would it mean, I thought, to come from a place where even the trees got to choose who touched them?

I brewed tea from fuzzy, stinging nettle leaves for Tommy's bad back, and from the little purple blossoms called self-heal for my anxiety and grief. I took pictures of rainbows until Tommy teased me about it enough that I stopped—you get rainbows almost every day in Ireland, after all. He said if I wanted to be anything other than a tourist, I'd stop noticing them.

I wanted that badly, of course. I wanted to belong to this place, its winding bramble-lined, shining-wet roads and fields. Tommy told me often that he was too poor to give me anything but Ireland. If we married, an idea we were starting to talk about fairly often, then after three years I could apply for naturalization through marriage and become an Irish citizen. If he could give me nothing else, he said, he'd love to give me that.

When I had been there a month or so, Tommy told me he'd seen a kitten hiding up in the hay loft, where the farm dogs couldn't reach it. I hurried to the tiny local shop for cat food. They didn't have any, but I got a tin of salmon and brought it to the barn. Almost as soon as I opened it I heard a keening meow. I set down the tin and stepped back.

A skinny black shadow wobbled down from the rafters. He plunged into the fish right away and leaned into my first cautious stroking of his fur. After he ate, I tucked him into the pocket of the flannel shirt I was wearing and secreted him across the yard, with its nippy rat-hunting terrier and growling sheepdog, and into the trailer.

He made himself at home right away. He never wanted to leave my pocket or, later, my lap. He was the most affectionately doglike cat I'd ever known. He was also loud: Tommy would often snap at him, "Ah, be quiet, you teapot!" when he yowled for more food. It was such a silly insult that I decided the best name for him, after all, was Teapot—especially after Tommy explained it was a slang word that could mean either "loud, annoying person" or "penis." Teapot became a fixture of the trailer, and his rumbling purr and warmth in my lap was a constant comfort as I wrote or read.

After Tommy read an early copy of *Tides*, he told me he loved it, and that he wanted to make sure I always had time and space to write. That was as heady and seductive as anything else he told me. I wrote, and I cuddled with Teapot and knitted and read books I checked out from the tiny local library, and I trailed after Tommy and watched him train horses. He stroked their heads and backs when he greeted them, speaking to them softly, and they pricked their ears and listened.

Sometimes he spoke to them less softly. The first time he invited me to watch a cross-country hunt—a fox-free event, just a preplanned route across fields for galloping and old stone walls for jumping, ending at the local pub where even the horses drank Guinness—I saw him beat a horse that refused a jump for twenty minutes, until its mouth and hide were frothing. Exhausted, finally, it went over. His friend, standing with me, told me not to pay it any mind, that it was just part of the job. I told myself the same thing and tried to forget the cold distance I'd seen in his face as he delivered the beating.

Most of the time, he and the friend explained to me afterward, he didn't have to beat his horses at all. He knew how to use his body to show dominance. He didn't have to hurt them when just the way he stood and moved and spoke showed them he could.

I woke up gasping from a nightmare one night to Tommy's solid body behind me, his rumbling brogue telling me I was all right, that nothing could hurt me.

"What if my dad shows up?" I whispered. "What if he knows I'm going to report him, and he comes out here to stop me?"

He didn't even pause to think. "Sure, Colm and I'd drop him in the bog." For a silent moment he let me imagine my father's body sinking into the peat, turning white and wrinkled as roots. "Plenty of bodies lost there for thousands of years. No one would ever know." His voice was low and menacing and completely serious.

I knew he'd really do it, him and Colm, the man who owned the stud farm. A teenager who worked with them was being bullied at school, and

Colm and Tommy left one night to pay a visit to the bullies' families. Tommy told me the kids changed schools after that. At any rate, the boy never heard from them again.

A man who can be violent, but is gentle with you: What had every story told me I should want but this?

I proposed to Tommy the day I went back to America again: June 4, 2013. *Tides* was being published that same day. I'd been counting down to it ever since I signed my book contract, as the day I'd dreamed of all my life, more than I'd ever dreamed of getting married: the day I would become a published author. I'd dreamed of that day since my mother taught me to read. If I ever did marry, I was going to elope and save my big celebrations for my books.

I had gotten a job teaching writing at a camp for gifted kids in New York for the summer, too, and that was money I'd need when I came back— money we'd both need. It was more than he made training horses for cash under the table or in exchange for a place to stay. He'd decided not to come back to the US with me after all: he said his horses couldn't spare him. I tried to push away the image I'd clung to of his hand in mine while I made the police report. I could do it alone, I told myself, if I could do it at all. But I didn't want to do anything without him anymore.

Tommy and I had talked about getting married a lot over the last few months, shared those dreams of an adventurous international brood of children that he'd care for while I wrote, but neither of us had officially asked the other. Being the one to propose, and on my publication day at that, made me feel more empowered than ever: like I was finally stepping into the life that was meant for me and leaving my frightening childhood behind. What a good story this will make, I thought.

We were lying on the worn brown couch cushions in the trailer, a tea light flickering over his hard golden skin, my head in his lap while he rubbed my shoulders. He was always giving me massages, usually at night and by candlelight—real deep-tissue massages, the likes of which no professional masseuse could touch. He got out knots I never knew were there, using what he'd learned from working out the knots on *racehorses*. When I told him I felt guilty about it, that I didn't want to tire him out when he'd already been doing physical labor all day, he would say that if he could do it for ten hours a day without tiring, "half a slip of a girl" was nothing to him. And all six feet and two hundred pounds of me would shiver deliciously and lean into the rough pressure of his touch.

"I'll miss you too much when you're gone, you know," he said. "You might not come back."

I rolled my eyes, then stopped when I turned and saw the look on his face. "Of course I'll come back," I said.

"I don't know," he said. "I'd want to kill myself if you left me, you know."

"That's not funny."

"Ah, it's not."

I looked up at him, his square jaw and shoulders in the candlelight, his beautiful dark eyes intent on me. "I'll marry you when I come back," I said.

He took a long, slow breath. "All right." He started to smile, and then he leaned down and kissed me. We broke the kiss to laugh, and we didn't stop kissing and laughing for the rest of that sweet night.

I left for America in the morning. I found *Tides* in New Hampshire bookstores and stared at it, astounded. I signed every copy I found.

I was a real writer, at last. And I was engaged. There was one more thing I knew I needed to do to open the portal to true adulthood, to a happily ever after, and step through.

I went back to the one aunt I'd told about my father, the one who'd disbelieved me. She had a young child by then and was planning to bring them for sleepovers at my parents' house that summer. I told her again what I had told her before, and I added Johanna's corroboration, a summary of the years of therapy I'd done in college, and my training as a rape crisis counselor. I told her I understood why it was so hard for her to believe me, and how it had hurt me that she hadn't, but that I was telling her again for her own child's sake.

This time, she did believe. And when I told her I was ready to make a report to the police, she said I could stay at her house while I did.

So I told my parents only that I was going to stay with my aunt for a little while, and that I'd be going back to Ireland after that, I wasn't sure for how long. I took as much as I could from my room without seeming like I was leaving forever: the stacks of journals I'd kept since I was thirteen, a couple precious boxes of favorite books. I swallowed down the nausea I always felt at their touch when they hugged me goodbye: they were off on the trip to Africa, at last, that my father had bartered with me over the year before. When I left my childhood home for the last time, my parents thought they'd see me again in a few months. We hadn't talked frequently in years, but they had always been able to reach me. That day I changed my phone number. I wondered how long it would take them to notice.

Later that day, I walked out of the interview with the police detective feeling untethered to earth. I was so light I thought I'd float away. I didn't know how I'd been walking under so much weight for so long.

In every dream I had, for the rest of my time in the US, I was a ghost. I was glad to be dead in those dreams. No one could touch me.

But I could scream. I screamed in every dream like the *bean sídhe* of the country I was running to—a word that in Irish really just means "woman fairy," but has come to mean the keening shade we know in English as banshee. I screamed all the screams I couldn't in the silent nightmares I'd suffered through all my life before.

When I got to the airport I ran to my gate, the same backpack I'd used when I'd first gone to Ireland bouncing between my shoulder blades. Someday I'd write a memoir about coming to Ireland, I thought, and running through the airport toward Tommy would be my happy ending. I'd call it *Coming of Age*, the story of how a writer travels to Ireland and grows up. Here I was, a published author, getting married, and I never had to let my parents touch me ever again. In a few years I'd be an Irish citizen through marriage, and Tommy and I would have children and travel and all the things we'd dreamed of. I couldn't see anything ahead but sweet brightness and a wide-open world.

I bounded off the bus and into his arms when he picked me up. "I'm never letting you leave again," he murmured into my hair.

I hugged him tighter. "You never have to," I said.

We eloped to Gretna Green a year to the day after we met.

Four

The Love of My Life

AUTUMN 2013–SUMMER 2016

for Sophie

When I look back now at a time when I thought I was happily married, it's like looking through a dark mirror, the queen's cursed mirror in *Snow White*. One of the hardest things about divorce is how it rewrites the story of your life. How did I see the things that happened, and the man I loved, back then? How do I see them now?

The night before we married, Tommy scolded me for not packing his toothbrush for him. I told him I wasn't his mother. He said being married means doing things for each other. I pointed out that he didn't pack my toothbrush, either. He got really close to me, his pointed finger in my face, shouted that he'd better not be marrying someone that selfish, and stormed out of the room.

We still got married. It's not like I wouldn't get married because of a toothbrush.

One thing Tommy gave me that I will always be grateful for was time—time to write, in a place so inexpensive we could scrape by for a year and more with just my book advance, some online tutoring, and his part-time horse training for cash—but most of all, time to heal from leaving my parents. I was finishing *Mechanica* by then, and writing my fictional heroine's liberation from her stepmother and the creation of her found family felt very much like writing my own.

We moved into a white stone cottage in the middle of nowhere, so remote I could cry or scream as loud as I wanted to and only the forest around us would hear me—and I did that. I got the crying or screaming out of me almost every day, while Tommy was with his horses. I went on long walks through the tumbling green fields and trees with only cows and robins and blinking hares for company.

And at the end of each day his strong arms, his dark eyes, his love.

Living so simply felt like another way of telling my wealthy, vanished parents I didn't need them anymore. Our little cottage was more than a hundred years old, with a wood-burning stove set into a hollow that had once been a hearth almost big enough to stand up in. Most mornings I would get up early, struggle to light a fire in the stove that was the cottage's only heat source, and then settle down to try harder to write. The fire required tending every forty-five minutes or less throughout the day, just to generate the small amount of heat that kept my fingers at the keyboard blue-nailed with cold but at least able to move. If I let the fire go out, by the time Tommy finally woke around lunchtime, he'd scold or shout at me. It was the same but worse when he came home from work. It was the job of the person who went out to work to bring home fuel, and the job of the person who stayed at home to keep the fire going. As little money as I made, it was more than he did right from the beginning, but it became my job to keep the fire burning, and over time to keep the laundry washed, and the rooms cleaned, too. His job, besides the horses, was doing dishes. He did them once or twice a week, and otherwise let the piles stink. If I wanted them done more frequently, he told me, I could do them.

I had been registered for the last two years with a housesitting agency, and a few months into our marriage I was sent an opportunity that sounded downright magical: maintaining a small castle in the Loire Valley over the

winter. They kept a few donkeys and horses there, so they needed someone who knew how to look after them, and they were ideally looking for a
couple who both spoke French. I showed Tommy the email as soon as I got
it, lightheaded with excitement. "It couldn't be more perfect for us!" I said.
I handed him my computer.

As he read through the listing, he started to frown. "Don't show me
things like that," he said.

My excited smile started to feel foolish, and I let it fade. "What do you
mean?" I asked.

"I have horses here to break. I can't be doing things like this. I'll never
be able to."

He never made more than a few hundred euros a month from his
horses, and he'd taken breaks from training them often enough to visit me
before we got married. He'd traveled plenty before then, too, I knew—he'd
told me about it. But somehow I didn't feel like I could point those things
out to him. I wouldn't have said back then that it didn't feel safe. I wouldn't
have used those words.

"Don't ask me to do anything like this again, Betsy," he said. "It hurts me
too much that I can't do it."

I wanted to cry, but I knew that would make him angry. I just nodded.

When I look back, I see patterns that I didn't want to see, that I worked not
to see, as they emerged.

Before I'd moved in with him, he promised he'd never smoke in a home
we shared. The first time a room in our house smelled like smoke, I asked
him about it. He told me it was disgusting how I wanted to control him, and
he could do what he liked in his own home.

In that house, when I complained of symptoms related to my birth control pills, he said there was no way in hell he'd get a vasectomy, and I'd better
not ever fucking think of asking him—when I hadn't brought it up in the
first place.

In that house he started pulling away from sex, and said I only wanted
it several times a week because I didn't exercise enough. The hurt that one

comment caused me, as a woman who had always felt so huge and so unfit, in every sense of the word, for male admiration—he knew exactly how much that would cut me, and I saw the sharpness in his eyes as he said it and watched me curl up. After that, he held sex over me, how much I wanted him. I felt too big and uncouth and ashamed to ask for it, so that when it happened, I came to feel as grateful as a mortal receiving a divine visitation. Sex became something he would give me in the wake of making me feel awful, to make me believe I was worthy and loved again.

I did leave him from that house. Once. He hadn't spoken to me for three days, since we'd had an argument—what I then thought of as an argument. When I finally tried to approach him in the kitchen while he made tea, reached out a hand to him carefully, hoping he would take it and smile in forgiveness—he squared his shoulders, as if to shake me off before I even touched him. And then his own hand shot out and his finger went into my ribs, hard enough that I knew it would bruise.

I went to a hostel in the Connemara wilderness. I wrote in my journal a lot in that time: how much I missed him, but for the sake of our marriage I knew I needed to show him he couldn't just treat me like I wasn't there.

A few days in, he apologized. I thought I'd shown him I could be even more stubborn than he was. I thought I'd shown him my strength.

He's mean sometimes, but he's not abusive or anything like that, I insisted in my journals. *Just . . . mean.*

I didn't write about the bruises. Poking wasn't hitting, of course. Nothing like it. Enough unlike it that it seemed childish even to notice it at all.

When I learned from the domestic violence center five years later that *poking* is absolutely included in the definition of physical abuse, enough so that you can be arrested and charged for it, it still felt absurd. Or I really, really wanted it to feel absurd. It was something he did, and something I brushed off, a lot.

Tommy was careful to stay on the side of some line, some line of things that he felt entitled to do. On the other side of that line, I think, was what his father had done to his mother. On the other side of my own line was my father, too. And Tommy wasn't like *that*. Not at all.

And yet: "Isn't it strange," he observed to me one day, quietly. He was smoking one of the inside cigarettes I'd come to feel too worn-down to argue with him about.

"What?" I asked.

"I'm a lot older than you are. I get angry sometimes, I scare you sometimes, even though I don't mean to. I just think it's a bit strange, how you married someone a small bit like your father after all."

I left him from that house once, but I came back a week later. I missed him, and missed our love story too much. What would have been the point of everything I had done, everything I had run from, all I had sacrificed, if I was wrong about him?

Every few months something would happen that I'd feel the need to call my friends about, to ask if it was normal. Back then I called it *having a big fight*, even though a fight implies an equality that was never there. Really it was him shouting at me, using his strength and body language to intimidate me, while I cried and shook, until he made it clear he'd do something worse if he stayed in the room, and stormed out. After all, we'd talked about the families we'd come from, and we had both agreed that if he ever hit me, I'd leave.

After a fight, he'd give me the silent treatment until I begged him to make peace. He loved it when I was desperate to earn his love. And I always was.

My friends, especially the older ones who'd been married more than a decade, told me this was all part of figuring out how to be married. The work of marriage for men, they said, is often learning how not to be an asshole, and the work of marriage for women is helping them, being patient while they learn.

My husband is the love of my life. I wrote that story, over and over, as the evidence of his unkindnesses accumulated.

Tommy noticed a knot in my right shoulder when we first met. He said it must have been there for years, a symptom of my chronic stress as a student and writer, or maybe even of my family trauma. It was strange, I thought, how I'd never noticed that pain was there until he pointed it out and started trying to help me cure it. But after we met, the pain seemed to get worse, not better, no matter how many massages he gave me, his touch so addictive for the way it temporarily soothed, even though he often pushed down so hard he had to hold me still to keep me from pulling away.

Finally, the knot got so bad that it distracted me from working. I felt like I was walking crooked, like a lame horse. When things were going well between us, he'd work on it for me every night. When they weren't, he didn't touch me at all, except for those sharp, bruising pokes.

"You should see John about it," he started to say. I'd always flush and shake my head. John was a folk healer, a man who worked as a butcher most of the time, but who had set up shop behind a pub once a week where, with the help of a bent piece of wire that he used like a divining rod, he cured horses, dogs, and people of their pains. There are still many people like him in Ireland, people with "the cure" who can heal different ailments. They are the seventh sons of seventh sons, babies born or baptized on particularly sacred days, or the custodians of holy wells or certain scraps of cloth that have been known to heal the sick for centuries.

It wasn't that I didn't believe John could help me. In our first months together, Tommy had brought a horse to him and I'd gone along, curious about the magical healer to whom he and the other gruff farmers I'd met so practically referred. The horse had colic, which Tommy told me was a death sentence—a very wealthy person with a very expensive horse might pay for abdominal surgery and its intensive aftercare, but most people where we lived were farmers who barely got by and kept one or two horses in the hope they might win a bit of money in a small race someday. With colic, this horse would never be worth the investment. It would die.

But Tommy said he'd bring the horse to John first, and I went along to see what would happen. We drove to a pub half an hour away, on a warm weekday afternoon, and joined a line of maybe a dozen patient men and horses. At the front of the line stood a middle-aged man who looked no different from any of the others, holding a bent piece of wire. The air was full of the good and bad smells of horses, but the gentle watery breeze that seemed like it always blew in east Galway kept either from getting too strong.

The next pair in line walked up, the man leading a horse with a bad limp. He and John chatted for a moment—for quite a few long moments, in fact, a good long chat being the crucial opening ceremony for any inter-action in rural Ireland—and then John held up a gentle fist for the horse to smell. (Tommy had taught me never to approach a horse, or any hoofed animal, with an open hand. They will read fingers as claws and see you as a predator. For some, he said, a fist means family.)

The horse sniffed and blew on John's fingers, and he blew back into its nostrils, having a different kind of chat. After a moment he nodded, moved to the horse's bad leg, and laid his hands on it. Finally he pulled back, shak-ing his hands as if to get mud off.

The horse's neck straightened. It placed its hoof gingerly down on the ground. Its owner made a quiet chucking sound, and it began to walk with no trace of a limp.

"Thank you, John," the man said, and led his horse to its trailer.

"You're staring," Tommy said.

"How could I not?"

"Aye, I know. But don't."

When it was our turn at the front of the line, Tommy introduced me to John and we talked for a few minutes about trivial things. I was learning the Irish chat rituals, too: one of the best things Tommy had told me was that the point of small talk in Ireland was not what you said, but just indicating to the other person that you thought they were worth talking to. Reframing it that way took all the pressure off my lifetime of social awkwardness. I was happy to talk about the weather, and to hear about it, when what we both were really saying was: *I see you and you're worthy of my attention.* Having a chat is just the longer, Irish version of the greeting I learned in yoga classes: namaste. *The sacred in me sees and honors the sacred in you.*

Of course, when Tommy taught me to understand conversation that way, it made his silent treatments that much more cruel, too.

So, I talked about nothing important with John, for only a few minutes. And yet, when he moved his attention from us to Tommy's horse, I found myself almost in tears.

For this horse, he took up his bent piece of wire. He ran it over the horse's belly and flanks, a few inches away from the skin, until it suddenly jumped in his hands. I thought of water-divining rods and electromagnetic fields. John placed his hand on the animal, as gently as he had with the limping horse, and we watched it relax under his touch, heard its frothy exhale as pain left its body.

Tommy brought that horse back to its owner colic-free. Death sentence gone.

"The thing is, it's not like the horses could be in on a scam," I said to him on the way home, wet patchwork fields unrolling past either side of the car. "The horses aren't pretending to limp or have colic. If it was people getting magically cured, I could think it was a racket, but . . . "

"Aye," Tommy said. "I saw the look in your eyes after he spoke to you too. The first time I met him it was just like that for me. It was the closest I've come to the feeling of meeting a saint."

I remembered the open ache I'd started to feel my heart becoming when he'd talked to me, when he'd turned away, even though he hadn't said anything in particular. "Yes. It was like he could see all the way inside me. I've never felt that from somebody before. And he doesn't even take money, you said!"

"Well, now, sometimes he does. But often he doesn't, if he likes you. You can tell he thinks someone's sound if he won't take payment from him. And I train horses for him sometimes, and some of the lads will bring him produce, or silage for his own animals. Payment in kind."

So when, a year or so later, Tommy suggested I go to John for the pain in my shoulder, I was scared. This person who brought some deep ache in my heart to the surface with just a few minutes of small talk—this man who could feel what's inside you and draw the pain up and out with a simple touch—what if he saw the darkness in me that I still feared was there? Despite having freed myself from my parents, despite the affirmation I'd gotten from Johanna, and from other people who later reached out to tell me I was right about my dad, to tell me about their own experiences with him—the fear that I was still a bad person somewhere deep within me remained. I had betrayed my first family, and sometimes I made Tommy so angry, without even knowing what I'd done, that I could watch him barely keep himself from hitting me. What if John saw that badness? What if he drew it out?

But eventually the pain in my shoulder won out, so I agreed to go.

I felt quite like a horse the day I waited in the line of animals and their men for John to heal me. We'd recently gotten two dairy goats (which would come with more backstory if I lived anywhere but rural Ireland, but it does in fact suffice to say that we'd casually acquired two goats) and I'd brought a box of goat's milk soap, cheese, and caramel, since I was trying my hand at all those things, in an effort to make the payment in kind that Tommy had mentioned. I also brought money, although I hadn't told Tommy that, tucked into my pocket just in case John saw that inner badness and asked for cash payment.

Tommy introduced me to John again and explained why I'd come. I'd told Tommy when we'd first met how shy I often felt, and he was always happy to take over and speak on my behalf. For all I'd learned about the sacrament of small talk, I was grateful for that, too.

John listened and nodded, watching me instead of looking at Tommy. Oh god, I thought, it was happening already.

When Tommy was done, John smiled and waved me closer to him, out of the line. "Is it all right if I touch you?" he asked.

That was why I'd come, I thought, but his asking made me relax. I nodded and smiled. He stepped back, but not far enough to leave my line of sight, then raised his hand and showed it to me before gently lifting my arm. I felt the ever-present tightness and pain intensify.

"Right," he said quietly. "Did you ever have an injury to this arm?"

"Um, not that I remember." Tommy had told me on the way there that he'd once seen John ask a man that question about his leg. He'd said no, but his mother had later told him that he'd broken that leg as a baby climbing out of his cot. The man had no memory of it, but John could tell with a touch.

I certainly had old injuries that were hard to remember. I wondered how many of them John could feel.

His touch felt kind. I closed my eyes and tried to figure out if I would call it magic.

He directed me to stand on an old plastic produce crate so that my shoulder would be at his eye level. He stood behind me and placed his hand flat on my back. Then he took his hand away, and—I promise—I felt him pull something out of me. I was so startled my breath caught.

He reminded me to keep breathing and put his hand on my back again. "Now lean back, slowly," he said.

I did, feeling the support of his hand against my back, until I'd leaned back so much that I had to step back off the crate. Then I was standing on the ground, his hand was gone, and so was the pain. Just . . . gone. Both my shoulders felt the same.

"Now, this is a two-part cure," he said. He looked over at Tommy, then back at me. "You need to rest that shoulder for at least a week. Don't do any housework at all. All right?"

I agreed, thanking him profusely. It turned out he wouldn't take payment, but I pressed the box of goat's cheese and soap and caramel into his hands, and he finally took it.

"Looks like your wife has many talents," he told Tommy.

"She's a laying hen," Tommy replied with a grin: he told me the same thing often, when I was writing or tutoring online. It meant I was a woman who could bring money into the house.

"Hmm," said John. And with a final look at me: "Remember, a whole week."

For a few days it was fine. On the third or fourth, Tommy shouted about my asking him to do the housework John had told me not to do, and he slammed through several doors and drove away. I was left shaking from the effort of staying upright through another fight, and I wanted to find something to do that would keep me from just sitting down and sniveling in a way I knew he'd think was pathetic. (I always felt like he was watching me, like I should act in a way his gaze would approve of, even when he was gone.)

I decided to clean the bathroom so neither of us would be angry about it anymore. It was a small job, I figured, and I'd be careful, but as I got on my knees to wipe the shower floor, I felt a deep twinge in my shoulder and with a rush, all the old pain and tightness came back.

I didn't tell Tommy what had happened at first. When he noticed me favoring the shoulder again a few days later, he shouted me down again for disobeying John.

I was too ashamed to go back and ask John for another cure after that. Tommy was right. I hadn't listened.

I started noting in my journal the things we talked about, and the things we did, in case he later accused me of not doing them or told me he'd said or done things differently than he had. But then, when those discrepancies filled my journals so much that I didn't like what they were starting to imply, I stopped.

After one of the things I called fights, when he hadn't spoken to me for days, I wrote that I knew I was getting older because I was starting to understand how people might become worn-out enough from life that death doesn't seem so scary anymore, that it seems like rest. I was twenty-six.

It was only about getting older, of course. My husband, I adored.

Five

The Selkie's Child

SUMMER 2016–WINTER 2018

for Martha

When we'd been married nearly three years, longing for a child overwhelmed me. We'd always wanted children—three of them, with five-year age gaps, plus foster kids. Tommy had told me right when we met that he wanted to do that someday, to give boys in particular a healthier example of masculinity than what he'd grown up with—and I had swooned at that.

Mechanica came out in 2015 and did well. It received good reviews and places on best-of-the-year lists, and even spent a week as a *New York Times* bestseller. Tommy told everyone we met that week just how much of a laying hen I was—and even though it didn't come with the big check we'd imagined it would, and that book wouldn't clear its $12,500 advance that year at all, it felt like a sign that I'd be able to support a family with my work as a writer, at least combined with the online tutoring and editing I was still doing.

I kept applying for every teaching and editing job I saw in Ireland, but most were too far away from the part of east Galway where Tommy knew farmers whose horses he could train. He'd told me when we were dating that, like me, he could work from anywhere training horses for cash, but after we were married, it seemed that he wasn't willing to go anywhere but where he already was.

My publisher paid me another advance, for a sequel to *Mechanica*, titled *Venturess*, and Tommy and I agreed that it might be a good time to start a family when I finished that book. By the time I delivered it to my publisher, my yearning for a child had grown so strong that I couldn't bear to keep swallowing my pill each morning.

We agreed to stop using birth control. I got pregnant the first month we tried.

I'd gotten a multipack of cheap pregnancy tests from the chemist, and I started testing days before they were supposed to work. I felt certain I could sense the beginning of something new inside myself, and I was talking to my baby as I went on my walks and did my chores, as I foraged wild strawberries at the side of the road, long before I saw those double lines.

I was so happy when I told Tommy. I wasn't expecting to watch his face pale with something like dread. He asked me, several times, if I was sure I was ready. Abortion was illegal in Ireland, but he could get us a ferry to England, he said, it wasn't a problem.

"No," I said, baffled. "I want this baby."

"All right," he said. "Then I do, too."

I didn't understand why we needed to have that conversation at all. When we'd agreed to get married, he'd said he only ever wanted to work part-time training horses, so he could spend the rest of the time minding his wife and children—the lifestyle I'd so radiantly described to my grandmother when I told her about him. But after he found out I was pregnant, he took the first full-time job he'd had since long before I'd known him, managing a horse yard an hour away, six days a week. I was suddenly in the middle of nowhere, alone with my growing belly from eight in the morning until seven at night. If I didn't have dinner ready when he got home, sometimes he'd laugh and say it didn't matter. Sometimes he wouldn't speak to me until the next day's dinner. Sometimes he'd shout at me about how I must care more about writing than my family. During that time I was mostly working on drafting a retelling of Robin Hood with a love interest I'd based on Tommy. That book was called *The Forest Queen*, and I dedicated it to our baby. When the book distracted me from housework, he said I'd better stop bullshitting and get my act together if I wanted to be a good mother.

He was anxious about fatherhood, I felt. The stories he told suggested that they'd been so poor he often didn't have food or heating as a child. I told myself he was breaking cycles by just yelling instead of hitting me, and by trying to work this job that he so suddenly felt he needed to work. He didn't want our child to be hungry or cold the way he had been—and, I started to think even then, he feared his child growing up in a house with an angry father.

My heart ached for him so hard when I thought of the fear I believed he carried. I told myself I needed to remember that fear, hold it for him, love him through it, no matter how much he sometimes scared me.

Our son Robin was born at three o'clock precisely on Good Friday afternoon. That was good luck, Tommy learned from a Belfast woman in the smoking area outside while he took a break from my labor. Her grandchild was being born the same day, and she told him that all Good Friday babies are lucky, but especially those born close to three p.m., the time of day that Jesus is meant to have died on the cross. And if a Good Friday baby is baptized on Easter Sunday, they will have "the touch"—magical healing powers.

"Well, we can't pass that up," I told Tommy as I lay in the hospital bed, nursing Robin, feeling radiant with the power of what I had just done and astounded by the child in my arms, so much like the man I loved and—it's true that this surprised me—so much like me, too.

Since we were both adamantly lapsed Christians, Tommy suggested a Celtic pagan baptism for the following Easter, on Inis Mór, where we met, and where we'd later celebrated our first anniversary with a handfasting ceremony.

Our first day home from the hospital, Tommy got out a *Twin Peaks* DVD he wanted us to watch together. A few minutes into the pilot, Robin wanted to nurse, and after nursing it took me a few minutes to settle him back into the moses basket we'd placed next to the bed. I took another minute, after he was settled, just to look at him, his little curling sleepy fists, his pouting baby mouth, his miracle eyelashes.

"Why should I bother if you won't even fucking pay attention?" Tommy's voice came through my reverie. He turned off the TV and threw the remote on the floor. "You don't care at all, do you?" And he stormed out. When I offered to watch it again with him the next day, he said he'd only do it if I paid attention, and when I said I would still need to mind, you know, the baby, he poked me hard and told me not to bother.

That night, Robin woke several times. Tommy was convinced he was too cold and told me I'd better hold him all night so he didn't get hypothermia. I put on a movie of my choice then, one neither of us had seen: *It Happened One Night*. "Sure I know the plot of this one," Tommy said. "He's taming her. I thought you were above that kind of shite." He grumbled over it for a while and eventually fell asleep. I stayed awake, afraid to put Robin down in case Tommy was right and he was too cold, but even more afraid of what would happen if I did, and then Tommy woke up and saw me sleeping.

There is a scene in that film where everyone on a bus sings "The Daring Young Man on the Flying Trapeze." I started singing along, softly, as I held Robin. At once it became his song, the one I knew I'd sing him to sleep with for years to come.

I quickly learned not to sing it in front of Tommy, though. I've never been able to carry a tune, and Tommy said he didn't want me to ruin the baby's musical ear. So after that first week, I only sang to him when we were alone.

Robin was a sweet and happy baby, but he had severe reflux and didn't sleep through the night for years. Sleep deprivation quickly turned me into a haggard ghost. When I asked Tommy to help with the baby early one morning, he picked Robin up quickly and changed his diaper while he started to cry, then pushed him into my arms so hard I felt as if I'd been shoved. "I have to fucking work today," he said, and slammed out of the room.

I was working again, too, by then, though neither of us mentioned that.

I'd finally gotten a part-time job teaching creative writing at the local university—they'd offered me the class two weeks after I found out I was pregnant. I started the semester by talking about classical story structure. I'd taught the same unit on it in graduate school and summer teaching programs for years: I spoke lovingly of how I started writing fairy tale retellings as a college student because my own teachers told me I was better at description than plot, and I had used these ancient, durable tales as training wheels to work past my own shortcomings.

When I'd run back to Ireland and into Tommy's arms after reporting my dad, I'd thought I had my happy ending. I thought my story, the story I'd tell Robin and our other children someday about what led me to them, was over.

Living in my happily ever after, Cinderella was on my mind even after I finished *Mechanica*. There is an important detail in that story that is often missed when we say "Cinderella story" and mean "rags-to-riches": what's missing is her beginning.

Before the cinders and stepsisters, Ella is the happy child of two kind, wealthy parents, who are, in many versions of the story, members of the aristocracy, or at least of the upper class. After her mother dies, her father marries a woman who is often depicted as a commoner or *nouveau riche*. Her stepmother's cardinal sin is not just that she is mistreating a fellow human being or a member of their family—she's placing herself above someone who was born superior to her. (No one worries about the other servants sleeping in the ashes.)

Similarly, at the ball, what the prince sees in Cinderella is not just beauty, or even goodness, but innate nobility. Marrying him does not raise her to new heights: it reaffirms her divine right.

The family I was born into was not kind, but they were wealthy. I was still reaping the benefits of that wealth, especially the education it had paid for and the doors my degrees now opened for me.

Tommy made a point to remind me often of all the opportunities I'd had that he had not. I hadn't been able to bear even the thought of my parents' eyes on a picture of my pregnant belly. But I could afford to have a baby in the first place, to have the life I had at all, because of gifts they'd long since given me.

I always made sure to teach that part of Cinderella, and to remember it: to remind myself, as Tommy did, that I was more privileged than special.

I taught fairy tales and then went home to what felt like a choice between silence and rage. When I woke up in the middle of the night with Robin yet again and stared into the darkness, unsure of whether I resented my husband for not waking up or feared that waking, I started to wonder if I knew what kind of story I was telling at all.

Whenever I voiced any concern about Tommy's behavior, he insisted that I had postpartum anxiety. I finally brought it up with my doctor—a happily married mother of six—and she said that, actually, it sounded like we needed marriage counseling. My husband screamed at me for asking him to go, but eventually agreed.

In our first joint session with the free Catholic Marriage Care Service, after having had private sessions with both of us, the counselor asked us to describe our last argument.

"I told a friend who was visiting that we were planning to buy our house," I said.

"No one needs to know that shite," Tommy said. "We're getting a deal, and we don't need anyone hearing about it."

"After our friend drove away, Tommy shouted at me that I was a fucking idiot." I felt like a snitch even saying that, like a little kid who shouldn't get their feelings hurt so easily. I felt like I used to feel when my dad yelled at me and then got angrier when I cried.

"I'll stop you right there," the marriage counselor said. "I cannot imagine"—she put her hand over her heart—"speaking to my spouse, the person I promised to honor and cherish, that way." She took a moment to look in both of our eyes, this woman with her artfully knotted silk scarf, her elegant gray updo. "What you are describing to me is not fighting. It is severe emotional abuse."

My skin prickled. I felt like a horror movie heroine when she realizes the call is coming from inside the house.

Tommy looked down at his hands. I watched him, longing, begging for him to look back at me, to give me some scrap of assurance that he was as horrified as I was by this diagnosis. I wanted him to reaffirm what we shared, the love on which I had staked my whole life. And now our son's life, too.

Such a huge part of my marriage was tied up in my escape from my abusive family. How could I have won that freedom only to stumble into another trap? I had trained as a rape crisis counselor and my husband as a social worker, and we both talked all the time about building a healthier family than the ones we came from.

How could I deserve a better family, if I hadn't been able to make one?

But I couldn't deny what the counselor was saying.

Tommy finally looked up. Not at me, not at the counselor. He stared into the middle distance for a moment, and I thought I could see him thinking quickly, a thousand thoughts passing behind the eyes I loved so much.

He took a deep, unsteady breath and squared his broad shoulders. "Right," he said. "How do we fix it?"

She referred Tommy to an abuser rehabilitation program called MOVE, and told me to get in touch with COPE, the local domestic violence center.

Those two acronyms still sound like commands: what he had to do next, and what I did. Change, and endure.

There is an idea that shows up over and over in fairy tales and romance novels, and in noir detective stories and action movies, too: that the love of a good woman can change a violent man. I write feminist stories for a living, but when I started going to an abused women's shelter, it was because I thought part of my job as a good wife was helping my husband figure out how not to hurt me. If I could love him well enough, I thought, he would get better.

When I started telling other people what was happening in my marriage, I could feel some of them thinking it, too.

It is hard to know that my father didn't love me well, and neither did my husband—and then to still believe I am worth loving anyway. I am worth loving even if my love doesn't make men stop hurting me. Even if my kiss won't turn a beast into a prince.

Years later, long after I learned to recognize it, I still get that feeling from married women sometimes: that they believe if I'd loved my husband as well as they love theirs, he wouldn't have hurt me, and he wouldn't want to keep hurting me now.

One January night, Tommy screamed at me in front of our baby while we drove home from the grocery store. Robin was nine months old. It was the *in front of our baby*, again, after all we'd tried to work through, that kept catching at me with its claws, impossible to ignore.

When we got home, I hid upstairs with the baby. The next day I told him he needed to spend a night somewhere else to cool down, that it wasn't okay for him to expose Robin to that kind of behavior. I asked my friends Irene and Jacinta to come over while I told him this over text, because I was worried about what he would do when he came back if they weren't there. I'd never told him not to come home before.

He wrote back that he shouldn't have married me, that he should have always known how horrible I am. He said he was done.

January is the Irish month that feels farthest from the land of the living. The days are lengthening in the wake of the solstice, but you can't yet tell. It's dark until nine in the morning.

After Tommy left that January, I stopped eating. For weeks I choked down one piece of dry toast a day so I wouldn't faint while caring for my baby, so my milk wouldn't dry up. I've always loved to eat, but after Tommy left, I hated even the taste of that plain toast. I lost two dress sizes in a month. People told me I looked great, when truly I was strained and haggard.

In fact, there is only one meal I remember eating with pleasure that whole winter. My friend Anna, who was living in Vermont and trying to scrap her way into journalism, flew out to see me just days after Tommy left the house: a last-minute transatlantic flight bought with her junior reporter pennies. A passionate vegan, Anna made me fried potatoes with cheese and bacon, and she held my baby and watched *Golden Girls* with him on her lap while I ate, then while I slept.

What does it mean to honor a commitment? To love someone for better or for worse, in sickness and in health, until death do you part?

Ask my friends. They're the ones who know.

I scrubbed the house that winter like I'd never done before, just to feel like I had some kind of power. I sustained myself on a brittle, flinching determination to prove I could do it all alone. I stacked the pile of turf outside into a perfect Jenga tower. I washed the floors every day. I forced myself to eat my toast even when it made me want to vomit. I danced to Queen's "Don't Stop Me Now" with Robin every night, smiled at him every time he woke up, even when I had no smiles for myself or anyone else, told him I loved him and I was so lucky to be his mommy when I couldn't bear to speak a word to anyone else all day.

When I was pregnant, I'd read so much about birthing styles, parenting styles, breastfeeding, homemade baby food. As that winter passed, my standards got a lot lower. When I put Robin to bed for the night, I decided, I would only ask myself two questions. Have I shown him I love him today? And: Have I kept him alive?

If so, I had succeeded. I unsubscribed from the baby development email lists, and I focused on love and survival.

Tommy kept texting me vague, cryptic condemnations that were violent in the ways they profoundly confused me, kept me longing and hopeless at once.

I would bring them to Saoirse, my support person at COPE, the domestic violence center in Galway City. Far from the sentimental hippie I'd imagined when the marriage counselor referred me to her, Saoirse felt more punk-rock with her short-cropped silver hair, Doc Martens, and clipped, no-nonsense Dublin accent. Saoirse seemed to have little interest in sentiment of any kind, in fact. She never pushed me to leave Tommy—which had been my other fear about going to COPE—and she listened respectfully when I spoke of how much I loved him, but she also always steered the conversation back to what I needed, or what my baby did. I thought I'd come to her to help Tommy, but she made it clear from day one that what she was most interested in was helping me.

I thought the confusing, painful texts Tommy kept sending could be a key to understanding him, to helping him get better. But Saoirse kept asking me if I really needed to read them all, if I needed to keep letting those lashing words into my heart.

When I'd asked Tommy to leave for that one night, he'd said he wouldn't be back and told me to pack a bag with his things that he could pick up the next day. I did it—I even put some money in the bag, in case he needed it. He had never carried a wallet or keys or bothered to learn our bank information. I think it helped him picture himself as a cowboy, a rogue, a wild rover. Later, Saoirse would say I should thank my lucky stars for it, but that day, it just made me worry about how he'd get by.

I also packed the thick socks I'd knitted him for Christmas. I wanted him to know that I still cared, that it wasn't over in my heart, that I would always love him and want him to be warm.

A few days later he asked how long I was going to drag it out before I took him back, because the B&B where he was staying was getting expensive. I asked if he agreed that he couldn't behave like he had around Robin. He said he guessed I wasn't ready for an adult conversation yet.

It was a week before he asked about Robin at all. How's my boy? the text finally came.

Robin had started laughing in his sleep again three nights after Tommy left. It had taken that sound returning for me to realize it had stopped.

I told Tommy that. I thought he ought to feel at least a little shame.

Eventually, one session, Saoirse looked me in the eye and held out her hand, stop. "I don't need to see these texts," she said. And while it took many more months, I would remember that motion, that simple, gentle raising of the hand, when I finally gave myself permission to block his number, too.

The same day Saoirse held up her hand, Tommy used the word "divorce" for the first time. (Until then, he'd vacillated constantly between wanting me back and angrily rejecting me again, no matter what I said or did not say in response.) I thought of the truism about never cutting your hair off or getting divorced in your baby's first year. Robin was nine months old when Tommy left. I'd always thought I was too big for short hair, but what did I care who thought I was beautiful now? Or who thought I had made bad decisions? I gave myself a rough pixie cut with my desk scissors, planning to pick up electric clippers at the chemist in the morning.

My hair was thick and long, dark and straight past my shoulders, and the weight that vanished as I lopped it away surprised me, the rush of blood tingling in my scalp. If you've ever worn a tight ponytail all day and then taken it out, you know how *good* that feeling is, that feeling of the top of your head waking up, so good it almost hurts. Cutting off the weight of my long hair was like that times a thousand.

It turned out I loved the way it looked. Just my face, with no long hair to hide behind.

I looked at myself in the mirror and thought that maybe I was making good decisions after all.

Six

Baptism

SPRING 2018

for Kathrin

Robin's baptism was approaching, and Tommy and I had been living apart for months. He'd refused to say whether he'd be there on the day, although I'd asked him several times.

"I don't want to play happy families," he said. "I don't want to fucking lie to people."

There would only be a few of our closest friends there, I told him. They would understand. And anyway, we wouldn't be pretending anything that wasn't true. We'd be Robin's parents, there to celebrate him. That would always be true, wouldn't it?

We had asked Johanna to be Robin's godmother when she had come to visit us shortly after his birth, bringing beautiful handmade baby clothes from her mother and a doll made from traditional fabrics in Kenya, where she had relocated for work.

When Johanna came back a few days before the baptism, I had to explain what had happened. She was furious with Tommy, in a way that I still loved him too much to allow myself to be. Other women's clear-sightedness, other women's anger, have saved my life time and time again, when I was too blind and bogged down by the conditioning of endless love and forgiveness to feel them myself. And yet, she still let me love him, listened to me when I talked about hope and redemption, didn't try to tamp down the light that still glowed in my eyes and heart for him.

Other women's grace: that has saved me too.

I was telling myself more stories about Tommy than perhaps I ever had. More even than when I was back in America with my parents, looking east to Ireland and my beautiful horse trainer as an escape. A week after he left me in January, he texted that he'd heard a song on the radio that made him think of me: Elbow's "Kindling (Fickle Flame)." I listened to the lovely abstraction of its lyrics endlessly, obsessively, and in my next meeting with Saoirse I began to tell her how I thought the song was a coded message—that he was trying to tell me he had a secret reason for leaving, a reason he couldn't tell me, and that his being so increasingly horrible after Robin's birth and then leaving us was actually an elaborate ploy to keep us safe. He'd told me he had friends in the IRA, there was a frightening-looking man who had come to the door looking for him a few weeks after he left, saying it was about money . . .

The conspiracy theory fell apart as I spoke the words aloud. Saoirse only listened, gently but without undue sentiment, as she always did.

"I know it sounds stupid," I said. "I know I'm being stupid." (That was a word Tommy often used for me. I hadn't yet noticed the habit I'd made of using it on myself.)

Saoirse leaned forward in her chair and glared at me. "Betsy." My name was a full sentence of admonishment. "You're not being stupid. It makes complete sense that you would want to believe that about someone you love."

When we drove to the ferry port in Ros an Mhíl for the baptism, it was an aquamarine April day, clear and salty-bright, and I was sure I'd see him there. He would be waiting for the ship that would take us to the island where we'd met, and where we were going to bless our baby and our family. It would be such a good moment, such a good story, I thought. He loved us. He would want to be there.

But the sidewalk down to the dock was a white line. He hadn't come.

On the boat my storytelling took over again, and I had visions of him on the Inis Mór pier as the ferry pulled in. Of course he wasn't in Ros an Mhíl, I told myself—he was on the island already, waiting for us, for me and for Robin, strapped so sweetly to my chest, as close to me as my own heart. He wanted me to long for him all the more, for the reunion to be all the sweeter, all the more tearful and loving: a baptism of our family anew, into a future of gentleness and care. A chance we were still living in a love story after all.

I longed for Tommy more fiercely on that ferry ride than I ever had, I think. If he had been there, maybe this story would be very different.

But the sunny pier was empty.

Johanna took my hand and brought us to the B&B she'd booked. And then she played with Robin on the floor by the beds, so that I could shower alone, and cry.

Still, I didn't stop waiting for Tommy. I thought he'd be in the bar when I went down to meet my friends who'd arrived from America for the ceremony. I thought he'd be on the late ferry, then on the early one the next morning. I dreamed, both waking and asleep, of our meeting on the pier. Just like we'd done before, when I hadn't believed he'd come back for me until he did.

Johanna agreed with me that he might come, although I don't know if she was just being kind. "What kind of father refuses to be there for his son because he's angry at his son's mother?" she asked.

I remembered looking at Saoirse, my eyes full of unbelieving tears, in our first session after Tommy told me he wasn't coming home, asking: "What kind of person leaves a nine-month-old baby?"

But Saoirse had none of my sentimental shock. "Lots of people," she said dryly. "Unfortunately, Betsy, people do that every day."

Her no-nonsense approach to that trauma, that heartbreak, thankfully snapped me out of worrying about how or why it had happened, and focused me on what to do about it now that it had.

At breakfast at the B&B the next morning, Robin, as always, beamed his huge baby smile at every person he met, gobbled brown bread with both hands and charmed the waitress into giving him two whole fresh-baked loaves, wrapped in tinfoil, to take home. All the while I thought surely Tommy would show up at any moment. When we took the mini bus with my friends, only my friends, the only people who had showed up, to the sacred well that would be the ceremony site, I thought at last that he might be there, waiting by that blessing water.

He wasn't, he wasn't, he wasn't.

But my baby's warmth was real and heavy in the carrier on my chest, his steady little heartbeat pressed to mine, and his fists gripped my clothes as his rich brown eyes, exactly halfway between the color of his father's and mine, looked up at me as if I were the whole world. Johanna's hand holding mine was strong and steady, too, still the big sister, determined to help me stand straight.

The blessing was beautiful. Dara Molloy, a Celtic monk who had converted from his Catholic priesthood to do this work, and who was a father of four himself, blessed Robin with the four elements, while his wife took photos and his teenage daughter played the harp. Johanna read from *Oh, the Places You'll Go!* Robin nursed through half the ceremony, squealed and giggled through the other half. When we all gathered for the last group photo, Robin sighed contentedly and laid his downy head against my collarbone. Friends surrounded me on every side, and I felt for the first time like no one was missing at all.

The ferry ride home was rough, and Johanna, in her seat next to me in the boat's dank belly, turned increasingly pale and green. I noticed Robin begin to watch her from his place in the baby carrier on my chest. After a few minutes, he reached out and placed his tiny, chubby hand over her heart.

Johanna's seasickness left her at once.

The baptism did what I longed for it to do. Our family was blessed and made anew—just without Tommy. I wasn't looking for him on the pier when we landed back on the mainland. I was holding Johanna's hand and looking at my baby.

I am your only parent, I thought, and he smiled up at me as if in answer and smeared a sloppy baby kiss across my shirt. *Maybe I really can be all the things that means.*

If Tommy had been there, maybe we could have healed with him. Instead, we started to heal around the hole left in his absence.

Magic powers, maybe, after all.

Saoirse always made sure to check in with me before holidays or important dates: our anniversary, Christmas, Valentine's Day. She said abusers often find ways to ruin special days. "We both make a point of not doing much for things like that," I'd always said, waving her off. I still didn't like to think of Tommy as an Abuser. I still saw him as someone I loved who was struggling, and it was my duty, in loving him, to understand that struggle. "We both grew up in families that were really performative about Christmas, and we think all that stuff is consumerist anyway."

I really was young and in love enough to believe we were reinventing the world. That no one had ever tried to live differently before. How often that trying fails.

"All right, well, any dates that are important to you, then," Saoirse said dryly.

The baptism had been the first. Saoirse was utterly unsurprised that he didn't come, and that he'd left me hanging as to whether he would or not. "That seems much more cruel than just outright refusing to go," she told me. "My heart aches to think of you looking for him from that boat." She was good at that, at articulating feelings that I couldn't give myself permission to feel, or to admit to feeling.

That made me want to defend him, of course. He was hurting, too.

"It's like we're both soldiers behind enemy lines," I said. "I can't abandon him. Not when we're both wounded in the same way." The enemy lines were our parents, our childhoods.

"But you have a baby," Saoirse said, more gently than usual. "And he's hurting you too."

•   •   •

Robin's birthday was our next important date. As it approached, I had no word from Tommy about it at all, and Saoirse cautioned me not to wait for one. "At some point you have to stop waiting for him," she said. "You have to make a life that's good for yourself and Robin. And this is the first anniversary of your giving birth to him. You should celebrate yourself, too. Do something *you* want to do."

I knew at once what that would be. I wanted to drive to Connemara: the rocky western expanse of County Galway, home to craggy glacial mountains dripping with heather and water, the country's only fjord, and a vastly gorgeous landscape that makes you feel like you're wandering through the opening shots of an epic romantic film. You want a shawl for your shoulders in Connemara, if only so that you can wrap it tragically around yourself while facing into the wind with your hair drifting behind you, dreaming of every love you've ever lost. I have never liked to drive, but Connemara is my only exception—so beautiful, and so different every time you see it. It's a landscape like a still-wet painting, fresh and lush and shining, a vista always ancient and nascent at once. The painter keeps changing her mind, too: the smallest change in weather, in time of year, can render the same landscape in an entirely new palette, different colors every day. Heather or gorse or grass, dappled mountains showing sun or cloud or shining snow.

I planned to drive through it with Robin, always a happy passenger, and to stop for a wander around Galway City on the way. That day, at least, would be a gift to myself and my baby, a day of peace when we weren't waiting for his father to come home.

The morning of Robin's birthday I woke up early, even after the nightly series of feedings that left me haggard. I was afraid of something, even then. Something hung in the air, something that told me not to be in that house much longer. I got up, twitching with the kind of nervous domestic energy I had been running on since he left, put in a load of laundry and set the delay timer so it would be freshly ready to hang when we came home. I mixed bread flour, soda and buttermilk into a dough and baked it hot and fast. I left the loaf on the counter, steaming and caraway scented. I had grown sick of soda bread since I came to Ireland, but I was sick of every food by then, and it was one of my baby's favorite things to eat. I forced down my own piece of dry multigrain sliced bread from the shop, still just about the only thing I could stomach.

When I locked the door to leave, I looked over my shoulder, still waiting for Tommy to be there.

We left early because I was afraid. I couldn't pretend that wasn't true. I knew I didn't want to have the altercation we'd have if we were home on Robin's birthday when Tommy got there.

A month prior I'd held the door closed, holding Robin, both of us crying, while it felt like he tried to force his way into the house as he shouted—at me, I know, but it feels like *at us* in my memory. A mother and a baby really are one being when the baby is that young. Try to hurt one and you hurt the other. There's no separation between them at all. That was one of the moments that it was clearest to me that I needed to save Robin, even as a baby, from the things his father did to me.

As we drove out, my phone pinged on the passenger seat. The sound of a text message had made a little wash of stress rush through my body for all the years I'd known Tommy, but I was always telling myself that was just because I *wasn't good at conflict.* That was the only reason I felt afraid every time I heard from my husband, had to steel myself to find out whether he'd written to me in love or anger.

But I didn't pull over to read it, even though when we were living together I would have. I had eked out that much freedom for myself. I was afraid he was finally asking to make plans for Robin's birthday, and I was afraid I would cave to whatever he said if I looked right away. So I didn't until we were in Galway City.

I got out of the car and settled Robin into his carrier. I'd never had a stroller, both because they were so expensive and because the bad rural roads where we lived were too pockmarked to push a stroller over anyways. Robin's reflux, too, meant that he slept better and longer upright, on me, than he ever did in his crib, or ever would in a pram. We were both more settled, more calm, when our heartbeats met each other while I wore him.

It weakened the rush of adrenaline that came from picking up my phone to read one of Tommy's texts, too, if I was wearing Robin while I did it.

Bring my boy to the pub. I want to see him on his birthday.

I took a deep breath, my nose in Robin's soft, sparse hair, the scent of his head filling me with the courage to do what Saoirse had warned me I'd have to. I heard her voice in my head along with my own, like a Greek chorus, while I typed my reply:

We can't come to the pub. We are out today for Robin's birthday. If you had let me know beforehand we could have made a plan, but we can't today.

No apology. No "I'll bring him tomorrow if that's okay." It was reasonable to have plans and not be able to change them immediately. It was reasonable. It was normal.

I was terrified.

Robin wanted to nurse as we walked into the Latin Quarter, and the rhythmic pull of milk out of my body into his helped slow my pulse down, too, helped replace the flood of fear with kinder feelings.

We walked through Galway's bright red-and-blue-lined streets, the same buskers who'd been there since I arrived five years before, the same murals on the walls and solid cobblestones. There was the tea house I'd always loved, festooned with so many fake flowers inside and out that it looked like a cloud or a coral reef; but my stomach didn't even want tea. We walked through the Spanish Arch, a gloomy cave of an archway where the TV vampire I'd crushed on as a teenager had met his fate (I still often wonder how much of the blame for my taste in brooding, dark-haired Galway men I can place at Angel's feet). I saw a small art gallery offering an exhibition on *Hidden Mothers*, and we walked in.

The gallery was in an old building. The rooms had small dimensions and rough stone walls like all old Irish buildings, but brightly white-painted and lit to make them feel bigger. The hidden mothers in question were Victorian photograph portraits of children. It took a moment to see the mothers: dark ghostly lumps in the furniture, mothers covered with drapery, heads bowed into humps, hands holding the children still while trying to hide behind their bodies. Early photographs took a long time, which is why even pictures of adults from the first days of the medium often look glum or blurry; it is hard for anyone to sit still that long. These photos would often be the only ones anyone had of a person, of their beloved child. So these mothers held their children still, and hid while holding them, so that there would be some version of them they could hold forever.

I have no pictures of Robin and me from when he was born. Tommy didn't take many, and those few were all on his phone. I have very few photos of the first months of his life. If I have a record, it is this writing.

We walked among the hidden mothers, Robin post-milk dozing on my chest, until I had taken enough deep breaths to be able to read Tommy's response. I knew he would say something cruel, but I was still completely unprepared for what I saw:

> If you refuse to bring him to me today I will get you sent back to the
> States and keep my boy with me in Ireland.

My vision speckled as I felt blood leave my head, my feet, my fingers. My hands came up to hold my baby closer, even as I struggled to stay standing. I felt like someone was going to walk up to me right that second and tear him out of my arms.

I knew that Tommy meant what he said: if I didn't obey him, he would try his best to separate me from Robin forever.

My head wouldn't stop buzzing. My hands wouldn't stop shaking. I pulled the straps on the baby carrier tighter, squeezing Robin closer to my heart. We weren't safe here, out in public, I suddenly felt sure—what if he came looking for us? What if he realized we were in Galway and came to find us? What if he was tracking my phone? He'd always gotten mad at me if I kept the password from him. It would have been easy for him to add something to it. Why had I never thought of that before? Why had I ever trusted him?

We couldn't stay here, and we couldn't go home. He would come there, I thought, and hurt me for disobeying him. It was all crystallizing, so clear to me what would happen next, and next, and next, suddenly obvious that it was always going to come to this, some crisis of obedience or disobedience that would lead him to genuinely believe it was his right to hurt me, it was right to hurt me. If I went back to the house, I wouldn't be physically safe, and therefore neither would my baby. The whole world turned in a moment into a place where my husband could find me and take my baby away.

There was only one place that was safe for us to go: the place that had listened and helped me and warned me this might happen, even when I hadn't wanted to believe it.

I started walking.

I still felt ready to faint, but I walked as quickly as I could, as if we were being chased. We crossed the Latin quarter of Galway, back the way we came, through the cobblestoned misty streets and past the brightly colored shop fronts that had all seemed so comforting a few minutes before. Now anyone we passed might have been someone who knew Tommy and could tell him where we were.

As soon as I saw the heavily locked door of COPE, I started crying with relief and shame.

There was a torn-off acrylic nail in the clear weatherproof plastic box I reached into to press the intercom. A relic of another woman who had possibly been even more frantic, even more afraid, than I was. I felt the ghosts of the other hands who had begged for this same help around mine. I didn't stop crying or shaking, but I felt them nonetheless.

"Hello?"

I knew from coming for counseling sessions that I had to identify myself and why I was there. "I'm Betsy, I come here to see Saoirse but I"—my words cut off in a big hiccupping wind-knocked-out sob—"I need help. I just need help now."

"Okay. Come on in." The buzz of the door unlocking, I twisted the heavy latch, and we vanished inside. Robin was waking up on my chest and starting to cry. I'd heard once that you should treat parenting a baby like being a flight attendant, and not show any turbulence ruffling you that could worry them, because they assume nothing can be wrong if you're calm. But I couldn't do that for him now.

"I'm sorry," I told him, and I was sorry for so many things.

The woman at reception, freckly and curly-haired in her early twenties, came out and saw both of our distress—Robin was ratcheting up to full-on wails by then—and suggested I leave him with their childminder while we talked. But I couldn't bear the idea of being separated from him, even by one room. I shook my head, still crying, and said I was sorry but I'd rather keep him with me. I had learned to add an apology to nearly every sentence by then.

So she sat me down in her office with Robin still wailing in his carrier, and I tried to explain to her over his growing sobs and my slowly receding ones what had happened. The smell of that space, I think more than anything, was helping me calm down: the antiseptic instant coffee smell of so many charity-adjacent places, the smell of each of the sessions I'd had with Saoirse, the smell of the only place where I'd been fully believed, fully safe. My child and I were both here now. There were four locks on the door outside, and they would not let Tommy through. As long as we were in this building, we would stay together.

"Actually, maybe it would be good to let him play upstairs for a while," I admitted at last, under his screams.

The girl smiled at me and nodded, and she made a quick call. "You can go on up to her," she said.

I stood with Robin at the bottom of the stairway that led up to the childcare room, and I texted Tommy. There was something I needed to know for sure.

You promised you wouldn't stop my citizenship application.

He texted back almost immediately. There will be no application for me to stop when you're deported. I've kept my word.

I clearly remembered the conversation we'd had about it, shortly after he started the abuser program. We were standing in our little cottage kitchen, Robin on my hip. Things were good between us that day, so I felt able to refer to the problems we'd been having as I didn't dare to when they were more present. "No matter what happens between us, I need you to promise me that you won't do anything to interfere with my citizenship application," I said.

He put his strong arms around me, our child held between our hearts, and looked at me with his beautiful eyes. I melted a little, as I always did, as he always knew I would. "I promise," he murmured in his gentlest voice. "I promise I would never do that to you."

I had held on to that so hard, one of the pieces of evidence that I presented in the courtroom of my mind to defend my husband's innocence until proven guilty, his status as an essentially decent person. Standing at the bottom of the painted concrete stairwell that day, I finally saw him differently. Even in that moment of seeming good faith he had been planning ways around his own promises, storing up things he could use against me.

I knew I could never trust him again.

The childminder came downstairs, radiating warmth and gentleness and safety, and my empty insides and my baby and I followed her upstairs and into a room scattered with soft toys. Robin would be safe and happy there, I knew, and I had to go downstairs and get help to deal with what had happened, for his sake. It was the *for his sake* that ultimately allowed my hands to leave his sides and let him go.

Downstairs the on-call support person and I talked through what had happened. "Is it safe for you to go home?"

I closed my eyes briefly. "No."

"I'm sorry to tell you all the rooms in the shelter are full," she told me. "We can book you a hotel room if you really need it."

As much as I'd felt shame at the idea of coming here as someone who needed to stay in one of the kind but dire little chipped-paint apartments with my baby, I realized then that I had longed for it, too. To retreat into what felt like a rabbit warren of women and children who knew what we knew, a beehive of survivors. I'd gone to a historically women's college, lived in an old-fashioned women's boarding house in Manhattan, spent the happiest summers of my life at nerdy camps on college campuses living in halls of other girls—they were my safest spaces. I didn't want to be alone. I wanted to be with other women who knew my story because it was theirs, too.

But I heard "if you really need it" and my pride kicked right in. I said no, I can pay for a hotel room. It would be with just about the last money I had—we had, my husband's and my money in our joint account—but what better use could it be put to than saving our child, even if he didn't see it that way?

She looked at me cautiously. "Are you sure?"

It felt like life-or-death to be nonchalant just then, not to show how much more I really needed when I'd already admitted I needed so much. "Oh, sure."

So she helped me find a hotel room. I said I didn't want to stay in my home area, or in Galway City. I thought he would know to look for me there.

"What about the Lady Gregory Hotel, in Gort?" she asked. "Is that far enough away?"

I had been there only once or twice, and it wasn't somewhere Tommy would think I'd go. The name Lady Gregory seemed like a sign: she was a writer, translator, re-teller of mythology, playwright, and patroness of the arts. She seemed like a good patroness for us, too.

"That's far enough," I said, unsure if it really was—but the price was right, so I gave her my bank card and she booked the room. I started to understand why Saoirse had said I should be grateful Tommy didn't bother with credit cards or any of our important documents—it wouldn't be quick or easy for him to access the statements, even though it was a joint account.

She told me to get my car and bring it back around and she'd give me changes of clothes and pajamas for Robin and myself, nappies and other things we might need. I started to say we didn't need it, but the money I'd just spent on the hotel room stopped my throat.

I got Robin, cooing happily at the childminder, from upstairs and the door buzzed us back onto the vulnerable street. I went furtively to the car, looking around for danger all the while, then drove back to collect our donated goods. She'd given Robin a toy among our necessities, a tags-still-on zippered bag full of soft fabric blocks. That pierced me the most of anything I'd seen that day: that they wanted to give us not just things we needed to survive, but something kind and gentle, too.

We made one more stop, at the local German discount grocery store, so I could fill my trunk with shelf-stable baby food and cheap crackers and cheese, since we couldn't go back to my kitchen, and I couldn't afford to eat out for dinner. At the checkout desk, the cashier cheerfully handed me a packet of lemon balm seeds and a little disc of dry compressed earth inside a tiny paper plant pot, a free promotion from the store. I took it, not able to look long at the photo of the garden on the packet. I had nowhere to plant seeds, nowhere safe to watch small things grow.

With the trunk full of the donations and clearance groceries that had become all we had in the world, I settled Robin into his car seat, took my own seat in the front, and looked at my hands on the steering wheel. My phone kept vibrating angrily, but I could give myself the gift of not looking at it right away.

"Okay, my love, let's go," I told my baby, and we drove.

Seven

The Lady Gregory

SPRING 2018

for Susan

The first night at the hotel I spent rewriting our story. Among the emergency supplies I'd bought was the cheapest notebook I could find. I knew I needed a record of what had happened.

Journaling suddenly felt higher-stakes than the emotional sorting system and beloved memory keeper it had been for me since I was thirteen. In case something happened to me, or to Robin, I needed to make it clear. My journals up until then had been full of longing for Tommy and me to make it through this, to heal. They had insisted with increasing desperation how much I adored him, how much I believed he would get better, that he would never really hurt me. There were plenty of things I knew I had omitted because I couldn't bear how clear they looked in writing—how writing forced me to see them clearly.

Now I was remembering more and more of the safety advice from COPE that I'd dismissed as not applying to me or my husband. Keep a record of everything. Judges care more about patterns than single incidents. And if you are gone, the writing will be there.

I wrote it all. How afraid I was of him, how frightening living in my own home had become. The time he'd threatened to kill me because he thought I hadn't built the fire high enough. I forced myself to write down other dangerous, frightening things he'd done that I'd explained away, ignored away, loved-him-too-much-to-see away: things that for legal reasons I can't even write here now.

The purpose of this book has never been to shame Tommy, or to punish him by airing my grievances. I want to write about what happened because I hope other people might recognize it, and maybe it will help them. For that reason, it hurts a lot that I cannot write everything that happened here.

But I wrote it then, and I know it to be true.

I had to look at Robin, watch his small belly move in and out for several breaths, after every sentence I wrote. It felt like living through that fear again, just putting it down. I told myself each word I wrote, each record, was working to keep him safe. An incantation.

I texted friends back in the US, too. I needed there to be a digital record that could not be destroyed the way a paper journal could. I understood that, as ashamed as I'd been of telling the full truth about my marriage, I needed to do that now. My friends were far enough away that they could hold these records with security, that Tommy could never erase them. His power seemed so huge to me then, capable even of separating me permanently from our child, but he could not reach into phones and computers on the other side of the world.

With the knowledge that I needed to tell people came the realization that it would be a comfort to do that, too.

Robin was a dream that weekend, squealing with pleasure in the hotel bathtub (the first real bathtub he'd ever been in), playing happily with those donated blocks, taking the longest nap of his life in a pool of spring sunshine in the middle of the bed. I watched him sleep, his tiny hands curling and relaxing as he dreamed, turning from baby to one-year-old as three p.m. passed between lines that were so hard to write. Watching him breathe slowly and gently while he slept made me breathe that way, too, a tidal echoing of soft currents in the spaces inside both of us. In and out. I could breathe because he could breathe, because I could watch him breathing.

I started to understand then that it was through saving Robin that I had also saved myself. In pulling his tiny vulnerable body and soul out of the deep water our house had become, I was dragged to the surface with him, sealskin around the selkie, because we were part of the same thing. At least for now, we both could breathe.

Looking after him kept me from coming apart with pain and fear. He pulled me into moments of peace. Having to find comfort to offer him meant I found it for myself, too.

He grounded me. He still does.

The next morning, I brought Robin for a walk. Gort is, for me, the quintessential Irish small town, a wobbly square of gray cobblestone with pastel-painted shop fronts and bright residential doors, supposedly because Queen Victoria once ordered all doors in Ireland to be painted black and the Irish rebelled in a riot of color.

We ate a very little breakfast in a sunny café, more money I told myself I shouldn't be spending, but I wanted to sit among people and feel welcomed, feel normal. I wanted to have someone make me a warm milky drink and bring it to me with a smile and a "now, loveen."

I posted a picture of the coffee glowing in a shaft of sun and wrote that it was a fresh new morning—and framing the words that way made me feel that it was. There was hope and possibility, now that I had finally realized I could not save both my marriage and my child. There was a freedom that I hadn't had when I was clinging, desperately heartbroken, to both. The sealskin in the child's outstretched hand.

Within minutes an account I'd never seen before commented: "It sure is." My stomach twisted: I knew it was Tommy. The handle was an Irish phrase I didn't recognize. When I put it through Google Translate, I got back "the rock of the murder."

Suddenly I couldn't stand to be in the café anymore, to be looked at by any of the people whose quiet company I'd longed for an hour earlier. I took Robin and left, back through the sunny gray square.

I still needed to hear a kind voice, so I called Jacinta, a friend who lived ten minutes away from the cottage, and asked her to pick up my little portable filing cabinet and my journal from home. The safety sheet I'd gotten from COPE had told me to keep important documents in my car, but once again, I hadn't thought it applied to me.

If you ever get advice from a domestic violence center, I'm begging you: follow it.

Jacinta said she was on it, then called me back a little later. "You sure you aren't still staying there?"

How many times can you run through clichés of physical fear in one day? My stomach had twisted, my blood ran cold; now I felt my heart drop. "No. Why do you ask?"

"I'm outside the house now, and I can hear the laundry machine spinning. And there's smoke coming out of the chimney."

"I'm not there. I haven't been there since yesterday morning. I didn't put on a fire." I took a breath. "Jacinta, don't go in there. Please. I can get the documents back another way."

"Ah sure Jaysus, it's not me he's mad at. Anyway, his car isn't in the drive. I think he's been and gone."

Tommy didn't have a key to the house, any more than he carried a wallet. I had triple-checked the doors were locked before I'd left. I wondered how he'd gotten in.

A few minutes later she called back to tell me she had my things, and some more of our clean clothes, and that I could meet her in the village to get them when I was ready. She said a loaf of my soda bread was out half-eaten on the counter, the exposed crumb still soft.

"And Betsy—" She hesitated before going on. "The back door was smashed open."

I felt a kind of flooding in my head. "Okay." I didn't know what else I could say.

She told me where and when to meet her. We hung up.

The walls of the Lady Gregory Hotel loomed up at us. I knew I couldn't afford to stay there much longer. I thought about the isolation of our little cottage, how I'd once savored the knowledge that I could scream or cry as loud as I wanted to and no one would hear me. I knew it wasn't safe to go back home, nor to ask any of my and Tommy's mutual friends in the nearby village if we could stay with them.

But I did have one local friend who wasn't his friend, too. Irene was the sister of Maeve, the grad school friend who'd told me I should go to the Aran Islands, that Ireland was where the world kept its magic. She lived twenty minutes away, and we met for tea and chats a few times a year—and, annually, for an expedition to Dublin's Knitting & Stitching Show, since we were both avid crafters.

Irene knew what had been happening with Tommy. On our Knitting & Stitching pilgrimage the previous year, I'd told her what the marriage counselor had said, and that he was in an abuser rehabilitation program, so I knew she'd believe me. When I asked her if we could stay, I was surprised to get the feeling she was proud of me. I didn't feel judged, despite her own long, successful marriage to a retired Irish Army officer named Cían.

"Cían's mother left his father, years ago," she said, "when no one did that sort of thing. Everyone looked down on her for it, but Cían was always glad. Of course you can stay here until your order comes."

I didn't think I was homeless then. I thought I'd be going home with Robin, once I got my safety order—the Irish version of a restraining order. So I packed Robin and our few things into the car, checked out of the hotel, and started driving toward Irene's house, confident—or wanting to think I was confident, not wanting to consider the yawning void of what we might have to do otherwise—that we would only be houseguests for a night or two.

I loved Irene and Cían's house, and I looked forward right away to going there. It was tidy and tasteful, with American quirks like closets and high-water-pressure showers and a big clothes dryer that Irene had to beg the builders to accommodate. They had two dogs and two cats, whom Robin already adored. Irene didn't have children of her own, but doted on her god-children and on Robin—and on me. Irene, as it happens, was born the exact same day as my mom.

My mothers in the world, thank goodness, have been many.

On the drive to Irene's house, Saoirse called.

I pulled over at the side of the road to take the call, glancing around, grateful I wasn't anywhere I might be overheard—sometimes it feels like everyone in Ireland knows everyone else. In our small town an hour away from Gort, everyone knew Tommy from birth, and me only as his slightly shy and strange young foreign wife. I didn't need to think about whose side they would take in all this.

"I heard what happened," Saoirse said gravely. "That you came in to us this weekend. Tell me about it."

Immediately I started sobbing. I hadn't cried since I'd left the COPE building two days ago. "He says he's going to have me deported and keep Robin here," I said. "I'll never see him again."

"No," Saoirse said.

"But what if he does? Saoirse, that's the scariest thing I've ever heard!"

"Betsy. Listen to me."

She took a slow breath. I made myself match it.

"I am going to ask you one question. Do you really think he wants to be a single dad?"

I thought of all the things I did for Robin, every day and every night. How I hadn't had a single good night's sleep since he was born, how I'd turned my body inside out to bear him, and how I did it again every hour to feed him, the evidence of it leaking through my shirt, reeking in the diaper bag, flooding my cracked-open, tired mind. Tommy had already told me in many of his texts and emails how glad he was to be a "free man" again. I thought of how my body hurt from tiredness. The love that would never let me leave Robin was the only thing that sustained me to do that tiring work every moment of every day, to give my heart and mind and body to keeping this small being alive and well.

No, he didn't want that. He didn't want our baby at all. He just wanted to hurt me.

Something settled into me then. Something made itself quite clear. "No," I whispered.

"No," Saoirse repeated, more clearly. "Now. What do you need?"

I couldn't afford to stay at the hotel any longer. There was no room at the women's shelter. It wasn't safe to go home while Tommy might be there, I was sure.

"I need a safety order," I said.

Saoirse was briefly quiet. "We would never tell anyone not to apply for a safety order," she said.

I frowned. "What do you mean?"

"Only that you need to understand the risks." She'd told me about them before, in the days when I thought the idea that I'd need such an order against my beloved husband was absurd. I'd been warned in the same way against getting a restraining order when I reported my dad, learning then what I remembered now: applying for any kind of legal protection often actually puts a survivor in greater danger, since the person you're applying against is informed before the order request is brought to a judge, so that they will have time to build a defense. If the judge decides you don't have enough evidence of danger to deserve the order, that person will take the decision as a permission slip to keep doing what they're doing to you, or even make it worse.

"Surely now, though," I said—now that I'd fled my own home with my baby in fear of my husband, I'd be able to get one.

Saoirse sighed. "We would never tell a survivor not to seek a safety order," she repeated, in a certain deliberate tone that made me see she was reciting it as some kind of rule. "But I've been working in domestic violence for a long time, Betsy, and I need you to know that the risks might outweigh the benefits. Unless there's hard evidence—a video recording, or something like that—of physical violence or the specific threat of it, those risks are really significant. Especially in a situation like yours where—and I know you know I don't mean anything minimizing here—where the abuse mostly hasn't been physical."

I heard what she was trying to say. "Okay." My eyes burned. I closed them, and then opened them quickly when not being able to see what was around me for more than a blink was too scary.

Robin snuffled in his sleep in the car seat. I told myself Saoirse was right. I didn't think Tommy wanted to be a single dad.

But I did think he wanted to punish me. I knew, too, that he didn't really understand what being a single parent meant, the cost of it in mind and heart and body, day and night.

And I wondered if he would learn that cost too late, after he had put an impassable barrier of immigration law and ocean between Robin and me.

"If you apply for a safety order and it fails, he'll think he's allowed to get even more controlling," Saoirse said. "I've seen it happen before. He'll get worse."

"He'll get worse anyway," I whispered.

I heard a soft rustle on the phone, and I could picture her nodding, her long statement earrings brushing a collar or a scarf. "Set up a meeting with a solicitor. She'll be able to help you with the divorce and custody, at least. Then the safest thing you can do, for yourself and your child, is just wait."

Family court records in Ireland are sealed. I cannot write about what any solicitor or barrister has told me, or what any judges, clerks, or court-appointed social workers said to me, in any of the days in court I've had since I fled home.

But I will say this: I know who benefits from that forced silence. It is not me, and it is not Robin. Silence does not safeguard any protective parent or their child. Silence only empowers and protects abusers.

I had an emergency in-person meeting with Saoirse the next day. When she asked me how I was, I launched right into the plans I'd been thinking through.

"We'll go somewhere. I need money to live, for Robin and me, and we need to be farther away to be safe if we can't get an order. We'll go somewhere he can't get to us. I probably need to go somewhere else to get a better job, anyway." I swallowed. Ireland had once been my sanctuary, the place I'd fled to for safety. Where could I go to save myself and my baby now? "Maybe an international school. Maybe a bigger city, I don't know—Cork, Dublin—" I'd been lucky to get even the pennies-paying, part-time adjunct teaching job I had at the local university. Writing jobs weren't exactly thick on the ground in rural Ireland. I'd thought of offering myself as a private tutor when I'd first moved here, but Tommy had shot it down: he told me that I'd never be able to compete with tutors who had Irish degrees, that no one would want an American to teach them English. He'd tossed out the flyer I was planning to photocopy at the library. I hadn't thought he'd have any reason to lie to me.

A few days before, I'd gotten an email from my MFA program's secretary about a job opening she thought I'd be particularly suited for, a tenure-track professorship in creative writing, specializing in children's literature, at a well-regarded American university. The pay started at $70,000. I'd made barely a third of that last year, or any of the years since I'd left school. I was going to have to provide for Robin entirely on my own, that was obvious to me right away: Tommy had always worked for cash and it seemed that he reviled the idea of paying taxes. He'd told me many times there was nothing he wouldn't do to keep from being one of those men who paid through the nose every week just to see his kid for a few hours. At the time I thought he meant he'd work hard to stay married.

Here, all I'd be able to offer my child was scraping by, which I'd barely been able to do on my earnings combined with Tommy's cash from training horses—even when our rent had only been €150 a month for our tiny cottage.

But the landlords had been willing to sell us that house. For €15,000. That was the same as the advance I was being paid on my next book, a retelling of Snow White and Rose Red set in a circus, called *The Circus Rose*. I'd been paid half of that advance when I signed the contract, and I'd get the other half when I delivered the manuscript.

My deadline was in July. It was April now. I had struggled to focus on the book, between new-parenting and what I had been thinking of as the "rough patch" in my marriage. Most of it still needed to be written. But I needed that money more than I'd ever needed it before. I was determined to meet the July deadline. And if I could sell one more book, I thought, maybe I could buy the cottage myself, just for Robin and me.

Besides, I didn't want to go back to America, to the home that had never felt safe to me, to the land of my parents. I wanted to keep that barrier of ocean between them and myself, and between them and my baby. I would have to stay in Ireland, and I would have to prove that I could take competent care of my child—financially and emotionally—if I wanted to keep him.

To keep him: any other option felt like death.

Saoirse took a quiet breath. "Betsy," she said, "I'm sorry. I don't think he can make you leave. I don't think, as I said, he even wants you to leave. But he can make you stay."

It took me a moment to be able to speak. "What?"

"I'm sorry," she said again. I could hear in her voice that she really was, that it was hard for her to say these words to me. "A child needs both parents' permission to move out of the country. Even out of the county."

I looked around at the close beige-painted walls of the little room where we were meeting.

How can you feel trapped, and desperate to stay in your trap, at the same time?

"How long do we need his permission?" I asked. "To leave at all? He can't really keep us just from—from leaving for a weekend, even, can he?"

Saoirse peered at me gently over her glasses. "I'm afraid he can," she said. "Until Robin is sixteen."

"Fifteen years?" It wasn't a question. I just needed to say the time out loud.

I was twenty-nine, and I wouldn't be able to leave Ireland until I was forty-four. It sounded like a life sentence.

"The solicitor agreed that I probably couldn't get a safety order," I said quietly.

Saoirse nodded. "I'm sorry."

"I'm here on a spousal visa," I said. "He can take that away. And then what?"

"I've looked into that a little for you. I think you can get a parental visa, since Robin was born here. It will take a while, but I think it's your best chance." The certainty she'd had in her voice on the phone, though, when she'd said Tommy didn't want to be a single dad, was gone. I could tell she wasn't any more sure than I was that I could stay.

"But my spousal visa is about to expire, and anyway I'm sure he's already trying to get it rescinded. Will it take more than, say, a month?"

Her wincing smile said it would. "Just try your best."

"It's not safe to leave, and it's not safe to stay," I said. "I'm stuck here for fifteen years, if I *can* stay, and I can't even get an order to keep Robin and me safe while I'm stuck here. What am I supposed to do?"

Saoirse said nothing. But she met my gaze, and didn't look away.

I knew at least that I needed to get back to the cottage, that my and Irene's friendship would not withstand too long a stay. I told Tommy he needed to leave the house again so that our baby could sleep in his own crib.

He refused. Unless I came to the house to talk to him, alone, he said he wasn't going anywhere.

I knew, deep in the gut Saoirse was always telling me to trust, what would happen if I met him alone in that house, out of screaming distance of even our elderly farmer neighbors.

I knew, and I still know.

The next time we talk in person will be with a licensed counselor present, I texted him.

He suggested a mutual friend who ran a pub. He's counseled plenty of marriages, he said.

I said no. A qualified, licensed, neutral third party.

Then it looks like I won't be leaving. Good luck finding somewhere else that will take you.

Back in the little closet of a private support room at COPE, I told Saoirse, "He can't just take over the house like a square on a chess board and sit there until I give him what he wants. I know it's not safe to go back there. I know it's not."

"So maybe don't go back," Saoirse said. "Maybe let it go."

"But I was going to buy the house! I was going to have a place to give my baby!" I heard myself and lowered my voice. "I can't afford anywhere else."

"You have a place to stay for a few nights, with your friend Irene," Saoirse said. "We both know it's safer there than in your family home. And you are not the only mother here to lose your house. You know that, too, right?"

"He can't just take it," I said.

She took a breath. "I'm afraid he can."

Eight

Tea in the Cloud

SPRING 2018

for Christina

Along with texting my friends, there was a larger group I knew I needed to tell, knew that the act of telling them alone would help keep me safe: Friday Tea. I'd attended, and adored, a historically women's college in the Pioneer Valley of western Massachusetts called Smith, where it was a tradition that every Friday after classes, students would gather to drink tea and talk about our weeks.

A few years before, a Smith alumna named Gina Ko had started a virtual Friday Tea gathering. The group had grown to twelve thousand alums from all over the world. Each Friday we'd post pictures of our cups of tea and describe the best and worst things that had happened to us that week. It connected me with friends I hadn't kept up with and gave me a window into the lives of Smith alums who were doing incredible things all over the world—in the sciences, arts, politics, any field you can think of—and who were at the same time dealing with family troubles, illness, grief, and heartache. The woman who had presented at the UN that week was also worried about her mother's cancer diagnosis; the one who had just scored her dream byline was also dealing with infertility. It was a refreshing break from the insistent positivity of most other social media.

I hadn't posted about my pregnancy on my public-facing online profiles at all, worried my parents would see them—but I had told Friday Tea
the same week I found out. I'd written about ultrasounds, cravings, and
Braxton-Hicks contractions there, given and received celebration and com-
miseration along every step of pregnancy and postpartum. I'd even written about the trouble in my marriage, although up until now I'd called his
abuser program an "anger management group," dreading, even then, the
starkness of what I knew I'd see if another person in Friday Tea talked about
trying to stay married to an abuser.

So I didn't feel afraid to write to this group of twelve thousand people,
most of them total strangers, and tell them about the scariest thing that had
ever happened to me.

I wrote out the bones of what had become the traditional Friday Tea
post format: the words *Tea*, *Best*, and *Worst*, with colons after them. I stared
at those blank spaces for a minute, and then I started writing.

Tea: black.

Worst (of a long time): My baby and I are staying with a friend because
my husband started threatening me, forced his way into our house (he
moved out a little while ago and we'd explicitly agreed he could only
be there when I'd specifically given permission) and is refusing to leave
unless I agree to talk to him alone. This all went down on our kid's first
birthday, part of which I spent crying in a domestic violence shelter, and
the rest checked into a hotel with my baby hoping he wouldn't find us.

I'm going to be a single mom in a country I've only lived in for a few
years, in a rural area with no family connections (I cut off my parents
years ago, definitely the right decision and like hell will this drag
me back to them) and I won't be able to look for the more lucrative,
baby-supporting work I know I could find outside Ireland unless my
husband's guardianship is stripped, which everyone tells me is basically
impossible.

Best: well, to be honest, he crossed enough lines that I'm finally able to
stop longing for his better self. I can focus on keeping myself and my
baby safe and well. I feel free of him, of the huge energy it took to keep
fighting for my marriage, at last.

Other bests:

Of any country to be theoretically stuck in for fifteen years, I really think I'd choose Ireland anyway.

And always, my baby, my baby, my baby.

It felt good to write it down. Writing put words like borders around a pain that had seemed boundless.

And then the loving words from other Smithies started pouring in.

Roshan Catalina:

So much love. Also, your name seemed familiar so I tried to find your books—imagine my surprise when I found one sitting on my shelf! I loved *Tides*, and I can't wait to read your newer stuff!

Gwen Stewart:

Sending love and strength! I will actually be in Dublin/Cork in mid-May if I can do anything helpful from there. In the meantime, buying your books and recommending them to others is a pleasure.

Jennifer Doe:

First, I'm so sorry that you spent your child's first birthday crying in a domestic violence shelter. I know that pain and no one should have to go through it.

But there is life after, and it seems to me you already have a grasp on that vision. And yes, Ireland is a lovely place to be "stuck." I've only visited once (stayed in Galway by the way) but fell in love with the beauty of the countryside. My daughter and I kept making my partner pull over and we would tumble out of the car to gaze on one green hillside dotted with sheep after another. If I could choose a place to seat my creative work, rural Ireland would be in the top five.

Sending you luck and strength as you move forward and away from the darkness of abuse.

Hallie Tolo:

All the love my dear. You are the strongest and such a fierce advocate for yourself and your baby. Little R is the luckiest baby alive to have you in his corner.

Ilana Shydlo Shupak:
> Sending much love and empathy your way. I hope that it is healing
> and fortifying to feel all the love radiating out toward you from
> Smithies all across the planet. You know you and your sweet son
> have a standing offer to stay at my place if you are in Brooklyn.

Rebecca Woolf:
> I'm in Dublin. PM me if you need ANYTHING.

I have a hard time, still, saying I was homeless, because my baby and I never slept on the street—just as I still have a hard time, sometimes, using the words *domestic violence* or *abuse* because my husband never hit me.

And because on that day, I found homes in all the hearts that reached out to hold mine.

The time we spent without a home, blessedly brief as it was, showed me how thin unto nonexistent the line that separates most people from homelessness truly is. If I didn't have one friend who didn't like Tommy, and a little money for that first frightened weekend hiding in an anonymous hotel room, my baby and I would have slept in my car for who knows how long. If I didn't have work I could do from a computer, and a computer to do it on, we wouldn't even have had the car. We could have been on the street, and maybe we'd still be there now.

I remember that every time I put my child to sleep in a bed, every time I see a homeless person. Maybe we'd still be there now.

I felt like the undead during the day, dragging myself through the things I had to do. I worked doggedly on my next book, the July delivery date when I'd next get paid a beacon in front of me. Every waking moment I didn't spend writing was another moment my baby and I didn't have that money.

At night, while Robin slept in a folding travel cot that I now knew we'd never actually take traveling, I soothed myself to sleep by reading real estate listings. I had a little over a thousand euros left, less than I'd need for just a deposit on most of the rentals I could find, but at night I scrolled through thatched cottages and regal stone buildings and converted old pubs for sale in Galway. I imagined living in Connemara, the wild landscape that had enraptured my hungry heart since my time on the Aran Islands. I clicked on a beacon-white lake house in Recess, a refurbished knitting factory in Carraroe. I rolled the names around in my mouth like hard candy and pictured myself and my baby free and safe inside those houses.

I was intensely grateful for Irene and her husband's hospitality and help, but I also knew that we were wearing out our welcome. Robin, never much of a sleeper, had been waking up to nurse even more since we left home. At the breakfast table in the mornings, my friend and her husband were tolerant and kind, but clearly worn down, dark circles under their eyes, fewer smiles for my baby's antics than they'd had before.

The only place for rent within a huge radius that I could even imagine affording was a falling-down old pub with holes in the walls and mold on every surface, flaking lead paint and faucets that ran mostly rust. As I walked through the many crumbling bedrooms, I imagined the place refurbished— it could be a bed and breakfast, or even a place to host group retreats. I'd always wanted to teach at writing retreats. There was so much I could do with that place, I thought.

If, that was, I had a few hundred thousand euros to buy and renovate it. As it was, it would fail any health code going.

After I looked at the pub, I came back to Irene's house and stared at her guest room wallpaper for four hours, unable to bear the thought that this was the only home I could offer my baby, a place where almost everything we'd touch was toxic.

I posted on every local online group I could find, describing myself as a quiet and responsible university teacher looking for any kind of accommodation for myself and my baby. Finally someone wrote to me about a little country bungalow that her son owned, and that she was thinking of renting out for him while he was working in Dubai.

I regretfully spent five euros on new flats at Penney's, since I only had the scuffed old shoes I'd left the house in, and still the landlady looked at me askance and asked if I worked.

"I teach at the university in Galway," I said, "and I write books. I have three published," I handed her a business card with the covers of those three books on it, "one coming out at the end of the summer, and another scheduled for 2020." All those things sounded like money more than they meant it, but it was enough for her to unfurrow her brows, and later to agree to give me a year's lease at €600 a month.

I looked at my bank account. After the deposit and first month's rent, I'd have less than ten euros left. My only truly predictable income was the €900 a month I made from teaching at the university, and that was only during the school year: it was May now, the semester had ended, and I wouldn't be paid again until September. I had renewed my online tutoring account, but that was neither predictable nor well-paid. I only made money from a book once every year or so at most, and there was never a guarantee that I would sell another. Any waitressing or shop-clerk job I could get would be a twenty-minute drive away at least from Robin, and would barely cover childcare anyway—besides which, I was still driving with only my US license, not an Irish one. I was going through the long process of getting that Irish license, made longer by the expense of the required private lessons that I could only afford now and then; until I got it, any driving I did was technically illegal. When I'd been with Tommy, I'd bought my own beat-up old car, but usually he drove it, and getting my Irish license hadn't seemed urgent. I could drive the back roads, to go to small grocery stores or to friends' farmhouses or Robin's childminder, without much fear; but driving to work every day would be a much bigger risk. (During the school year, I took the bus to the university once a week.) Now, if I did work I had to drive on main roads to get to—work I only qualified for with the spousal visa I was sure Tommy was already trying to get revoked—his threat of deportation could come true.

I had work I could do from home, on my own schedule. I didn't need Saoirse to tell me how lucky I was in that.

The deadline for *The Circus Rose* was in two months' time. Saoirse had warned me not to take on too much when I'd talked about using that money to buy the house we'd lived in with Tommy. Now that home was lost to us.

I remembered a time when Robin was a few days old, just home from the hospital, and Tommy took him from me to hold while I ate dinner. Robin started to cry. With that noise in my ears, I couldn't force myself to swallow—my body wouldn't let me feed myself while my baby cried. I took him back and ate while he nursed. Tommy said it made him understand some mares he'd seen, who refused to leave their foals no matter how you beat them.

I was going to take every hour of tutoring I could, and look for any other online work I could find, too. And I was going to make that July deadline. I would provide for my son and keep him safe. My body understood no other option.

We moved in two weeks later. We'd been without a home for barely a month, but the memory of being unable to provide a place for my baby would always stay with me.

Nine

The Bungalow

SUMMER 2018

for Natalia

The bungalow was a narrow yellow rectangle on a small country lane, stuck between farmers' fields divided by low stone walls. There was an apple tree in the yard, a yard that the house itself hid from the road. I could play with Robin outside without worrying that Tommy would drive by and see us. Our closest neighbors were cows and horses.

Every time we moved, I worried about what the instability was doing to Robin. After I paid that deposit and first month's rent, I took my remaining eight euros grocery shopping. Robin was still nursing, so I kept faith he at least was getting all the vitamins he needed, and I turned those euros into bread made from the cheapest buttermilk, flour, and oats I could find. I imagined Rumpelstiltskin in reverse, turning the last of my gold back into wheat.

Irene and Cían brought me back to our house—to Tommy's house—with their flat-bed trailer. Tommy was in the middle of a workday an hour away, and I had those two friends with me, but my hands still shook and my pulse buzzed in my ears as I gathered my and Robin's things.

When I went into the kitchen, I saw the smashed-open lock in the back door. I thought: Tommy would have still broken down that door if my baby and I were home.

I found Teapot hiding under our bed. He'd always been affectionate and brave, and I wondered what had frightened him so much since Robin and I had left that he'd need to hide. I would never have thought Tommy capable of being cruel to an animal just because he was angry with me—but then, there were so many things I would never have thought he'd do.

I begged him to come out so I could bring him to the bungalow with us, while Irene and John waited outside and every minute that ticked away brought an increased risk of Tommy returning.

When Teapot finally came to me, I cried into his fur.

I stringently took only my and Robin's things, and left the cookware and television I'd bought for the house—I still hated to think of depriving Tommy of anything. I even left some books that I'd bought because he'd mentioned wanting to read them. The next day Tommy texted me to say that if I came back to the house while he was gone again, he'd report me to the police for theft.

Tommy had never had his own social media. In the last few years he'd gotten into Instagram, but always on my account, on my phone. He got angry whenever I changed my phone's password, which strangely enough was one of the things that forced me to admit there was something wrong with his behavior, even when I was deep in denial about far worse things, only because that particular form of control has shown up in too many PSAs to ignore.

I'd helped him set up his own Facebook profile and Instagram account months ago and sent him a friend request, but he'd never accepted it, never touched his own accounts again. Instead he'd given me the silent treatment for a few days until I decided it wasn't worth it and changed the password back—he was my husband, and he was trying, and this was a small thing, I told myself.

The day we moved into the bungalow I saw he'd accepted that months-old friend request. I knew he was trying to find out where we'd gone. I blocked him right away, but I couldn't block out the feeling of his eyes on me.

I couldn't bear to delete my own social media. My presence there was part of my work as a writer—recommending books, promoting my own, connecting with readers—but more than that, the internet was where most of my far-flung friends lived.

And there was Friday Tea, a haven at the end of every week.

Tea: Hot chocolate in my new house.

Best: Baby, cat, and I are moved into our rental. It smells like fresh paint and my New Hampshire candle. It has a big yard and three tiny bedrooms and a huge ugly couch that I have covered with a blue-and-white bedspread my friend Irene gave me.

Worst: I keep imagining talking about everything that's happened with Tommy, the husband who loved me, and I can perfectly imagine all the things he'd say, how horrified he'd be, if this were happening to someone else. Or so I thought.

I have no doubt and no regret about leaving the man he's become. I just miss the man he was. Or the man I thought he was. The husband I thought I had is vanishing. It feels like I'm mourning a death.

It is so strange that less than two years ago we decided to have a baby together because we adored each other so much and had so much faith in each other. As a former crisis counselor, I know this can happen to anyone, but I was still smug enough in my choices to think, "not me."

Katharine Beutner:
    I'm so sorry, Betsy. My first husband was not violent, but I remember that feeling of losing the person I'd loved as his behavior changed, and wishing for the best friend I'd had in the partner from our early days. Wishing you calm and peace and love with your wonderful baby.

Catherine Carr:
    You are not alone in marrying an illusion. Walk through your grief and we will be waiting to celebrate when you're ready.

Anna St Lorenz:

> I empathize mourning a death that will never be treated as such. No neighbor will bring you casserole, no time off work to process this, no insurance to take care of sudden costs and no funeral to say goodbye. You'll always be regarded as a divorcée, but feel kindred with widows. And the worst part is you now have this strange new person you have to manage on top of it all.

Every comment was comfort: a kind voice that felt like a reassuring touch, even if it was thousands of miles away. The well of nurturing I drew from to offer my baby, because of those college friends and strangers, never went completely dry. Those tiny acts of mothering, mostly, but not entirely from women, allowed me to mother my child in turn. They kept me from feeling alone in the task before me. They kept us alive.

I took every online job I could find: tutoring, freelance editing, conversation with English language learners. I started as soon as Robin woke me, around five most mornings, and I kept at it after I put him to bed at night. I did all my work at my desk in the bungalow's living room, which faced the road so I could be vigilant as I worked, as I always was, for Tommy's car.

Our new place was only twenty minutes from the cottage where we'd lived with Tommy. For my own sake I would have run farther, but I wanted to keep Robin's childminder, Brigid. I told myself that if he still went to her, she'd be able to give him some sense of continuity that I knew I'd failed to provide myself. Brigid took just two babies, Robin and a little girl two months younger than him, and looked after them at home with her own children. She was quiet and kind, and I often wondered if Robin liked her more than me—but I was so grateful that I couldn't feel much jealousy.

After Tommy had first left the house, I'd never considered stopping childcare: I would have had no hope of making the money I needed to keep us afloat without it. After the cataclysm of Robin's birthday, that was even more true. Saoirse kept reminding me I needed the time to keep myself sane, too, time to grieve openly when Robin wouldn't be around to see it, time to rest during the day now and then since I was still up with him so often at night. She reminded me that other single mothers she worked with lived near their parents or other

extended family who could help with childcare. I had none of that. My friend
Jacinta had ghosted me after getting my things from the cottage—she and her
husband were Tommy's friends, too, after all. I'd figured I would lose our mutual friends when I left him, since they had all known him so much longer.
But it still hurt. And I couldn't bear to ask Irene for any more help than she'd
already given. I would have given my last penny to Brigid, and I often did.

When I walked up to her house the January morning after Tommy first
left home, she had opened the door with a bright smile and a hug for Robin,
as usual. When she saw the expression on my face, she straightened. "Are
you all right?"

I took a deep breath. "Tommy left. I have to ask you not to let him pick
up Robin anymore. I don't think he will, but—don't. Please." My voice and
hands had both been shaking.

She looked at me, my baby in her arms. I watched her understand that I
was going to cry if I said one more word.

"Of course I won't," she said. "Don't worry about that. Mind yourself,
Betsy."

I smiled a tight, wet smile of immense gratitude and hurried back to
my car.

When I came back later that day, Robin was napping, and she invited
me for tea in her kitchen. She asked if I wanted to tell her about what had
happened.

"Um—yes and no," I said.

She stroked a finger across her mug. "A friend of mine was in an abusive
marriage," she said.

There was no way to keep the tears from coming now. "How did you
know?"

She looked at me, shook her head, opened her mouth, paused. I shook
my head back. I remembered so many little things she must have seen.
Tommy had just told me he was going to stop defending me when people in
the village said I was crazy. He'd never mentioned doing that until he said he
was going to stop, and I'd started to wonder who was really defending me,
and who was accusing.

Robin had come home from Brigid's one day when he was seven months old, a month after she had started looking after him, with an infinitesimal scratch on his forehead. Brigid had told me exactly what happened: despite her coffee table's baby-proofed corner guards, Robin had still managed to fall into it in a way that left a slight mark, one I wasn't sure even Tommy or I would have noticed if Brigid hadn't pointed it out. But Tommy worked himself up to screaming that night, about how the scratch meant that Brigid was obviously abusing Robin, and I was, too, if I didn't give up everything to stay home with him right away. He'd already started trying to convince me that we couldn't trust anyone else to take care of Robin, that I needed to give up both my work and the few hours of respite that kept me sane.

He'd once said all he wanted was to look after a wife and child himself, and that it would be his great honor to give me time and space to write. I told myself that he must really believe Robin was in danger if he had changed his mind so thoroughly.

But then, I wondered why there seemed to be no chance of him giving up the long hours of his own job for Robin's sake. Even though my income was less predictable, I had still been the household's breadwinner. I didn't dare say that aloud, though.

Tommy made me promise to question Brigid about the scratch thoroughly the next morning.

"Those questions I asked you—about the scratch—" I said, my cheeks burning. "He made me say those things. I'm sorry."

"I knew that when you said them," Brigid said.

"Oh," I said. "Right." I took a wobbly sip of tea.

"My friend's son is grown up now," she said, "and he's wonderful. He knows exactly what his father's like, without my friend ever having to tell him. His actions bore it out. Robin will understand someday, too. You'll see."

Those words were a magic spell. They conjured up a vision of a future where my baby was okay, despite all the ways I'd failed him.

"Sam was raised by a single mum, too," Brigid went on, referring to her husband. "I've always thought he's a better man, a better father, for it."

The vision kept getting brighter.

So, no, I could not bear to give up Brigid, no matter what I had to do to be able to pay her. As the drama of that winter and spring wore on, Brigid was always sweet and tender with my baby and with me.

When we fled the cottage, Tommy came to her and demanded to know where we were. Brigid said she didn't know, and that she'd have him arrested if he showed up at her house again. He didn't, but I started driving different routes to and from her house every day, keeping an eye out for Tommy's car, an old unregistered red Volkswagen. I took back roads, drove behind buildings, trying to make sure he didn't see us, hoping he'd believed Brigid that she didn't know where we had gone.

When I apologized for my husband's behavior, Brigid told me I didn't have to, that she understood. She gave me gentle witness as I wept and shook and cried. She made me endless cups of tea in her kitchen, the real Irish benediction.

Brigid and Sam were putting an extension on their house so that her mother-in-law—a warm and glamorous woman who swept around the place in cream-colored cashmere, a single mother herself whom Brigid whispered to me had dated a famous musician—could move in and spend more time with their children. We drank our tea on a kitchen counter laden with blueprints, wooden slats, tiles, and building tools. I often caught myself looking at them wistfully. Not only was I a single parent now, one who could barely afford the cheapest rental I could find, but I was self-employed, low-income, and an immigrant. I couldn't imagine ever being able to afford a house of our own for Robin and me, one I could choose tiles for, one that would be *ours* enough that I could put my hands to it and change it.

Brigid caught me in those wistful looks, too. "Thank god for the chalet," she said. "We'd never have been able to buy this place without it."

"What do you mean?" They'd run a holiday ski chalet in France before moving to Ireland; that was all I knew about it.

"Oh, it was totally run-down when we got there. It had been for sale for years but no one was interested and it was in total disrepair, in the middle of this snowy forest . . . " She smiled at the memory. "Sam and I offered to rent for a few years, fix it up and run it as a business, if in exchange we'd have the chance to buy once the business had made us enough money."

I stared at her. The tea was dark and rich in my mouth. "You can do that?" My mind flooded with desperate, longing ideas for businesses I could run from a home Robin and I lived in: a bed and breakfast, a bookstore, a writing retreat center . . .

She laughed and shrugged. "We didn't know if we could or not. But it worked. We bought the chalet two years later, and a few years after that we sold the business and used the money to move back home. And here we are."

I looked around at the safe home she had given her children, and that she shared with me and mine. Around it I imagined the ghost of a dilapidated, forest-bound chalet, a home no one had wanted, that she and her husband had transformed as if by magic into the house where we sat now.

"Here you are."

I lay in bed on the night of June 4 thinking about how five years previously I had asked Tommy to marry me, and remembering the warmth and joy and sweetness of that moment as I listened to the wind outside, cold in my bed. I imagined driving back to the cottage, knocking on the door, and telling Tommy I was sorry. I would say I knew it was all a misunderstanding and I knew he was trying so hard and I still loved him and I knew we could make it better, and he would sweep me up and kiss me and bring me back across the threshold of our home, and I would have him again, even if only for a little while . . .

My body started to pull me out of bed with longing for him. But then I thought: I'd have to put Robin in the car seat.

And I couldn't do that. I couldn't bring my baby back to that house after all it had taken to leave.

If it had been just me, I would have gone. Let me be clear about that: I would not have been strong enough to stay away on my own. But for my baby, I broke my heart all over again.

Journal: June 6, 2018

I keep catching myself talking about Tommy in the past tense. "He was a
horse trainer." "He really was a gorgeous man." "He always said . . . "
    & now that it's summer & warm I keep missing the days when I
would go with him when he trained horses, & wander the fields taking
pictures, or sit reading on the hood of his car, or lean on a gate & just watch
him, his serious, thoughtful beauty, his muscles moving in time with the
animal's. I think I worshipped him a little. That probably would have had
to die no matter what. But it does feel like the man he was is gone.

I was still seeing Saoirse every week. After I finished getting moved into the
bungalow, though, she told me she thought I was ready to meet the group.

"It's only for women who've definitely left their relationship," she said.
"I'm sure you can understand why."

I nodded. If I'd gone into a group of survivors before I left Tommy,
I'd have talked to them the way I'd talked to Saoirse: full of love and longing and hope for my husband's redemption. I understood immediately how
painful that would be to hear now. How it might start to lure me back into
those thoughts myself, how often those thoughts cast their own lures as it
was.

"They're a good network," she said. "The other moms are there for each
other in ways I can't be, in ways the ethics code of this job won't let me be.
They'll be good for you. And I think you'll be good for them. And I facilitate the group, so you'll still see me."

A good network: ever since Tommy first left the house we shared, people had started asking me in a pitying way if I had one.

"Oh yes," I'd say. It was a lie every time. I didn't have local family, and
the most any of my faraway ones had offered when they found out what
happened to me were a few long-distance phone calls.

I'd lost most of my Irish friends with my marriage, and beyond that,
Tommy had always made a point of reinforcing my fear that I wasn't good at

making friends. He reminded me when he thought I'd said something weird to someone, encouraging me to lean on him and his social graces. Layer that over the paranoia that coming to fear the person I'd trusted most had created in me about everyone, and I was isolated.

I had Irene, and I had Brigid. They were each my friends. But my relationship with Irene had already reached its limits, and Brigid I paid. I didn't really know anyone else. Outside of working hours, it was just me and Robin.

I had Saoirse, of course, and our sessions at COPE that did so much to save me. But when she brought me into the fold of the survivors' group at COPE she saved me again, in a hundred thousand ways.

The first time I joined, they were having what Saoirse called a "healing day out." So I drove to a crunchy community center half an hour outside Galway City, where for the first time I met, in person, other women who had been through the same thing I had.

The first thing I noticed was that they—that we—were all quite different from each other. At twenty-nine, I was one of the youngest women there. The oldest was in her eighties. Only a slight majority had Irish accents. One wore a headscarf, another an undercut. Many of us had nothing else in common—nationality, class, race—except domestic violence.

More than a few women had matching triangular notches ripped out of their earlobes. It took me a few moments to realize why.

We were led through a yoga session and some art therapy, and we shared a lunch of vegan curry. As we ate, the woman in her eighties told us about how she had left her sixty-year marriage that year, and just last week she had gotten her own car for the first time in her life. Her children were angry with her, she said, but she had finally realized that she didn't want to spend the rest of her life feeling afraid in her own home—and so she left.

"I'm amazed at all of ye young women," she said in her thick country accent, "being brave enough to leave so much earlier than I did."

We all stared at her, amazed right back, certain that none of us were as brave as she.

•   •   •

I was still striving toward the July deadline for *The Circus Rose*. I wrote in short snatches between my online gigs, between Robin's naps and nursing, or with him on my lap and *Puffin Rock* playing on half the screen. I was waking up with Robin three to five times a night, working every minute I could, while Robin was with Brigid and while he was at home, working at the gigs I'd found and working at finding more. I pitched a podcast to a quarterly American magazine called *Parabola* that I'd written for a couple times, and they agreed to pay me $100 an episode, once a month. Not being paid to teach in the summer hadn't been a problem when I'd been with Tommy, whose work was seasonal and at its best in summer. But now the $7650 I'd get when I delivered *The Circus Rose*, and all the gigs I could scrape together until then, were all that stood between my baby and me and eviction.

So I wrote, even when I was so tired my eyes couldn't focus on the screen. I kept thinking, like a prayer or incantation: *let me leave my whole bleeding heart on the page*. I felt like it was all I had to offer. When I couldn't plan a chapter or a scene, when I couldn't even think to string a sentence together, I'd make myself write half a line and leave it dangling, then go back to Robin, or to searching for more jobs.

I'd wanted to be a writer all my life. If I lost sight of writing now, if I didn't prove I could still do it even when life was so hard, I felt sure I'd lose it forever. So I wrote, and hoped the words would lead us somewhere better than where we were.

The Circus Rose was going to be my fifth book. My fourth, the Robin Hood retelling called *The Forest Queen*, was coming out in August. I hadn't thought of it much at all since the day, when we were staying at Irene's house, that I'd written to my editor and asked if I could change the mention of my loving husband in the book's acknowledgments to thanking COPE. The manuscript had been about to go to press, she told me. I was just in time.

There is a single mother in *The Forest Queen*: an analogue of Little John called Little Jane, a hugely tall girl whom no one believes could have been raped by her child's father. The scene where she gives birth, and names her baby after the girl Robin Hood who saves her, was always the emotional center of the story for me. Looking back on that book from a year later, it was the only scene I could bear to reread—much of the rest of them concern the heroine's romance with a hero I modeled after Tommy, when I thought of him differently.

For all my other books, the extent of my publicity work had been typing out answers to interview questions for blog posts. Moving to Ireland had landed me squarely outside my publisher's or my own budget for in-person events. But my books had gotten good reviews, and this time a real event was suddenly presented to me: participation in a panel of young adult novelists writing feminist takes on old stories. All of them were better-known than me, and I knew without my publishers having to tell me that it was a coup for me to be invited at all.

Even before I finished reading the email my heart was aching with the wish to do it and the knowledge that I couldn't. I was thinking through the best way to tell them that I had neither the money to travel to the panel nor a single person who could take care of my baby for me while I did it.

But at the end of the email I saw that the panel would be online. Two years before COVID lockdowns and the proliferation of Zoom, it felt like a miracle. *Yes*, I wrote back. *I'm so thrilled that I can do this.*

And I was, but as the panel approached, I became so anxious about it that I wanted to scratch off my own skin. Because of the time difference, the US-based panel would take place during Irish dinner time, when my always hungry and chatty baby could be relied upon to be extremely, well, hungry and chatty. I splurged on a punnet of strawberries, his favorite food, and hid them like a box of rubies, higher in the fridge than he could reach. One minute before I was due to sign on for the panel, I arranged him in his high chair next to me and spread out the berries in front of him. When it came to strawberries, he was a slow and utterly enraptured eater, and if all went well, they'd give me half an hour before he demanded any other kind of entertainment. I'd asked the facilitator if it was all right to have my baby with me in the room, and what I'd be asked to talk about and for how long. She assured me it was fine and that I'd be talking about my own book for ten minutes or less, and the rest of the time I could mute myself while the other authors spoke. (It went without saying that most of the questions would likely be for them.)

I had never done an online panel before. I had assumed it would begin at the time I was told to log on. Instead, the facilitator greeted me and the other authors, then told us we'd be waiting in a virtual green room together for half an hour until the panel started.

Robin already had his strawberries. Taking them away now would cause a nuclear meltdown. The countdown was on.

In the end, I got through the panel. Robin remained happy to watch the faces on my computer screen for a good ten minutes after the strawberries were gone, which was a small miracle in itself, and a few more courses of teething biscuit and oatmeal I'd stashed away kept him entertained a little longer. Finally he demanded to be held, and to nurse, so I finished the panel doing that, too.

Afterward, I dragged us both into bed, my cheeks burning. I'd dreamed of being on a panel like that almost as long as I'd dreamed of being a writer. I was sure, after that day's showing, that I'd never be invited on another. The small talk I'd made with the other panelists had been painfully awkward, and I'd felt unprepared despite my notes and too distracted to pay attention to what anyone else had said. Already I could barely remember it, which only made me more sure I'd disgraced myself. I could hear all the times Tommy had scolded me for saying the wrong thing under the guise of constructive feedback, and I writhed.

Robin fell asleep quickly, his snickerdoodle-colored baby curls drifting on his forehead with each tiny breath. I was exhausted, but I couldn't sleep. The memory of embarrassing myself at the panel chased me up and out of bed, back to my computer by the windows.

I closed the blinds every night so no one could see inside from the road. Still, whenever I turned a switch on or off, I always saw the house from outside in quick flashes, the lines of light at the edges of the windows a map that could tell someone watching where I was. I always left the lights on in more than one room, and often overnight. I didn't want Tommy ever to know for sure I was asleep and unwary.

I meant to work on *The Circus Rose*. Every night, after Robin was down, I opened my word processor and wrote what I could, in between online tutoring appointments or scrolling through Friday Tea and the online parenting groups that had become the closest thing I had to community. I was so tired I could barely focus on the screen, but I knew I'd hate myself too much to sleep if I didn't manage to do something that brought me closer to bringing some money into the house before I went back to bed.

I stared at the draft for a few minutes, writing half-lines now and then, all of which I hated. I clicked over to my email and saw a forwarded list of artists' residencies from my MFA program.

I knew I was just torturing myself, but I read through all of them. Space and time just to write, and to rest . . . almost all of them had fees bigger than my rent. Not one allowed writers to bring their children with them.

I qualified for those residencies. I knew I did, I thought stubbornly, angrily. I'd published more than anyone else in my MFA's year, and I was teaching at a university. I knew I could probably get accepted to most of them.

But I also knew I'd never be able to go. Never mind the astronomical fees, there was no one with whom I could leave my kid. Not that I'd even want to. And if I did bring him, it would be into a space, like the panel I'd just done, that wouldn't really work for someone like me.

Was there any place in the world, I wondered, that let you be an artist and a single mother at the same time?

At the COPE survivors' group meetings, we started by taking turns talking about our weeks. It was a lot like Friday Tea, really, in its way. These were single moms like me, many still dealing with post-separation abuse years after they left their children's fathers, carrying extra phones, scraping by on welfare or working multiple jobs, waiting years for court-ordered child support that never came.

In my first session I sobbed as soon as I tried to speak, and then felt so embarrassed, I told myself I wouldn't go back.

I had lost count of the number of strangers I'd cried in front of since my marriage ended—cashiers, taxi drivers, women who smiled at my baby on the street—I felt ashamed every time. But at the survivors' group no one was surprised or bothered by tears. Soon enough I learned that someone cried there every week. I didn't have to explain myself, or defend the boundaries I'd put up against my ex.

More than that, I started to understand something in my heart that before I'd only known intellectually: there was nothing wrong with these women. There was nothing broken about them that invited any mistreatment. In fact, hearing their stories of survival and resilience and protection of their children, I quickly came to see single mothers as the most remarkable women I knew.

And then I had to admit that there might not be anything wrong with me.

Before I knew my marriage would break down, I'd offered to host a Notre Dame undergrad at our home and provide writing mentorship in exchange for some part-time assistant work and childcare. Natalia showed up in late June, a willowy Mexican girl who was going to spend her first months with American citizenship by flying to Ireland to live with me—to live with a writer, something she had always wanted to be. I still struggled to see myself as a real writer sometimes: my books were only published in another country, a place I both missed and feared being forced back to, and when I told people I wrote young adult fantasy I could almost see the phrase "not a real writer" flicker inside their heads. (Or maybe it was just flickering in mine.) I'd always imagined that when I was a real writer, I'd host college students for summer internships and writing time of their own, the kind of thing I would have killed for as a student myself. In that dream I was elegant, eccentric, elderly, and wealthy, and had a house with a pool and accompanying pool boy for my intern to fall in love with—clearly a fantasy left over from a time when I wrote love stories.

Once in a while I would look at the slowly growing shelf of my own books and chide myself that I *was* a real writer now, pool boy or no. It was in one of those moments that I had originally agreed to this exchange the previous autumn, when I imagined Natalia would be coming to live in the cottage, with Tommy, Robin, and me.

Why hadn't I canceled on Natalia when things started going badly? What does "going badly" mean? When we got our diagnosis of emotional abuse from the marriage counselor? Looking back, that's when I think I should have done it, if I was being responsible. When Tommy left the house? No, then I needed someone to help me more than ever.

She wrote to me about signing off on her summer internship funding the weekend I stayed at the Lady Gregory Hotel. Then? I was sure I'd be going back to the cottage then.

And in the weeks of our brush with homelessness? I should be ashamed to say that I didn't think of her once in those weeks of panic and fear. But I am not. Writing back to that time now, I am not ashamed of anything I did or did not do. I kept my baby alive and I found us a roof. Everything else is dust.

She sent me her flight details a week after we moved into the bungalow, and I was startled into remembering she was coming.

I'd never given her a specific street address, I realized. Just said I lived in a small house in east Galway where she'd have her own room. That was still true. The only difference was that my husband wasn't there.

Will I even tell her? I thought as I drove to Ballinasloe to pick her up. She stood on the edge of the green where two hundred years ago Napoleon had bought his horses, so my husband had told me, and where for five years I had watched him sell his. She had a backpack and a roller suitcase that looked bigger than she did. I wondered when college students had started looking like children to me.

I put down my car window and called to Natalia to put her things into the trunk.

I'd thought I could be mysterious, keep things buttoned up, and not burden her with everything that had happened. What this means, of course, is that within five minutes of the car ride home I had told her I was getting divorced.

I managed not to cry, at least. Soon I would stop counting the number of strangers I'd cry in front of that year, but not yet.

I was horribly ashamed about getting divorced. My family had always been religious, and with Natalia coming from Notre Dame I was expecting someone who, like most of the undergraduates there, attended Mass every week and had no problem living with a nun and staying out of the boys' dorms after ten p.m. and signing the student code of conduct, which forbids sexual activity on or off campus. *Maybe she won't even want to stay with me*, I thought. I told her that I was embarrassed to tell her, even. I have always been an open book.

"Oh, please," she said. "Nearly everyone in my family has gotten divorced, so I'll feel right at home."

We both laughed, and I thought maybe the summer was going to be okay, after all.

Natalia was so many things to us that summer, but mostly she became someone who loved us. She became one of the first people to teach me, to reteach me, that some people are happy to be kind, that for some people kindness makes them happy. In some ways she was as wide-eyed and sheltered as only a student at a religious college can be, but she was also quick-witted, dryly funny, and had a wry practicality that meant she was equally happy helping me with filing, changing diapers, or waking with Robin on a Saturday so I could get a little sleep. I liked her at once, and so did Robin, who learned the word "besos" from her and started demanding them immediately. She bought a football to kick back and forth with him, made horchata for us to drink together on Independence Day, asked if Robin would call her Tía Natalia and if we would like her to show us Mexico City someday, when we could travel and had money from the movies my books would obviously someday become. (The answer to both those questions, of course, was yes, and although the movies have shockingly still not arrived, she is one of the people who keeps the faith that they will—which is something every writer needs.)

She heard me cry on the baby monitor as I sang Robin to sleep every night, cry on the phone to companies whose bills I couldn't pay, just cry endlessly. I couldn't be brave all the time in my own home. She knew and understood and held that for me without ever saying anything about it.

• • •

At the COPE survivors' group, I quickly came to see myself as lucky. There were things I would never have imagined one day counting as luck: that I was fluent in the dominant language of the country I lived in; that I was able to find some kind of work, any kind at all, that I could do and also take care of my child; that I had housing and was not living long-term in a homeless shelter or hotel room or my car—that, at least I knew I would always count lucky, and be grateful for.

I was lucky, too, I learned, in my child's father. The more horror stories I heard from other mothers about the emotional and physical wounds their children bore on return from time with their fathers, the more I understood how lucky I was that Tommy had rejected us so thoroughly when we'd left him, and that we'd managed to hide from him since then. I was lucky, too, that he didn't have money—money for an aggressive legal team, money to bribe police and officials, money and the ineffable power and connections that come with it. What a happy ending it had once seemed, to many of the women in the group, to have a child with a successful, powerful man, only to have that same power turned against them and used to tear them from their children.

There was Mairéad, who was court-ordered to leave her own house on the weekend so that her alcoholic ex-husband could have overnight visits with their three daughters, because a judge had deemed him too unstable to have the girls over to his new place.

Imagine: coming home after a night at a hotel or back at your parents' house as if you're a wayward teenager and smelling the smoke of your ex's cigarettes in your bedsheets, knowing he could rifle through your drawers and shelves at his leisure, use your bathroom, lay his head on your pillow. And then having to help your kids recover emotionally from being spoken to unkindly, mocked and neglected, in their own home—where, from their point of view, their mother had abandoned them to their father.

Then there was Aisling, whose ex tells her children he does pay child support, but that their mother spends it on beauty treatments and that's why she can't afford their schoolbooks or new shoes. Whose ex then tells those same children to steal money from their mother's purse to fund his gambling habit, tells them it's his money by right—and probably really believes it is, as recompense for her leaving him, for the indignity of even being asked to pay that nonexistent child support in the first place.

There was Kelly, who left a controlling partner when her son was a baby and raised him with family in America for years, until her ex used the courts to drag her and her child back to Ireland—where she now has to adhere so rigidly to the access schedule he set that she is unable to hold down a job or keep her son in naíonra, because twice a week they spend seven hours round-trip on a bus to Belfast to see her (car-owning) ex at his convenience, all approved by the courts.

The women whose children report physical and sexual abuse by their fathers, but who are accused of lying and parental alienation when they bring those reports to court. Women the world sees as bitter, as scorned, who are just trying to keep their children safe.

Listening to their stories I so often wanted to scream. Sometimes we did: sometimes Saoirse would end a meeting by having us stand up and throw out our arms and let out whatever noises we needed to make. It reminded me of an old Smith tradition called Primal Scream: at midnight before the first day of exams, everyone opened their dorm room windows and howled all their fears into the night. It reminded me of banshees, too.

Screaming helped. So did crying. But just telling our stories helped the most.

What I talked about, in my first months with the COPE group, was often immigration. It was taking months of paperwork to inch toward getting the parental visa that I hoped would replace my spousal visa and let me remain in Ireland. Until then I was an undocumented immigrant—but I was also almost always the only white person in the waiting room at the immigration centers and Garda stations where I waited to have my papers filed and refiled, and it was absurdly obvious how much better I was treated because of that: because of my skin color, because I spoke English, and with an educated US accent at that. And despite all that I still found the endless hoop-jumping and convoluted forms upon forms I needed to fill out to get my visa desperately confusing and draining, the officers I met with full of a vague contempt that made me feel dirty and ashamed and unworthy, only to watch that vagueness sharpen into hatred when the next person in line after me had dark skin. One of those officers, early on, had winked at me and backdated a form, a small act of grace and kindness that made me have to hold my breath to keep from weeping, even as I wondered—without really wondering—why she'd decided I was the person in the room that day who deserved her taking that risk.

Natalia's church had lost half their congregation in the last few years, she'd just told me, to deportation. Family separation at the US–Mexico border was in the news, my home country's government acting out the same threat my husband had given me.

Yes, I learned quickly, I was very, very lucky.

The first of July came and I couldn't make rent. The money from my online gigs had gone to luxuries like electricity and food. The deadline for *The Circus Rose* and the money that would follow hadn't come yet, and I was afraid I wouldn't finish in time. After the panic attack that followed looking at my bank account, I turned to Friday Tea. I knew at least that I could tell them about it and they wouldn't judge me. Along with my weekly best and worst, I listed some freelance editorial services I could provide and wrote that if anyone would be willing to buy them, I'd be extremely grateful. I felt ashamed of sullying the sacredness of Friday Tea by asking for work, but I didn't know what else to do.

Several people did take me up on editorial jobs, but more, far more, sent me something I couldn't have imagined receiving, let alone asking for: money for nothing. They sent me enough money to cover July's rent entirely, plus half of August's, and the rest came from freelance jobs and selling signed copies of my books.

I sat at the little table in the bungalow's living room absolutely stunned. This meant my rent was paid until I started teaching again in September, until I had my regular paycheck back. I couldn't remember ever having received money without any expectations in return—certainly not from my parents or my husband. This was money from strangers and near-strangers on the other side of the world, who would never get any silence or compliance or submission from me in return, who simply and genuinely wanted to help. It baffled my worn-out heart.

The Friday Tea group's spontaneous crowdfunding helped me imagine something else, too. I kept thinking about Brigid's story of renting the run-down chalet and starting the business there that allowed them to buy it. Maybe the Smithies would believe in a project like that, I thought. Maybe they'd help me get it started. I was still scrolling through real estate websites when I couldn't sleep, replacing dreams with pictures of houses for sale.

I kept thinking of all the shame I'd felt after that book panel, feeling it again every time I recalled it. I thought of all the residencies I'd never even applied for because they were too expensive or couldn't account for childcare. I thought of the acrylic nail broken off into the intercom box at COPE. I thought of other women's hands.

Maybe I could make the kind of place I longed for—a place that welcomed single mothers, that honored and centered us instead of letting the basic facts of our lives—financial hardship, constant caretaking—exclude us.

I would never have dared to think that so many people would want to help me. I could never have imagined asking for such a thing. But it had already happened.

Maybe, if I found the right place, it could happen again.

When I dropped Natalia off at the train station at the end of her internship, the last thing she said to me was: "You're a good mom. And a good writer. I need you to hear that."

"You are, too," I said. We were both crying then.

She hugged me and walked away without another word.

After Natalia left, it took me a few days to remember how I'd lived without her. No one else doing anything around the house, no one else taking any early mornings, no one else with an adult vocabulary to talk to? Before I had those things, I hadn't seen—hadn't let myself see—how hard it was to go without them. It felt impossible for a few days, until that seeing closed up again, until I made myself close it up.

I felt my vigilance, too, in a way I hadn't when Natalia was there. I was the only person protecting Robin again. I was the only person at the house, should Tommy find us.

I started working later into the night, partly chasing the delivery payment for *The Circus Rose*, but partly, too, so I could keep a later watch. When I stayed up past midnight, night after night, knowing Robin would have me awake again at five or earlier, I told myself it was for the sake of my deadline. But I played my writing music quietly enough that I could hear passing footsteps outside. Sometimes I thought I did.

I mostly hated the book I was writing. I thought I was too scraped-out, too broken and brokenhearted, to write anything worthwhile. I couldn't even manage to write full sentences most of the time. I was sure it was the worst book I'd ever written.

But it didn't need to be good, I told myself, almost believing it. It just needed to house us. I pictured the pages open above us like a roof. I might write good books later, if I could just make us survive long enough to get there. One bad book was a small price to pay for feeding and housing my child.

It finally occurred to me, late one night, to let my half-lines break. I didn't have it in me to do anything more. If that was all I could do, I gave myself permission to do it.

With that permission, those half-lines turned, slowly, into a pattern of their own. *The Circus Rose* became something I might never have dared to write if I had felt more whole, more safe: a novel in verse.

Finally, late one summer night, I finished that book. I looked up from my screen at the dark line between the edge of the blind and the window frame, at the darkness outside. I felt like my eyes and fingernails were bleeding. But I'd met my deadline.

Robin had demanded to sleep in my bed that night. I dragged myself under the covers with him, curled against his small warmth, and fell asleep knowing I'd kept us fed and housed for a few more months.

Ten

Herd Animals

AUTUMN 2018

for Leah

One morning, driving home from the grocery store, I stopped to take a picture of the view: fields tumbling like bolts of green silk down the hill, tiny winding roads among the patchwork landscape, east Galway wrapping the sky up like a quilt. I still saw Ireland the way I had when I first moved here: a land of miraculous wetness and greenness, a sanctuary as sacred as a church, and as protective from the forces that had driven me to it.

And then I thought I saw Tommy drive by.

I thought I'd seen him a million times before. I told myself this wasn't any different, the eyes I thought I knew looking back at me in the rearview mirror for that split second as he went by. He didn't even slow down.

It couldn't have been him. He still didn't know where I was. He still didn't know where we lived.

Robin was with Brigid, at least. I would be safer in my car, and then safer in my house. It probably wasn't even him.

I drove home. The driveway was empty.

I backed into it, the way the safety plan from COPE had taught me. I parked and looked at my phone: no messages.

I got out of the car, still looking at my phone, wondering if I should call Brigid and make sure Robin was okay, wondering how neurotic that would sound.

When I looked up, Tommy's car was blocking the way out.

He was standing in front of it in his wide horse-trainer stance, staring at me.

I managed to stand straight and stay still. I kept my phone in my hand.

We looked at each other.

I hated my body and heart for wanting him as much as I feared him.

"I want to see him," Tommy said. "Get him out of the car."

"He's not with me," I said.

His glance flicked to the back of my car, to its empty car seat. Thank god, thank god, thank god.

He didn't move.

"You're not welcome here," I said. "You're not welcome at my house."

He kept staring at me. "This is a public road." His feet in their beat-up boots were, I saw, just touching the far side of the groove the gate made in my driveway. I was sure he'd made certain of that.

"If you don't leave, I'll call the guards," I said—the Irish term for the police.

"You're being fucking stupid now. You're pathetic."

I put my other hand to my phone to make the call. "Please leave."

He kept staring.

It wasn't 911 here—999 was the Irish number, I thought, and 111 was the EU one. Or was it the other way around? It didn't matter, I should call either one. I should have the local Garda station number saved in my phone. Why didn't I? Why was I so stupid? Why was I so fucking stupid? Pathetic.

I pressed the first nine. Tommy scoffed at me, walked around his car, and got back in. He kept watching me from the driver's seat.

I pressed the second nine. He drove away.

I triple-checked my car was locked, went inside, closed all the blinds, and sobbed.

Then I called Brigid and told her I wanted to pick up Robin early.

When I got there, she asked what was wrong.

I held out my arms for Robin first, and she gave him to me. I buried my nose in his hair and felt the trembling in my body start to ebb.

"I let Tommy see me," I said. "He followed me home. He knows where we live now." I took another breath of Robin's smell, felt the direct line it made to my heartbeat, slowing it down. "I'm sorry, Brigid. I'm so stupid."

"What do you mean, you let him see you?"

"I got out of the car on the side of the Ballinasloe road to take a picture. I didn't need that picture. I know he takes that road sometimes. I should have thought."

"Oh my goodness," Brigid piped, in the same tone she'd have used if one of the babies in her care was being naughty. "You can't be thinking about hiding every minute of your life. Don't be silly, now."

I tried to laugh. Of course I had to think about hiding, about keeping my baby safe, every single minute. If I didn't, anything that happened to him would be my fault.

She looked at me another moment, and I could tell she understood what I was thinking, and also understood that she would not be able to persuade me otherwise. "Will you have a cup of tea, before you go?" she asked.

I said I would, and then Robin wanted to nurse. So we were both refreshed, and calmer, by the time we went on the road again.

After that day I never got out of the car to take pictures, remembering with bitterness Tommy's instructions to stop photographing rainbows. I stopped looking for things to notice.

The next week, Brigid's husband Sam ran out of the house to stop me as I was getting in the car after dropping off Robin in the morning.

"Your car is leaking brake fluid," he said.

I followed his pointing finger to a dribbling trail of dark liquid leading from my car to the road.

"When's the last time you got it serviced?"

"Um." I didn't know but had the familiar man-is-going-to-yell-at-me-if-I-tell-the-truth feeling in my gut. "A while ago."

"Right. You need to get that fixed today. Today. Drive straight to a garage and sign up for a service while you're there. It's really dangerous."

He said it kindly, no hint of angry-dad or angry-husband in his voice, but I still felt that miserable girl-in-trouble feeling that I got whenever anyone saw that I'd made any kind of mistake at all.

I drove to the nearest garage and asked them to check my brake fluid. They did, told me I was lucky I'd made it there without dying, and charged me €600 I didn't have to fix it.

J. Courtney Sullivan, a fellow Smith alumna writer with several bestsellers to her name, had written to me the week before, after another Friday Tea post where my "worst of the week" was, as always, money woes. If I ever needed to borrow money to make ends meet, she said, I should let her know. I wrote to her then and asked for the €600 for car repair. She lent me that and then some. I booked the service and was able to go grocery shopping and pay Brigid for the week's childcare. Most miraculously of all, I was able not to hyperventilate while I did any of those things.

After my car service the following week, the mechanic took me aside. "Did you know your wheels were about to come off?" he asked.

"Um." The same feeling again. Would I ever not panic when a man told me I'd done something wrong? "No."

"It didn't feel strange, maybe when you were driving fast? Like the wheels were wobbling?"

My stomach dropped. "Yes. Sometimes."

He nodded. "Don't touch them again yourself, just bring the car in here. People shouldn't be messing with their wheels if they don't know what they're doing."

I had never touched the wheels, but I just nodded. Voicing that would have led him to ask a question that I didn't want to ask myself: had someone else?

If the wheels came off at high speed, I would be dead. And Tommy had just found out where we lived.

I don't know. I'll never know.

That's one of the strangest things about emotional abuse: there are so many things I'll never know for sure. Just like I'll never know for sure what happened to the cash from the sale of my last car—cash that Tommy had blamed me for losing when it vanished after I was sure I'd put it in my purse. He'd had a strange amount of cash himself, the following weeks, but how dare I suspect the husband I loved? He was always theorizing aloud about what kinds of deaths might be quick and painless—carbon monoxide poisoning, a gunshot to the head. There were so many moments that scared me in ways I didn't want to admit, that scared me so much I had to explain them away to survive. The further away I got from those memories, the more frightening they became.

Saoirse had once told me that the most accurate predictor of whether an abusive man will become homicidal after the end of a relationship is not his history of violence, not even whether the relationship itself was previously physically violent—it is the woman's gut feeling about how dangerous he is. *She* is the most accurate predictor of what he will do.

I don't know. I will never know.

But I have a feeling.

A field across the road from the bungalow housed a skinny dun mare. Her mane was falling out, and her hide was raw in the places she had bitten off her own fur. You could always see the whites of her eyes.

One of the many things Tommy taught me is that a horse kept alone in a field will never thrive. It won't sleep, will go off its feed, will even start pulling out its own hair. But if you put any other herd animal in the field with it—it doesn't have to be another horse, it can be a cow or sheep or goat or donkey—they'll get on just fine.

This is because in a herd, animals take turns being lookout. One animal watches for danger while the others rest and eat. A herd animal by itself, or by itself with its baby, is always watching for danger. It won't lower its head long enough to eat much or feel safe enough to sleep deeply.

I felt for that horse. I felt like her, too.

After Tommy found the bungalow, I started waking up even more often—not just for Robin, who was still nowhere near sleeping through the night, but anytime there was a strange noise outside or anytime I, dreaming, thought there was. We lived deep in the countryside, surrounded by fields and bogs and woodlands. Any noise that might be human could be my husband, who had become the wolf again—this time one I was running from, not toward.

I still wasn't eating well. So many people had congratulated me on my weight loss, as if it were proof that it was healthy for me to have left my relationship, as if I was preparing to go back on the market at a higher value, as if I were cattle myself. I hadn't been trying to lose that weight, but I still couldn't make myself eat. Couldn't make myself sleep. Their congratulations made me want to scream.

Waking up with Robin at night, at least I could hold him, nurse him, feel that I was doing something good. Staring alone into the darkness, into my own fear and vigilance, was so much worse. Ever since I'd given birth, I'd often get to the morning astounded that there were people in the world who had slept through those endless nights, who had not even noticed time passing at all, when it felt like years had gone by for me before dawn. I already felt about a decade older than I had when Robin was born.

But those nights also gave me an unexpected gift. I had friends on the other side of the world, and when I was slogging through endless dark it was the afternoon for them, or the bright morning. There were people who could speak to me from the land of sunlight and reassure me it was still there.

And, it turned out, I could do the same for at least one of them. Claire was a girl I'd known in high school back in Maine, two years older than me. While we'd run in the same artsy groups, I'd always thought she was far too pretty and cool to really be my friend. We'd both done the musicals, for instance, but in *Grease* she was leading lady and I was stage manager. I'd watched her kiss the cute boy from backstage while I told the spotlight to queue up. She did Pilates after school and always had the right lip gloss. You get the idea.

Claire had moved to Arizona with a husband who had some mysterious lucrative job I didn't understand, and she had her first baby six months after I did. We vaguely followed each other online, the way you do with people you liked in school but didn't know well.

One morning, after Robin woke me at five yet again, I opened Instagram to see a grainy selfie she'd posted, holding her wakeful baby in a dark nursery, just a few minutes ago. Something about the worn look in her eyes made me reply.

I messaged her: The nights feel endless sometimes, don't they?

My phone pinged right back.

> Claire:
> Truly. Like they'll last forever and no
> one else is awake in the world.

Me:
Yeah, I know. It sucks. It's morning here but
it's still dark. My kid wakes up at five, and in
winter the sun doesn't come up till nine.

> Claire:
> Jesus. I took Irish Studies in college
> and they never told me that.

Me:
It's brutal.

> Claire:
> This kid waking up five times a night is brutal.

Me:
Ugh. Absolutely. I'm sorry.

> Claire:
> But at least I have someone to talk to now.

Me:
Same.

We were eight hours apart, and we quickly realized that we could be awake for each other when no one more local was, at the exact hours when each of us most needed a friend. Claire and I talked about our babies, our sleep deprivation, our frustrations and our worries—we talked about mutual crushes past and present, boys from high school and Hozier—we talked about *Buffy the Vampire Slayer* and fantasy novels and our heartaches over our husbands. She was trying hard to stand by hers, but he was an addict and a serial cheater, and her pain at his behavior often matched mine over

Tommy's. She was far more of a kindred spirit than I'd ever given her credit for when I had been so sure she was a too-cool-for-me girl in high school.

It also turned out she was raised by a single mom. I'd never known that. Her dad was, to a bizarre degree, like Tommy. And she knew exactly who had been there for her, and who hadn't, when she was growing up.

Claire was telling me a story, with just the fact of who she was, of someone who was raised by a single mom and turned out okay—turned out, in fact, to be one of the most wonderful people I know. She was telling me a story with the friendship that she showed me, with the endless conversation we've kept up in between working and looking after our babies since then. It was a story I retold myself every time I felt the stigma all single moms feel—one that told me my family, and my child, could be *good*. As good as this woman I'd long thought was too good for me, but who turned out to be as good a friend as I have ever had.

After a nighttime vigil with her, I always slept a little deeper.

When a heavy cardboard box arrived with our post one day, it scared me a little. I'd come to dread every piece of mail I got, in case it was an overdue bill or something equally unpleasant from my lawyer, from the courts, from immigration, from Tommy.

Then I looked at the return address: it was from my publisher. A box of finished copies of *The Forest Queen*. I touched their satiny green covers as cautiously as if they'd arrived from another planet.

Somehow, even with the work I'd been doing for its launch, I kept forgetting this book was coming out. The person I'd been when I'd written *The Forest Queen*, before Robin was even born, was someone I didn't recognize anymore. These books should have arrived back at the cottage, for her. I felt like I didn't even know what to do with them now.

I had a COPE group meeting that day and I brought a few copies along. When it was my turn I dug them out of my bag with a shrug and said I didn't know if anyone would want them but they could have them if they did.

They all rushed on the books, exclaiming and arguing over them. I blushed and laughed and said I'd bring more next time. When Saoirse asked me why I'd thought no one would want them, why they wouldn't be proud of me, I suddenly couldn't speak at all.

A year ago, I'd booked a reading at a Galway bookstore for the launch. That, I could talk about. "I've been thinking of canceling," I said. "I'm afraid Tommy will be there. What if he tries to hurt me there? What if he tries to hurt other people? How can I ask anybody to come, and risk that?"

Saoirse looked at me steadily. "He didn't come to the baptism," she said. "He doesn't pay child support, he hasn't looked for custody. He strikes me as the lazy kind of abuser. I don't think he'll show up."

"He shows up at the house now," I whispered. "He did it again just the other day."

Saoirse nodded, holding my gaze. "You're right," she said. "I'm sorry." She thought silently for a long moment. Saoirse always seemed confident in her silences, something I was trying to learn from. I'd started to realize I was always hurrying to explain myself, or to speak out loud. Tommy used to say that when women paused while speaking, it meant that they were planning their next lie.

"Could you show the staff a picture of him?" she asked. "They could keep a lookout."

"Oh. Right. I should have thought of that."

Saoirse frowned. "I want you to stop using the word *should* so much," she said. She looked around at the group. "I want that for all of you. Should just makes us feel inadequate."

Aisling, whose eyes always glimmered with good humor even through the worst, raised a hand. "You're telling us we should stop, so, Saoirse?"

We all laughed.

"Maybe he won't come," I said, "but I'm not sure who else will. I lost most of our friends when I left him."

The women looked at each other, and I realized what I'd said. "I wasn't fishing," I said, "I really wasn't! Ugh, I'm sorry. Please don't feel obliged."

"I'm going to ask you again, Betsy," Saoirse said, almost severely, "why you're so sure that we don't want to."

So when the reading came, I walked into Charlie Byrne's to see nearly every seat filled. Some of my current and former students were there, but mostly it was women I'd met through COPE, women I would never have known if it weren't for the crises that had brought us together.

In grad school, we'd had to do readings on campus every semester. The professors told us that if we got nervous, we should choose one person in the room, one kind-looking face, and read to them alone.

Saoirse was there, in the center of the front row, watching me proudly through her bright-colored glasses, a signed copy of my book in her lap. Every time I looked up from my words, I saw her smile.

Eleven

The Castle

AUTUMN 2018–SPRING 2019

for Friday Tea

Every year, Irene and I went to the Knitting & Stitching Show in Dublin: a cornucopia of yarn and fabric suppliers, craft demonstrations, and textile art exhibits, plus a hefty number of booths advertising arthritis pills and back massagers, because they knew their audience. We called it Old Lady Heaven even though both of us—I was thirty and Irene in her fifties—were among the show's youngest clientele. Irene, an accomplished embroiderer, had a tremor in her hand that, for some reason, stitchwork stilled. I learned to knit at eight and have done it ever since, the closest thing to both meditation and math that I enjoy.

The previous year, in 2017, it was on the train to Dublin that I had confessed to Irene that Tommy was in an abuser program and I was getting help from COPE. Six-month-old Robin rode in his carrier on my chest. At the time, I hadn't known at all what Irene would say: Irene, who had a sharp-witted judgment for every coworker, family member, and friend; Irene, who loved gossip with her Gemini incisiveness; Irene, who was born the exact same day as my mother. "Well, I'm proud of you," she had said matter-of-factly. "I'm proud of both of you. And, you know, this time next year, hopefully you'll be able to tell me you're in a better place."

That had comforted me. Robin would be toddling the next year, instead of riding in his carrier. What would he see? What would I? How much happier and healthier, surely, would my marriage be from all the work Tommy and I were doing?

This year, in 2018, it felt like I had utterly failed. Irene had insisted that I deserved this day out, this time off work. I found the idea of deserving anything hard to comprehend. What I deserved was to keep my baby safe, and I earned that by working every minute I was awake, staying vigilant through the nights, nursing him as long as he wanted to nurse, breastfeeding him even through food poisoning. (When I told Saoirse about that, she nodded and said that's when you learn what single parenting really is.)

On the three-hour train ride up to the Knitting & Stitching Show, I talked of nothing but houses. Every night after Robin's first waking, I was unable to go back to sleep: I woke up overthinking and could never turn it off, and I kept thinking I heard footsteps outside the window. So I was back to reading real estate listings on my phone.

I showed my favorites to Irene, tiny rural cottages under €150,000— still unimaginably out of my price range, and ten times what my old landlords had said they'd sell the cottage for, before Tommy took it back over, but still low enough that I could at least fantasize about them. Even though a cottage and a mansion were equally unattainable, I didn't dare dream about somewhere too expensive.

Irene had been a lawyer in the US and was now an office manager. She had never had trouble financing a house, with her Irish military husband and their two stable jobs, and she clicked her tongue at the idea that I would.

"It's not like you're unemployed," she said. "My goodness, you're working, what, nine different jobs now? Just go into a bank and ask how much you qualify for, and then you can start house-shopping for real."

When I laughed at that, she frowned.

By then we were in the conference center, sighing over a box of recycled sari silks.

"Well, what if you write a book about a house, and sell the book?" she said. "You know, like *Under the Tuscan Sun*?"

I snorted. "Yeah, *Under the Irish Rain*. Have you seen any sun-drenched villas in Galway?"

Irene laughed. "No, but I mean, you know how Americans get about old Irish cottages. You could find some worn-out place and write about fixing it up. Some old damp house no Irish person wants, something unusual enough to write about. Think of all the things Americans love here. Thatched roofs. Sheep." She waved a hank of wool. "What's that old film we Yanks love? *The Quiet Man*. You could be 'The Quiet Woman.' That's what you could call the book." She laughed again, as if she hadn't just violently woken up my heart with foolish hope.

I had about half a second of scoffing left in me, of pretending my imagination wasn't already sweeping me off my feet into this fantasy. A snarky reply died in my throat, and I found myself trying not to cry.

Write a book, I thought, *to buy a house . . .*

I remembered how the only way I'd managed to finish *The Circus Rose* was by imagining its pages as a roof over Robin's head. I remembered Brigid's story of the chalet, and the writing retreat business I'd pictured for myself, how I'd imagined a place that could offer free retreats to single mothers, too.

Write a book to buy a house. I had written five books. I was a writer, something that had seemed an impossible dream all my life until I made it come true. After all, I thought, writing a book to buy a house was less far-fetched than a mortgage broker offering me a single euro. I could write my way into a stable home for myself and Robin and never have to face the howling wind of homelessness again. A place, maybe, that I could turn into a business the way Brigid and Sam had done—a place for writers and artists, or even just a little B&B. A place that was my own, that Tommy could not take away. Somewhere no one could ever make us leave.

On the taxi back to the train station that afternoon, I saw a listing that took my breath away: a castle.

Well—a small run-down tower house with three dimly lit bedrooms, a cramped kitchen, and an ancient toilet that clearly had moss growing out of the bowl even in the listing photos, but still, an honest-to-God castle, built in the 1500s by descendants of William the Conqueror. Its name and thick walls sang of fortification, the kind of safety that could see out a siege. Just like Irene said, it was old, damp, and certainly unusual. It had been on the market for years without a sale.

Surely, I thought, it's been waiting for me.

On the train ride home from the knitting show, I wasn't staring at my phone and sighing anymore—I was writing furiously in my journal, in between increasingly excited talks with Irene about what the book could look like. It was true, we both knew, that Galway was no less gorgeous than Tuscany, the yellow sunshine and ruddy wines of Italy no more romantic than Ireland's cool mists, nubbly Aran yarns, whispering turf fires, and luscious, chocolate-rich Guinness. Hadn't we both been seduced away from our whole lives, not just by our husbands, but by Ireland itself?

Tea: Instead of tea, look at these juicy recycled silks I saw today at the Knitting & Stitching Show.

Best: OK, this is a complete fantasy, but there is this tumbledown castle ruin near where I live. Part of it was restored as a small three-bedroom house years ago, so it's old-fashioned but livable. It's for sale right now. For the same price as other deeply boring non-castle houses in the area. I was with my friend Irene at the knitting show today and she said that I should propose a memoir about moving into this castle as a single mom coming out of an abusive marriage and chronicle my first year in it, fixing it up and empowering myself as a woman ET CETERA.

The thing is, if someone else wrote that book I would read the ever-loving HELL out of it. And that is usually my barometer for the kinds of books I should write.

Maybe a publisher would want to buy this book for down payment type money. I think I might start writing a tiny proposal.

Writing that post, for the first time in months I felt full of energy, happy to stay up and write after Robin went to sleep, instead of dragging myself between my desk and bed until the next time he or I woke up. That feeling was as seductive as the idea of a real home: a dream I could really reach for, among all the slog and fear of simply trying to survive.

My Friday Tea post blew up. Scores of comments told me it was a brilliant idea, I should go for it, don't let anyone stop me.

Megan Perry:
I was delightfully surprised when I saw those silks and the wonderful good time that you had—that it was written by the same person who has gone through what you have this past year or so. Not that you are obligated to feel good or okay for any length of time, but this doesn't seem that. This to me is a person who is burning too brightly to get taken over by someone else's awfulness for too terribly long.

MaryAlice Fernandez:
Betsy, I would read the hell out of that book, too! Your idea just made my morning. I'd love to meet you sometime!

Monique Holtz:
Yes you should buy the crap out of this house and write the crap out of that book, and for the record, in the event that you want a section on doing house renos with long distance friends, you will be hard pressed to convince me NOT to show up.

Dara Kaye:
If your literary agent doesn't do much nonfiction, I would donate an hour to look over your proposal. It's what I do all day long.

Their disembodied voices filled me with a faith and strength I hadn't felt in a long time. All these smart people believing in this dream made it start to feel less absurd. If they believed it could happen, maybe it really could.

Betsy Cornwell:
OK Smithies: I wrote to the estate agent and I'm going to call them on Monday. Meanwhile I'll start working on the proposal. I think a Kickstarter would be ideal for funding renovations and updates, and maybe even part of the down payment—hopefully I'll get a viewing this week and have a better idea if this is really workable.

Thank you for believing in this idea that made me laugh at myself, but also caught my heart.

I didn't hear back from the estate agent that Monday, and I kept not hearing back for days and days—and yet I kept believing, with a deep certainty that fell somewhere between romantic obsession and religious mania, that it was going to happen. I couldn't afford despair any more than I could a down payment.

When I finally heard back a week later, I booked a viewing and walked through, unable to keep myself from trembling with excitement even as I saw that there wasn't just moss in the toilet, but a fairy ring of mushrooms, too. The rooms were small—less total square footage than the bungalow, if much more romantically distributed—and moldy and cold and damp, to a disturbing degree, even in the context of every other old Irish house I'd lived in. The castle had collected its damp for half a millennium. Its cold had history. Its mold had depth.

But it was a *castle*. I told myself it was destiny that we would mend and heal each other. I tried not to think about how I'd once believed that of Tommy.

Besides, there were good surprises, too: a real suit of armor in the entryway, canopy beds, a huge claw-foot bathtub in a stone alcove in the biggest bedroom. I wanted a bath there like I wanted air to breathe. I would have lived in that bathtub. I would have taken all my author photos in it. Even a selkie, I thought, might give up her sealskin for a bath in that alcove tub.

I thanked the realtor for the tour and tried to seem blasé, though I'm sure he could see me drooling.

I asked Brigid how she and her husband made the rent-to-own offer on their chalet. She said I should have my solicitor write the offer letter, and make sure to lowball them at first, so I did: I offered €50,000 under the asking price, which I said I would pay after two years of renting to own.

Then I waited.

In between drafting pieces of my next novel—a revenge-themed sequel to *Jane Eyre* that I called *Reader, I Murdered Him* and found deeply cathartic for some mysterious reason—working my many freelance gigs, and singing along with my Muppet-loving toddler to "Something Better," I daydreamed about renovating the castle. As I shuttled Robin quickly from our blinds-drawn bungalow to the car in the winter rain and sludge, I thought about how we could plant hazel and elder trees in the garden and build a little shed next to the wild snarl of overgrown roses in the corner.

When Robin woke me at night yet again, and I stared into the darkness while I soothed him back to sleep, I pictured covering the castle walls with tapestries—maybe I could find a loom and weave them myself. I thought of the friends who wrote messages of strength and support to me online, and imagined sewing their names into those tapestries, a way to surround ourselves with their warmth.

I didn't hear back. Over the next six months, I sent the realtor higher and higher bids, telling myself the numbers didn't matter because I didn't have them yet anyway.

My solicitor warned me that if the owner agreed to a sale, I'd need five grand to get in escrow, and then I'd have a month to raise the rest. I told Claire that in one of our late-night texting sessions.

Send me the book proposal, she wrote. I've always wanted an Irish castle.

Her husband was relapsing again. She needed a dream, too.

An hour later, after she'd read it: Honey, this is real magic. I'm in. Send me your bank details and I'll get you that five grand.

I was astounded. It was an unfathomable amount of money to be able to just *send* in my mind. Oh my god, Claire, really? It's too much. I can't let you do that.

You can. There's only one thing I want in exchange.

I would have sliced off my hands for her, for a chance at the castle. I would have given her my skin. Name it. Do you want to move to Ireland? Do you want me to marry you?

I won't rule it out. But no. When this book gets made into a movie, I want to be your date to the premiere. ˙

Every now and then, just when I started to hope he had stopped, Tommy would come to the house. Usually in the evening, banging on the door, slurring his speech. Saoirse was certain he was a drinker when we were together, but I didn't think he was: we were both homebodies most of the time, he'd go to the pub maybe once every couple months—and he'd come home seeming drunk, and sometimes telling stories of getting into fistfights, but it wasn't more often than that.

I did think he'd started to drink after we left. A lot of his most bizarre, ranting emails and texts were sent between midnight and dawn. When he started driving to the bungalow and banging on the door, he always seemed clearly drunk.

While he grew increasingly angry outside, I would repeat what I had rehearsed over and over with Saoirse. "I am no longer willing to speak with you privately. Anything you need to discuss with me you can say to my solicitor." Finally I would tell him that if he didn't leave, I was going to call the guards. He would dare me to, and only when he heard the ringing from my phone speaker would he dash back to the car and peel out of the driveway. The guards would always get angry with me when they finally picked up and I had to explain that he was already gone. They told me to stop calling unless I was in real danger.

While Tommy pounded on the flimsy hardware-store door of the bungalow, I would hold Robin, close my eyes, and think hard about the castle. What I longed for most wasn't its fairy-tale glamour, but its thick walls. Six feet of stone, six hundred years old, guarding us from the world outside. With those slit-narrow windows you can shoot arrows through.

A week before Christmas, my car broke down completely. I had to tell Brigid I couldn't bring Robin to her anymore, which was secretly a relief, because already I'd had to delay her payments for weeks, waiting for one of my many gigs to send money that I wouldn't immediately need to dump into rent or electricity or food.

I didn't tell her my car broke down and I couldn't afford to replace it; that was too embarrassing. Besides, we were about to have two weeks off from childcare for the holidays, which stretched out frighteningly before me, since there was never a day when I wasn't working, wasn't thinking about work and trying to scrape enough out of my hollowed insides to make it through the next month. Having no one to take on any childcare was only going to make that harder.

Robin decided to wean himself that week, too. I woke up what felt like a million times a night with sore and overflowing breasts, my body convinced that because it wasn't feeding my baby anymore he must be dead, my scraps of sleep full of nightmare images of him strangling on electrical cords or drowning himself in the sink. I pushed his stroller to the shop in the freezing rain because we didn't have a car, and as we passed the nativity scenes that lined the road I wondered if it had ever occurred to the wise men that a mother stuck in a barn might want, not frankincense and myrrh, but a ride and a babysitter.

For Christmas itself, I swallowed my pride and asked Irene if we could stay with her and Cían. I was sure Tommy would come to the house on Christmas. Irene warmly agreed. She picked us up on Christmas Eve and I hauled the car seat and travel cot into her car. We slept in the same guest room where we'd spent those first frightening weeks after Robin's birthday.

Saoirse had taken me through the overstuffed storage room where COPE kept their Christmas toy donations—never enough cash donations, always too many toys—and pressed me to choose a dinosaur and play computer for Robin, even as I kept insisting that other families needed them more. Irene and Cían got him a beautifully carved wooden bear-and-block set that I recognized from a German children's boutique in Galway City. I had admired the display window but never stepped inside, knowing I couldn't afford it.

I had wrapped some toys I'd found in charity shops, and one little sand-filled lizard I'd bought new from the gift shop outside the aquarium Robin and I both loved so much. I'd gotten a year's membership when he was born, and renewed it shortly before his birthday, when I thought I could do things like that.

When Tommy started showing up at the house, I started taking Robin out as much as I could. The aquarium was something free—or at least, already paid for—that we could both enjoy. We spent whole days there, wandering through the moody, swirling, water-filtered light inside. Robin crawled and toddled and even ran for the first time on the aquarium's slightly damp and gritty floor. He loved every fish equally, but my favorites were in a small display on the top floor, empty except for a string hung with mermaid's purses. The egg cases of sharks, mermaid's purses are translucent little amber-colored rectangles with delicate swirling curlicues at each corner, to help the eggs hook on to seaweed while the babies grow. The tank was lit so that you could see—a miracle every time—the thrumming rhythmic movements of the unhatched sharks, swimming in their tiny private oceans, waiting to be born.

I didn't spend much time walking outside in Galway City anymore, still worried that Tommy could find us there. But I always felt safe in the aquarium.

I hated that I couldn't buy Robin more than charity shop toys and that €4 aquarium lizard for Christmas. I thanked Irene and Cían endlessly for taking us in, walked their dogs through the bronze hills ringed with frost-edged dry ferns, helped make pumpkin pie with filling from Irene's recipe and crust from mine. And I was jealous of all of it: their warm safe home that they didn't have to panic daily to heat and light, their custom bookshelves and Jacuzzi tub, the toy they gave my child and the lovely earrings they gave me. I sat with Robin on the floor by the tasteful, beautiful Christmas tree, envying the same generosity I was the grateful recipient of, and hating myself for it.

Robin, in the grand tradition of babies, loved the wrapping paper more than any gift.

Next year, I told myself, I'd host them for Christmas in the castle. I'd invite some of the moms from the COPE group, too, the ones who didn't have their kids for the holiday. I would give all the things Irene and Cían were giving me. Telling myself that was the only way I could manage to accept it.

In early spring, the final answer arrived from the castle's realtor: no.

He told me in a terse email that the owner had realized he wanted to hold on to the property and would be taking it off the market altogether. I got the distinct impression that my eager interest made him realize the castle was more valuable than he'd thought it was, at least to eccentric Americans.

I was devastated.

This was shortly after I had talked about the castle on social media, outside of Friday Tea, for the first time. Tommy was always closely watching everything I posted publicly—I knew that from things he said in the angry, rambling emails and texts he sent, as well as from the flood tide of harassment from anonymous burner accounts I was getting, that I believed were him, too.

Sometimes it felt like all the men in east Galway knew each other. I still wonder if Tommy got in touch with the castle's owner and told him not to trust me. I still think that sounds paranoid, too.

Really, it doesn't matter if Tommy had a hand in it. It vanished from me either way.

I closed the email and stood up from my desk, then unlocked the door and walked out onto the lawn. It was an unseasonably warm and sunny day, snowdrops nodding in sweet little groups by the fence. I squished my fingers down into the springy, moss-knitted grass and decided it was dry enough to take off my shoes and sit outside.

I took advantage of the sun and wind to dry a load of Robin's laundry. Every time I did that I remembered the midwife who had told me, as I lay in the maternity ward just after Robin was born, that if I ever started to resent my husband and child, I should go outside and hang laundry. "You'll peg up those tiny clothes and your husband's socks, him you love so much, and before long you'll be thinking to yourself, *sure aren't I the luckiest mammy in the world*," she said.

I hadn't been able to hang a single load without thinking of that damn line ever since.

I never washed Robin's laundry together with mine. Seeing our clothes tangled up, or drying next to each other, reminded me too much of all the boundaries my parents had crossed with me. The idea of my underwear touching his clothes made me nauseous.

I finished the laundry, not feeling particularly lucky, and went inside to get my journal and a cup of tea. It was so strangely warm out that I didn't even need the cup to warm my hands enough to write, the way I had all winter.

I flipped open my journal and said goodbye to the castle.

I wrote about all the things I'd imagined doing there: hanging tapestries on the cold walls of the ground-floor living room, draping my winter coat around the suit of armor that was rusting by the entryway, setting up bunk beds for group writing retreats on the next floor up. Baths in that glorious ancient claw-foot tub. I could imagine waking up in the canopy bed in one of the two little top-floor bedrooms, gathering Robin from the other, drinking our morning coffee and milk on the crenelated battlements, as clearly as if we'd already done it: a memory of a future that would never be.

The silver new-spring sun warmed up my notebook and the back of my neck. The old moth-eaten velvet of that canopy bed, the lichen-covered stone of the battlements, felt no further from my senses than the noontime light.

I had lived in the castle all winter. I saw that, then, sitting on the grass, breathing air full of the scents of budding leaves and laundry soap. When the place where we were felt too scary and bleak, I'd had a dream to retreat to instead. The castle had done for me what I'd needed it to.

The castle was a dream that didn't come true. But I cannot say it wasn't magic, not when it paved the way for everything that came next.

Twelve

Dreaming

SPRING–AUTUMN 2019

for my grandmothers

The endless-feeling process of getting a parental visa presented me with another hoop to jump through: I had to get a passport for Robin to prove that
my child was an Irish citizen. A birth certificate wasn't enough. But both
parents have to sign a child's passport application.

To get Tommy to sign, I agreed to meet him for visits with Robin in a
café near the bungalow. They were supposed to be hour-long visits for the
first eight weeks, with me there, and then graduate to two hours at a time
without my supervision going forward.

Tommy showed up late every week and left early. While he was
there, he sat with his legs and arms spread, elbows leaning on the table
behind him, and watched not Robin, but me. My heart whirred like a
prey animal's every second his eyes were on me, but I still had to encourage Robin toward him, had to *facilitate their bond*, as people kept telling
me, if I wanted his consent for the passport I needed to stay in Ireland
with Robin.

The first time I was supposed to leave Robin alone with Tommy, as fate
would have it, was his second birthday.

I was completely unable to sleep the night before, and I was sweating through my dress by the time I walked through the door of the café with my newly minted toddler. It was the perfect opportunity for Tommy to punish me, I was sure, by taking Robin away and not bringing him back. In his mind it would only be fair, considering what I'd done to him one year before.

But the drop-off time passed without Tommy showing up. He was always late, so it took the whole first hour for me to start to suspect the only possibility I would never have predicted: he wasn't coming at all.

The waitress, who had watched us closely every week and seemed to know exactly what was happening without my having ever said a word, came over to ask if we were all right.

"I think so," I said. "I don't think he's coming." Robin beamed at her from his booster seat. "It's his birthday," I muttered.

"What!" An exclamation, not a question. "Lord save us, we'll have to do something about that, now." She hurried away and brought back a massive slab of chocolate cake with a candle in it. Robin, who had not even noticed that the man who usually came and lurked in the corner to stare at his mother had not arrived, ate until he could eat no more.

Seeing through the waitress's eyes, I felt like Robin and I were acting out a maudlin movie cliché. The poor brave child whose father didn't even show up for a quick visit on his birthday. I hated it.

But I did eat the rest of the cake.

After that day, Saoirse told me I shouldn't have to facilitate those visits anymore. I texted Tommy that I would no longer be meeting him privately, and that instead I would start bringing Robin to a supervised access center in Galway every Sunday, designed for families where one parent was afraid of the other. He could still see Robin every week, but it would be with a social worker present, and I would be waiting in a separate room.

There's no way I'm seeing my boy at that fucking place, he told me. I won't have him growing up thinking of me like that.

That hurt as much as anything he'd said before. Didn't he know that was the last thing I'd wanted, too?

• • •

A few weeks went by after Robin's birthday with no word from Tommy. In that unexpected peace, I actually started to sleep more deeply. There were even a few nights when Robin did, too.

But one night, a few hours after I went to sleep, I heard my grandmother whisper, "Wake up."

I sat up in the midnight darkness, heart pounding. I hardly need to tell you that my grandmother was not in my room. In fact, she was both in America, and dead.

Still, I couldn't shake off the conviction that she'd woken me, nor could I go back to sleep. Guiltily as always, I opened my phone, lecturing myself about blue light and attention span but seeking the soothing shutoff it gave my brain anyway.

There was a comment on one of my Instagram posts from another username I didn't recognize.

> @powerhour258: search on YouTube: Tommy video for boy Robin . . . for anyone who's interested. She didn't let them meet for a whole year . . .
> no wonder he left her . . .

I felt the familiar cold hands and stomachache that reading Tommy's words always gave me. I knew I needed to know what was on that video, but I also knew I couldn't bear to watch it myself.

But there was a green active-now light next to one of my friends' names: Eleanor Lane, a fellow Smithie writer who had helped me so much with my own work, someone who was also an abuse survivor and understood the kind of fear and sickness I felt just then well enough that I wouldn't have to explain it to her.

Hey, I just got this weird comment, I wrote. Would you be willing to watch this video for me? I'm sorry to ask, I just can't handle it right now.

Of course, she replied.

A few minutes later: OK, I've watched it, and I've downloaded it to my computer in case he deletes it. I can tell you what's in it if you want, but mostly I think you need to bring it to the police tomorrow. Ugh, he's such an asshole. I'm so sorry.

What is it about?

It's a video he made of himself driving to your house and banging on the
door. He's obviously driving drunk. You ask him if he has a gun.

I remembered the exact day. I'd seen his silhouette through the fake
stained-glass window in the bungalow door, holding up an angular black
object, and the first thing I'd done was ask him if it was a gun. Now, here
is the thing: I'd thought it was a recording phone. But if he was recording
me, I wanted to make it clear how afraid of him I was. And now I had. And
he had uploaded it, his own drunk-driving harassment video, to the public
internet of his own free will.

Thank god, I thought. Maybe now I can finally get a safety order.

The video is handled, Eleanor wrote. It's not going anywhere. Take a screen-
shot of that comment and try to go to sleep.

Thank you, I replied. You're a good friend.

You are, too, she said. Now sleep.

And even though I always struggled with going back to sleep, even
though it usually took me several miserable hours tamping down my overthinking brain no matter how tired I was, that night I slipped back into
sleep as peacefully as I ever have and slept through until the morning without dreaming.

When I woke up, the comment was gone.

I don't know, honestly, if when it comes down to it I really believe
such things are possible. But I do know that if I hadn't woken that night,
certain I'd heard my grandmother's voice, I would never have known
about the video that was, indeed, what finally allowed me to get the safety
order I'd needed for over a year. In the end, Tommy provided the evidence
himself.

As much of a relief as the safety order was, I knew it would do very little actually to keep us safe in the moment if Tommy came to the house again. As
important as Friday Tea and the COPE group were to me, I often felt alone

in my field, as full of the hypervigilance of loneliness as the mare across the road. I still looked over my shoulder all the time, still felt the wolf outside my window late at night.

On a rare real phone call with Claire one day—instead of our usual texts—she asked me if I'd consider moving to another rental, somewhere farther away from Tommy.

I was caulking the windows against slug invasions, a Sisyphean task in any old Irish house, while we talked. I sighed and set the gun down. "It would be great," I said. "I'd have to get permission from a judge to leave County Galway, though, and I have my job at the university here anyway. It doesn't pay much, but I like it, I like my students, and teaching third-level makes people think I'm respectable. You know, people like judges." I stared out the window, at the road I was always watching for his car, his unregistered car, that he drove with an expired license. There were only small country lanes between our houses now. Just one motorway, I thought, one highly policed road, would be more effective than a safety order—or a castle moat.

"Ah, it's okay," I told Claire, trying to pretend it was. "I don't have the energy to pack all my stuff and move anyway."

"Shut up. Do you need me to fly out there and help you? Because I will. Or I would, if I had someone safe to leave my kids with right now."

"I know, honey." Drew had been in rehab for over a month. In his last relapse, he'd used while he was supposed to be taking care of their children.

We were both quiet for a moment. I said something I didn't say too often, both because she already knew I thought it and because I knew from my own experience that it wouldn't do much good. "You deserve better."

"I know I do," she said, her voice going hard. "I know what I deserve. What I deserve is Drew, when he's sober. He's my person then. I can't leave him, because what I deserve is Drew at his best."

"I know," I said. "I felt the same. I still do, kind of. Tommy at his best"—a rush of memories I had to shove away—"is still the person I would always choose if I could." I swallowed. "But I can't choose that person." I had to remind myself as much as her. "That person doesn't exist, because Tommy isn't choosing to be him. It got to a point where I couldn't wait for him to choose that version of himself, too, while he was continuing to hurt us. You can't stay married alone."

"I don't feel alone in it yet," she said. "He's in rehab again. He's trying."

It was the first time she'd said *yet*. Like she knew it was coming.

"Anyway, you really can't move anywhere farther away without permission?" she asked. "Like, what's the farthest away you can go and still be in the county?"

I thought of Connemara: the remote western part of County Galway, the place Irish people called their Wild West, the same region that holds the Aran Islands. I remembered how the eighteenth-century writer James Berry had described it: "impregnable, inaccessible citadel of the wilds of Iar-Connacht . . . when you reached it you were as safe as if you had taken refuge in the moon."

Refuge in the moon, in a cold, far-off circle of nighttime light, a safeguarding outer-space ocean between you and the unsafe world.

Longing swept through me like sea breeze. Connemara was the part of Ireland I fell for before I ever met my husband: a raw glacial mountainscape of rocky peaks and windy shores, where a unicorn or selkie would feel right at home. Hadn't it already been a sanctuary, a ring of salt around me, when I'd first come to Inis Mór longing for anywhere in the world where I would feel safe from my parents?

Connemara could keep me safe from the man I'd thought had saved me from my parents, too: it was two hours away from Tommy by car, separated by magic-barrier motorways, thick with Gardaí.

And it was still in County Galway. We wouldn't need permission to move there.

With Claire still on the phone, I pulled up the real estate website that had gotten me through many sleepless nights. There were exactly nine houses listed for rent in Connemara, the cheapest of which was €900 a month, half again as much as the rent for the bungalow.

Just a few weeks before, though, *Parabola* had offered me a freelance position as a digital editor at $2000 a month. Now that I had that better job, how much would I pay for space from Tommy, for peace and freedom—as much as custody laws would allow me?

"You should do it," Claire said. "You'll be safer there. Use some of the castle money for your deposit." She'd told me to hold on to it when the castle fell through. It was because I had that money in my account that I'd been able to get a €4000 loan for another car, and I could drive again—I'd just passed the test for my Irish driver's license, at last, in that car. I already couldn't count the ways she'd saved me.

"You're right," I told Claire. "You always know what I should do."

She laughed a little sadly. "We both do, about each other."

I wrote to the cheapest listing's landlord right then and started packing to move the next week.

The day we left the bungalow for the last time, to drive two hours to Connemara, I felt like I was leaving Tommy all over again. I'd thought I was only staying in east Galway for Robin, so that he could keep going to Brigid, and his little life would be only minimally disrupted.

I knew we would be safer farther away. But when I pulled out of the driveway that Tommy's car had blocked so many times, I couldn't bear to leave quite yet. I stopped, foot on the brake, and let the car idle for a moment, staring at the bungalow. The Chicks' "Cold Day in July" came on my shuffle, and I found myself crying.

I never thought I'd leave him. Often, when we were dating and when we were married, he told me I'd leave him someday. "Someday you'll figure out you're too good for me," he'd say. "You're too good for the middle of nowhere. I'll just enjoy you until that day comes."

I would wrap my arms around him and try to hold him so close he'd understand, see how much I loved him, how much his words hurt me. "Never," I'd always say. "I'll never leave you."

"There are things that would make you leave me," he'd insist, his mouth on my neck, in my hair.

I would kiss him anywhere I could reach and say: "Well, it would take a lot." And then there would be no more talking.

There were small sour apples in the tree behind the bungalow that would be heavy and fat and juicy in three months' time. We'd made those apples into golden-pink jelly last fall, but we'd eaten and given away all of it by spring. I wondered if the next people to live there would cook with those apples. I wondered if they grew in Connemara.

It wasn't just that Robin's life would be disrupted, I finally saw. It was that I was still waiting for Tommy to get better.

Now we'd be too far away for him to hurt us, or to find us.

It was good. We would be safer. It was good.

"I'm sorry, Tommy," I whispered, and we left.

Thirteen

Connemara

AUTUMN–WINTER 2019

for the survivors' group

The little Connemara cottage we moved into sat just up the road from An Trá Mhór, "the big beach" in Irish, on a postcard bóithrín—little road—a road so small and rural that grass grows down its center.

The cottage was a tiny box-shaped thing, but it felt so open, like an empty seashell perched at the edge of the ocean. I danced around the living room with Robin the first night, with the blinds up, moving lightly in the knowledge that no wolves were watching us. I loved the big square window in my bedroom, and the even bigger one in the living room that faced full west, where if you stood at the right angle you could see Inis Mór on the horizon, the first place I'd loved in Ireland. It felt like coming home to that first love in a way that none of my east Galway homes had, with or without Tommy.

The cottage smelled like sea and sun. It was summer when we moved, and I kept the windows open almost all the time: not just to catch the breeze, but because I was far enough away from Tommy that I felt like I could. The rooms were small, but I got some cheap decorations—a garland of tissue-paper jellyfish, an apple-scented candle—and decorated it as I liked. A jade plant Irene had given me years before Robin was born thrived next to the fireplace, facing the western window.

Inside, the house was sweet and lovely, though the outside was a little desolate: weedy uneven ground full of sharp rocks, the odd old broken bottle or rusty nail popping out of the ground. I figured that was why the rent was low. The landlord was horrid, and the ground around the house felt like him, but the inside felt like Robin and me.

I think it was the first home where I felt safe.

The cottage was in a Gaeltacht—the name for the parts of Ireland where the primary language is Irish, not English—and I enrolled Robin in an Irish-language preschool called a naíonra and started stumbling over "go raibh maith agat" and "slán" at the grocery store. I got to know my pretty neighbor Fedelma, who had a son a month older than Robin. We were both shy, but exchanging smiles when we passed each other on walks to the beach did more for my heart and my sense of home than I could have guessed.

I could make that walk from our doorstep to the silvery length of the shoreline in four minutes, and Robin and I did it every day. On clear days we could see Inis Mór and the Cliffs of Moher away on the gray horizon. I stretched and wandered and let my toes sift down into the cool wet sand while Robin ran and shrieked and clambered over rocks. We both stared endlessly at the cockles and limpets and infinite other tiny lives we found onshore. Robin loved to eat seaweed right out of the water, which I took as confirmation that he was part selkie. We breathed the sea air every day, and finally, finally, I felt able to make a fresh start.

Of course, it helped that I had started sexting with a twenty-three-year-old Olympic rugby player.

I'd signed up for dating apps for the first time when we moved. I'd met Tommy before they'd really taken off, so my only experience with online dating had been a little experimentation with OkCupid in New York City back around 2011—which had gotten me two tepid dates and a lot of creeps. Like any married person, I was morbidly curious about the apps, and I felt young again using them.

I didn't want a serious relationship, though. After all the fear and horror of my last one—and maybe some lingering shame about being disloyal to my marriage vows, as absurd as it might sound—I couldn't see myself ever wanting another.

But I was also still struggling not to think about Tommy when I touched myself, my imagination being somehow even more loyal than my heart. We'd had the best sex of my life, and I was convinced I'd never have it that good again: the crazy chemistry, the romance-novel fireworks. When I caught myself wishing I could have Tommy back for just an hour a week (and unable to speak), I knew I needed to start retraining my heart and body in new directions.

So the apps first brought me a too-young Olympian, who was searingly hot, but also made me realize I really didn't want to date someone whose brain wasn't done developing.

They also brought me, a month after we moved to Connemara, my first real date with a woman. I'd had, I don't know, *moments* with women before, the odd flirtation or make-out session, but nothing so formal as a date. I'd been monogamously dating a man my whole time at Smith, and queer women my age were thin on the ground, to say the least, at Notre Dame. Then I'd met Tommy so quickly after I was done with school.

But I matched with a gorgeous woman in Galway City who took me to a group ukulele lesson, and then to drinks. She walked me to my car and we kissed good night. By the time I got home, she'd sent me a song that she said reminded her of me. Then she asked me on a second date: to a slam poetry reading.

And herein lies the part of the story where I messed things up with the only other out, bi, single woman my age I'd met in Galway. The thing is, I promised myself I would never again pretend to like something I didn't actually like for the sake of a romantic prospect.

And I really, really hate slam poetry.

I never heard from her again.

All the other women I met on the apps turned out to have boyfriends and were trolling for threesomes. I thought about it. But none of the boyfriends were appealing at all—if they were, they would of course have been in those profiles, too.

Men, on the other hand, are so easy to find. Yet somehow people are still so impressed with you when you find one. The merit badge of being with a man, the proof that you're attractive to the people with the power after all, is pretty heady. That had lured me to men over women more than any other factor when I was last single, I realized.

That didn't make it any easier to meet more women, though. I found a trans-inclusive queer dating app that sounded great, signed up, and said I was looking for people five years to either side of my own age and up to fifty miles away . . . and was informed by a sad little pop-up box that there were zero people on the app who met those criteria.

Meanwhile dozens of Bumble men wanted to buy me dinner.

So blow the winds of fate, I guess.

At least I got to share my new foibles online, in Friday Tea, which became at least as fun as the foibles themselves.

Tea: I am taking a bath as I write this, so I am the tea?

Best: Oh lots.

I have come to a place of being very glad & relieved to have gotten myself out of an emotionally abusive marriage, but there was one thing I still really missed: sex with my ex-husband. I just thought that was something I had to give up to get out & get safe, & of course it doesn't compare in importance, but I thought I'd never have sex that great again.

This week I learned I was very wrong. There are so many other great people out there, & half that great sex? It was coming from me.

A few weeks after I moved to Connemara, I got a call from the guards in east Galway, saying I'd been reported for kidnapping my child. The number was saved in my phone, the same local Garda station that had refused to ever come to my house when I felt in danger from my ex. Now they were calling on his behalf, because he'd come to the bungalow looking for us—which the safety order was supposed to prevent—and found it empty.

"We left because—" I started, and was crying before I could finish my sentence. I knew from the other COPE moms' stories that crying was one of the worst things you could do in front of a guard or a social worker or a judge or anyone else in a position to decide if you were fit to keep your child. "I'm sorry," I forced out. "I'm sorry, please."

"Take a minute," the woman guard's voice said dryly.

I did, a few breaths, enough to swallow my fear and stop my arms from aching without Robin to hold. "We left because we weren't safe. It's the same reason we left the house we shared with him."

"We just need to know where you are, like." She sounded annoyed, impatient.

"I—we haven't even left the county. I promise. Just, please—if I tell you our address, are you going to give it to him?"

She sighed.

"We have an active safety order against him," I said. "I decided to move when I applied for the order."

"Hmm," she said. "He didn't mention that, now."

No kidding.

"I just need the address to write down," she said. "I won't tell your husband what it is."

It hurt that she called him my husband. But we'd lived apart for less than two years, and four years of separation were required before divorce in Ireland—and that was only since 1996, when divorce became legal at all. I swallowed my tears again and told her.

"Glad to hear you haven't left the county," she said, and hung up.

I looked around the living room of the little cottage, thinking about how safe and free and clean of my ex I'd felt when we moved in, knowing he didn't know where we were. I knew I couldn't trust the guards not to tell him. In all my social media I'd tried to make it look like we were living a few towns away. I liked to post about the beach, but all the Connemara beaches looked the same. I knew, in any case, that he'd always have had to find out eventually.

My paper strand of pink jellyfish rustled in the breeze from the open window. I got up and latched it closed.

A week later I got a letter from TUSLA, the Irish child welfare service that every single mother I knew feared. I opened the letter with cold hands in the cottage's sun-filled entryway.

The letter informed me that TUSLA had received an anonymous report that I was an unfit mother due to mental illness and suicide risk. The reporter had mentioned my social media posts as proof. They had investigated my online presence, they wrote—and found nothing of concern. The letter was to inform me that they were closing a case I'd never known was open.

Anonymous report, my ass, I thought.

Robin wasn't in the house. I let myself scream.

We were still going to the supervised access center every Sunday. It felt a little like going to church: wake up early, make sure my kid and I have tidy and respectable outfits, and head to a big building to visit a father who never appeared. We spoke with the clergy, though, about him: social workers who were trained to "neutrality" above all else. When I'd first heard about the supervised access center it seemed like a miracle, a place that, like COPE, was there to help keep survivors safe.

I quickly learned they were actually there for the dads. They spoke of the sacred father-child bond as worshipfully as priests speak about their god. Any mother who feared that a father would hurt their child simply because he'd hurt *her* was contemptibly shortsighted and selfish. Plenty of abusers made good parents in their eyes. They looked at me with scorn as soon as they saw me.

Week after week, though, as Tommy kept refusing to come, I started to earn a little grudging sympathy.

"Sure, look," said the manager, a few months in, "I'm sorry, but I don't think you should keep coming in. We need the rooms for fathers who show up."

"I need to sign in every week," I said. "COPE told me I need a paper trail showing I keep bringing Robin to meet him. He's already saying I'm keeping them apart. I'm sure he's going to argue that in court, and I need evidence it isn't true."

"All right. Well, how about this: you drive into town on Sundays, same as today, and leave us a voicemail to say that you've arrived. If he ever does come here, we'll let you know."

I felt my shoulders sag with relief. I was never quite convinced he wouldn't be there some Sunday, and preparing for that each week filled my body with fear. Not having to risk sharing space with him, even supervised, was a reprieve.

We started going to the aquarium every Sunday instead. As soon as we got there, I'd head to the giant ocean tank, its floor at my feet and the water's surface high above my head, and leave the message while Robin traced the stingray's wing patterns with his eyes.

That felt like church, too: sitting in quiet contemplation, windowed by strange, floating, illuminated beings, glowing through glass. I thought of Abraham and Isaac and sacrifice. I was praying two prayers at once: the one I spoke into the phone—*I have brought my son here although I know the danger*, and the one in my heart—*please don't take him from me.*

Despite the safety order, despite the distance I'd paid for so dearly, I started to understand that Tommy was still watching me. I kept getting weird comments on social media from burner accounts that felt, to me, just like him—written in his cruelest and most critical voice, knowing things about me and my kid that only he would know—which should have been a violation of the safety order. Dozens of anonymous handles left me cryptic comments, warning me about the dangers of bringing children near water when I posted a photo of a seashell, telling me a new coat made me look masculine, criticizing the way I talked to Robin about the rock pool in a video I posted, saying that my telling him to be gentle with the minnows was prioritizing their lives over my child's. I blocked all of them as soon as they popped up, and then five minutes later I'd get a new alert: "your contact Tommy is on

Instagram as @whatever." I deleted my Twitter, despite the fact that it was my biggest platform for marketing my books—a few thousand followers, nothing really, but something I knew had sold at least a few copies, and a place where I'd made some genuine friends—because that "anonymous" harassment had become so incessant I couldn't bear it.

No one would help me. Nothing he said—nothing whoever it was said—was a specific physical threat, and without one of those, EU data protection laws kept anyone from investigating the real identity of those accounts.

Still, when I'd amassed about seventy screenshots, I brought them to the local Garda station, hoping that together they would paint a clearer picture of why I still felt afraid enough to flinch when I closed my curtains each night, why I still couldn't really sleep deeply.

The guard on duty was an older man who needed me to explain, several times, what Twitter and Instagram were in the first place. He asked me to print out my screenshots and come back so he could read them. When I did, he told me there was nothing he could do.

"Can you at least keep them on file? For the safety order?" I asked.

He shook his head. "Sure, there's no point."

I was angry, but I knew showing it wouldn't help my cause. I'd heard enough horror stories from the other single moms at COPE about how the powers of law and order reacted to women's anger.

"Okay, but I should keep taking the screenshots, right?"

He stood up. He wasn't laughing anymore. He seemed annoyed, impatient. "Don't waste your time." I knew he was really saying: unless you get some real threats, don't waste ours, either.

I threw the printouts I'd paid for in his wastebasket on the way out. In anger I deleted them from my phone, too. *Sure, there's no point*, the guard's voice kept saying in my head.

When I told Johanna about that visit to the station, she was outraged and said it would be different in Germany. I wasn't so sure. I'd met enough domestic violence and stalking survivors online to know that all over the world, no one with power actually seemed to care. Whatever country we were in, people from other countries liked to tell themselves that ours only worked that way because it was backward. But the problems I encountered in Ireland were mirrored in the experiences of friends in the US, the UK, Australia, and all over the world. It wasn't a matter of a behind-the-times society or government. It was everywhere.

I was sure Tommy knew exactly where the line was, what he could say without getting arrested—or better still, in his eyes, what he could say that would make me sound most irrational if I reported it. Before I'd applied for the safety order, he'd sent me a barrage of long texts, angry and pleading and threatening in turns, and when I'd stopped responding to those, a series of increasingly erratic emails where he told me strange stories, attached photos of naked women in our marriage bed, and finally, when he received the safety order application, told me to go ahead and try it because "no order could keep you safe from yourself."

God only knew what that meant. It was far from the only line of his that didn't make sense, that felt more like a convoluted, drunken rant than a coherent thought. Saoirse had told me over and over again not to think about why an abuser says or does something, because that's what they want: to keep you guessing about, and more important, sympathizing with, their motivations. Don't think about why they're hurting you anymore, just respond to the hurt in ways that will protect you and your children.

It's good advice. But for some reason, as the anonymous harassment piled up and I understood more and more how unwilling to protect my child and me the guards and the courts really were, that line of his kept sticking with me. Every time I saw a man who looked like him and did a double take, every time I hurried through an errand in a place where we might cross paths, every time my fear of him clouded my days. I thought about how he'd say I was foolish, irrational, crazy, to be afraid of him in the first place. He'd say it was my own, made-up fear I wasn't safe from. The guards who wouldn't help me seemed to agree.

He doesn't know where we are, I told myself like a litany. I had stopped him from showing up and banging on my door, stopped him from knowing where my car was parked at night, at least for now. But part of me kept wondering if stopping that outlet for his hatred only meant I'd patched a leak that would spring, unpredictable and maybe even more dangerous, somewhere else.

The rest of the litany went like this: he's choosing not to see Robin. We have a safety order. The moment he actually shows up he'll be arrested.

I told myself those things a hundred times a day. I worked my jobs, worked on *Reader, I Murdered Him* (with, I admit, increasing secondhand pleasure in my heroine's vengeful vigilantism), took Robin to the beach every day after naíonra, rain or shine (mostly rain). I wrote on Tea a lot, told my fun stories about dating, commented on the posts of dozens of friends I was making there, sent a little money to people who wrote about their crises, remembering my own and trying to believe the worst was past. In my own posts I tried to focus the group's attention, and my own, on the parts of my heart I was learning to reclaim.

And, in the back of my mind, I kept dreaming about a home I'd own, one I could share as a retreat for other single moms—a place where I could help them feel safe and rested, even if there wasn't a single day when I really felt that way myself. I wasn't done dreaming of castles.

I can feel a whole ocean between my hips, I wrote in my journal one night, *and I'd forgotten it was there.* Like a gift from the universe, I thought, I had better sex than I'd ever had with Tommy the first time I slept with someone after him—and then I had to amend what "best" meant yet again when it was even better with the person after that.

Then I realized it wasn't a gift from the universe. It was just growing up. It turned out Tommy wasn't a sex god after all: he was just the first person in his thirties that twenty-four-year-old me had slept with, and he'd been doing it longer. Now they all knew a thing or two—and so did I. And, very generally speaking, people were kinder and more self-aware and gentler than my early-twenties peers had been back then—or, indeed, than the thirty-somethings who preferred to date younger. As I grew toward the age that Tommy had been when he met me, I understood less and less how he could possibly have wanted to marry a twenty-four-year-old. A silly fling with that Olympian—why not? But I began to see how easy it would be to manipulate someone so much younger, how very much not a peer relationship it had been between my decade-older romance novel hero and myself. While I still wasn't interested in anything serious, I began to seek out gentle, sweet people my own age, with whom I could enjoy equal exchanges while we talked, and not just while we did those other things. Talking to people didn't scare me as much anymore as it had when I met Tommy, when I just wanted to get him back into bed so that he wouldn't see how boring I was outside of it.

Friday Tea, opening up to people online, was one of the major things that had helped me see I was worthy of care and conversation without touch—something that I hadn't learned from either my husband, despite our great first date, or even my father. The COPE survivors' group helped, too. They reminded me that I had value besides being an embodied possession. Those women were part of that learning, and the people I dated were, too, as easily as they drifted in and out of my life. Their care and gentleness, however casual, was sacred, as I hope mine was for them.

When we'd moved, Brigid had offered to take Robin for the weekend once a month or so, at a rate discounted steeply enough that I could just about afford it. The first weekend I spent storing up on lost sleep. The second, I still slept a lot—but I spent my nights awake, and in good company. I had more dates, more sex, and slowly I found and recentered the delight of mingling my mind and body's edges with another.

One of those people, quietly, stuck around and made his way past my heart's edges, too.

> Tea: Scotch whisky at a lovely pub here in Cork City earlier. Thai takeaway and ice cream now.
>
> Best: I brought my kid to his old childminder for the weekend and am now visiting a new man and being treated like a queen.
>
> Worst: nope.

Séamus, called Shay: tall and lanky with a brown beard and a lip ring and a boring office job, with an English accent despite his Irish name, since even though his family was from Sligo he'd grown up in the UK. We met on the apps while he and his friend were road-tripping the Wild Atlantic Way, sent each other deeply millennial flirtatious GIFs and talked about books. His profile said he loved learning new facts, and I asked him what his favorite fact was. He said he couldn't choose, but a lot of them were about the moon.

The moon was closer in the time of the dinosaurs, he said. It gets a few centimeters farther from earth every year—doesn't that kind of break your heart, like losing a mother all over again? I asked—but imagine how the moon would have looked to a T. rex, Shay said. How big and bright and beautiful, how detailed all the craters and the pocks.

Shay said he was an atheist, but today the moon is exactly four hundred times closer to earth than the sun, and exactly four hundred times smaller, so that during an eclipse they cover each other perfectly. That's incredibly rare anywhere in the known universe, he said: it's the kind of thing that would be a tourist attraction for aliens. And isn't it a miracle, an actual miracle, that the only time such an unfathomably unlikely and unimaginably beautiful thing happens in the universe, there are sentient beings here on earth to see it, and to love it? It's the only thing that almost makes me believe in God, it's such a gift.

I think I'm starting to like this boy, I texted Claire after he told me that.

After every date I thought to myself, like the Dread Pirate Roberts in *The Princess Bride*, "Good work today, Shay, I'll probably break up with you in the morning." I didn't want to care about anyone, certainly not—the horror!—another heterosexual man. But there he was: cheerful and tender, gentle and generous, not asking for anything but the chance to care about me.

When I started dating again, I went to the local reproductive health clinic to get an STI test. Tommy was still the only man I'd ever slept with without a condom, and I wanted that part of my loyalty to him to get scrubbed away, too. I'd always been fastidious, almost neurotic, about safe sex, which I think was partly just common sense, but was also a remnant of my mother's conditioning about saving yourself for marriage filtering through, despite my best efforts to the contrary. That was one thing, at least, that I'd saved for my husband. Even though I reviled the idea of saving anything. Even though, if you count what happened in my childhood, nothing was saved at all.

So I marched myself one day to the clinic in Galway, the same place where I'd gotten my diaphragm fitted after Robin was born, after an attempt to go back on the pill had left me, I thought at the time, acutely depressed—although I had started to wonder if it was, like Tommy's claim that I had postpartum anxiety, more a rational response to his worsening behavior than hormone-fueled feminine irrationality. I wonder how many women believe they have postpartum depression or anxiety when what they really have are abusive husbands. I am sure that many of the emotional problems women spend our lives feeling shame over are actually reasonable reactions to the horrible outside stimuli that are passed off as normal lifestyle features for us.

I had forgotten, mostly, that the clinic was the same place I had come to when I'd believed Tommy was the last man I'd ever sleep with. Or I hadn't thought that I would care. But as I sat in the white, clean-lit waiting room, I remembered with sensory immediacy what it had been like to come there the last time, with baby Robin in tow just two months old, looking forward so much to having back a part of Tommy's and my life together that had always been so entwined with the happiness that we could give each other.

Now, even our first night together had changed in my memory. He had asked me then, when he was already inside me, if he could feel me without the condom for a minute. I had stiffened and said no right away—no one had ever asked me that before—and he'd apologized for asking. When it was over, it turned out the condom had fallen off inside me. That had never happened to me before, either. I'd panicked and cried, and he had been so caring, had sworn over and over with absolute believability that it was an accident, had showered with me and held me and stayed with me to make sure I was okay getting the morning-after pill the next morning—something else I'd never had to do before. His sensitivity and kindness in that moment had been one of the things that had drawn me to him.

It was only in that clinic, long afterward, that I allowed myself to revisit that night, and to wonder.

To wonder if he had violated me, had lied to me, right from the very start.

I sat in the waiting room, half of me back in that first night with Tommy wondering if I should have pushed him off me and screamed and never seen him again, wondering how naïve I could have been to have believed him, and half of me back two years previously, holding newborn Robin in my arms and feeling so excited to reconnect with my beloved husband in this way.

So almost none of me at all was there in the present moment when the nurse called me in for my tests.

She was, it turned out, the same woman who had fitted my diaphragm. She flashed a generic smile at me and skimmed my chart. "Don't have your lovely baby with you today, or that handsome husband?" she chirped.

I felt my chest constrict. "Not today."

"And you're here for an STI screen?" She raised her eyebrows.

"Um, yes. We're not together anymore. I wanted to get tested because, um, I've started seeing someone else." Oh god, I thought, now it sounded like I'd cheated and left him for another man. "We split up not long after the last time I saw you, I mean. It was, um, domestic violence." I was trying to get more used to saying those words out loud.

Her forehead puckered. "Oh." She cleared her throat and gestured for me to lie back on the table. "I'm sorry to hear that. Have you . . . gotten help?"

At that point—as I was opening my legs for her to do the swab—I remembered that she was probably a mandatory reporter. "Oh yes," I said quickly. "I get a lot of support from COPE. And we're out now. We're okay. He hasn't seen our baby in over a year. At all."

The sour look on her face intensified. She finished the swab and indicated with a brisk nod that I could put my clothes back on. "He doesn't get to see him at all?" she asked. With every word her voice got higher and higher.

I swung my feet back to the floor. Now I was sure she thought I was a harpy, one of those scorned women that are always compared unfavorably to hell's fury, and that I was keeping my husband's child from him out of spite.

"It's his choice," I said. "I bring him to access every week, and he refuses to show up. Every week. He doesn't pay child support, either." God, when would I learn to shut up? How many kinds of horrible or pathetic could I seem to this woman in the space of five minutes?

She let out a quick breath that was almost a whistle. She opened the curtains she'd pulled around the exam table just enough so that she could step through. "Well," she said, half her body already out of sight, "I'm sure someday he'll tell you that he's sorry."

She was gone quickly enough that she didn't see me flinch.

Suddenly I was crying again, and I thought maybe I had spent more time crying than not crying, all told, if you added up every instant since the last time I had been there. I wasn't sobbing, wasn't even moving. I could just feel the tears rolling down my face, coming out of the wound she'd just dealt me, as if she'd stabbed me and I was bleeding.

Tommy would never be sorry. He might say it—at the right times he said it a lot, and with great sincerity—but saying sorry and meaning it would mean that he understood the immensity of all the things he had to be sorry for, and that was never going to happen. The things he had done, and failed to do, had taken years off my life: I was going to die sooner because of what he had put me through. I understood that, in that pristine medical room, immediately and for the first time, feeling my heart stutter with the pain of her words, so casual and assured, and knowing how untrue they were. My heart had been shuddering and stuttering for years, trying to live through loving someone who hated me so much: he may have never hit me, but he had hurt me, over and over, constantly, enough that my heart had fewer steady beats left before it stopped. I was sure of it.

And I was sure he would never be sorry for that.

When I started going to the survivors' group, I worried that what I'd been through wasn't bad enough for me to deserve to join, but Saoirse assured me that not everyone there had experienced physical abuse. While there were other scars besides those notches from ripped-out earrings (one woman showed us a dent in her skull left by her husband's hammer), I quickly learned that most of the women had dealt with other kinds of abuse, as I had: emotional, verbal, financial, psychological. I did know, at least, from my father, that those can leave even more lasting wounds than the kinds of physical or sexual abuse that tend to be the face of violent relationships in people's minds. It was the sexual abuse that I'd reported to the police, but it was the hundred thousand subtler things that took so much longer for me even to name or begin to recover from. This group helped me see that clearly, too.

Tommy had told me stories from the abuser rehabilitation program when we were still together, stories about the other men he met there. Every one of them, he said, believed that a *real abuser* was someone who did things the next step worse than what he did himself.

He never laid a hand on her.

He pushed or pinched or poked her, but he never hit.

He only struck her with an open hand.

He never hit her hard enough to bruise.

He never broke the skin.

My god, but he would never use a weapon.

He would never knock her out.

He would never hurt her badly enough to have to go to the hospital.

He would never kill her.

He would never kill again.

Too many victims tell ourselves the same story: a real abuser would do something worse than what he does to me. I love this man. I can excuse the things he does.

One of the hardest things I've learned to say is: this is bad enough. This is bad enough to leave.

Saying that to yourself can save your life.

Fourteen

The Old Knitting Factory

WINTER–SPRING 2020

for Eleanor

One rainy day, I got my parental visa in the mail and found myself undocumented no more. But the government letter informing me of my new immigration status was cold and hostile in its tone, warning me that a condition of my being allowed to remain in Ireland as the parent of an Irish national was that I do my utmost not to rely on the state financially.

Several people had told me I just needed to wait for that visa to come through to get welfare: single-parent family benefits, low-income benefits. I stared at that letter sitting on my dining table and knew they had been wrong, knew that the frenetic, ever-shifting workload I'd scraped together wasn't going to abate. The price for staying in Ireland with my child was that I would continue to career through anxiety as my money inevitably ran out before each month did, as I switched between job and job and childcare each day, trying to carve out an impossible space for writing, too, in my heart and head, space that I nonetheless needed to write the books that patched together the rest of our living.

At the same time, I knew I was much better off than I had been. My new digital editor job was in many ways a huge relief: a predictable $2000 a month before taxes, even in summer. During the school year that came close to $3000, which would have been an unimaginable sum to rely on even a year before. I stopped some of my online gigs and my tally of jobs dropped to four: the magazine, teaching at the university, writing reader's reports for an Irish literary scout, and reviewing books for an American trade publication.

It astounded me, though, how that much more money still seemed to vanish as soon as I made it. Robin's naíonra cost a thousand euros a month, rent nine hundred, not including utilities. The cottage was on a top-up electricity plan, and it cost more than double what I'd paid at the bungalow, even though that had been a bigger building. The day after I switched to a cheaper level-pay company I got a call from my landlord, and as soon as I picked up the phone he was sobbing and shouting down the line, insisting that I remain with the company he preferred. He called again and again, crying and yelling, and he started having his family members call me too. They said they'd gotten a secret special rate from the top-up company, that it was under the table and technically illegal, and that if I switched they'd never get it back. None of the receipts I showed them seemed to matter. Eventually I just gave it up and ate the additional cost, even though it meant less money for groceries and diapers and heating fuel—the cottage was old and drafty, cold as soon as the boiler switched off. Robin always needed clothes and shoes, I did occasionally, too, gas and insurance for the car, re-payments on the car itself, good internet so I could do my job, legal fees that seemed to eat up any book money as soon as I got it. The housing crisis in Ireland was on the rise, too. Even my partnered, childless friends with stable jobs were struggling to make ends meet. The only people my age I knew who owned homes had gotten help from their parents.

I still worked from when Robin woke me at five in the morning until long after he was in bed—often until his first waking, because at two he still was rarely sleeping through the night no matter what I tried. At the end of each day I felt cracked-open with exhaustion, and still at the end of each month I was lucky to have any money left. Every time I caught a cold, I fought through it to keep working, knowing that even one bad bout with illness could mean I wouldn't be able to pay our rent; my landlord had shown me his colors enough that I knew there'd be no sympathy from him. The day we'd fled home, and the day I'd learned I had no home to return to, sometimes felt present still, a cycle I'd never be able truly to break, a memory of my and Robin's future as well as our past. At the same time, I knew how much better off I was than most of the single moms in the survivors' group at COPE, many of whom were stuck on welfare because they couldn't find work that would even cover childcare, or because the combination of sole caring and post-separation abuse from their exes left them too depleted to work. I feared both those fates.

I looked back on my dream of the castle, sometimes, with contempt. I had a better job now and I was still barely treading water, and most people in Ireland, most people all over the world, I knew, had it the same or worse. How dare I have thought I deserved to own a house, much less a castle? Sometimes it seemed like I despised myself as much as Tommy or my father ever had. Sometimes it seemed like I was taking that job over in their absence. Contempt was a home I'd lived in a long time.

But then I'd go to the survivors' group, and they would talk about their own varied struggles, and I'd think: every one of them deserves a castle.

And sometimes I looked back on the castle with a longing that felt like homesickness. I'd had a home in hope for a while, too.

"You know, last year I tried to buy a castle," I told Shay on one of our early dates. We were walking on the beach at An Trá Mhór, just on the shoreline, our feet slipping in and out of the edges of tingling-cold waves.

Shay laughed—but the laugh was gentle. "What?"

I told him all about it. In the telling, I started to remember the parts I'd forgotten when I focused on how that dream had failed: how hard I'd worked, all the planning I'd done—learning how to make a business plan, meeting online with Smithies who had offered possible mentorship and funding, writing a book proposal in addition to working on my next novel and doing all my other jobs and single parenting.

We wandered a bit farther into the water. A little flatfish fluttered out of the way of one of my steps, brushing my toes with a feather-soft fin.

"I don't know how you do all this," Shay said. "I mean just the parenting alone. My parents had me when they were at uni, and I was partly raised by my grandmothers while they studied. I don't know how any two people raise children without help, let alone one."

I shook that off; I never liked to talk about parenting being hard, at least not to anyone who wasn't also a single mom. It felt disloyal to Robin, and it was also dangerous: I still needed to make it clear, to everyone, that this was a job I could do well. My divorce wouldn't be for at least another year. If I didn't prove that, I still feared Robin could be taken from me.

"The funny thing is," I said, "I miss it."

"The castle?"

"No." I realized that as I said it out loud, too. "The dream."

An old school friend recommended a book called *Pleasure Activism* by adrienne maree brown. When I finally started reading it, the book kept leaping out of my fingers with the electric sparks it sent right up my arms—I had to put it down every few paragraphs and take deep breaths or give little screams of excitement, of longing.

"Pleasure activism includes work and life lived in the realms of satisfaction, joy, and erotic aliveness that brings about social and political change. Ultimately, pleasure activism is us learning to make justice and liberation the most pleasurable experiences we can have on this planet."

"Yes is a future."

I remembered how I'd stayed up late and woken up early in the months I was dreaming of the castle, not in pain and dragging myself from task to task because my child needed care and there was no one else willing to give it—or not just because of those things—but because my heart was beating *yes, yes, yes*, toward the future the castle allowed me to imagine. How it was always a future not just for me to live in, but for other single moms, the artist-mothers I'd dreamed of giving the funded residency time I kept longing for myself. It had been pleasure even to dream of it, even to try to make it real, whether or not the dream ever came true. I needed pleasure so much. The other moms I knew did, too.

Pleasure Activism made the connection for me that my pleasure really could be theirs.

Adrienne maree brown told me I didn't have to miss the dream of a future that made me feel alive right where I was.

One full-moon night that spring, I couldn't sleep.

Every time I lost sleep for any reason other than Robin, I felt a rage bordering on murderous intent. Robin was nearly three by then, still rarely sleeping through the night and waking at a pitch-black five o'clock each morning, so it was genuinely strange for me to struggle to fall asleep at night.

But that night, with moonlight reflecting bright on the line of ocean at the horizon, I didn't even feel tired. I was strangely energized, excited, humming with some kind of bracing happiness that didn't seem to come from inside me—that must have been pouring into me from somewhere in the future or past, some other self who had extra energy to lend. Whatever was keeping me awake reminded me a little bit of when I'd woken to my grandmother's voice the year before: urgent, directing me toward something vital, and yet full of love.

I gave up on sleeping by midnight, and until four or so I read books and watched old favorite TV shows and luxuriated in bed, feeling bizarrely wonderful, while Robin slept on as soundly as he ever had. It felt as if I'd been given time off, a bouquet of hours just for me, a little pocket dimension I'd been allowed to enter for a night where I didn't have to do any childcare or work or errands, where no one was even awake to expect anything of me at all.

It occurred to me at some point in that revelry to visit my old friend the real estate website. I scrolled through converted pubs, remote farms, and dozens of "Tiger Houses," the half-completed new builds abandoned when the Celtic Tiger's economic bubble burst. I sighed over a couple castles, bigger and grander and in better repair than the sweet little tower house I'd fallen for.

And then I saw a house that I remembered. I'd clicked on it in my first confused and frightened days at Irene's house, its name, the Old Knitting Factory, calling to me a little—I'd always liked to knit—but I'd thought it was too remote, far out in the reaches of Connemara, and anyway once I'd seen the castle I had eyes for nothing else.

But that night, something about it spoke to me. The listing showed a long white-and-yellow house nestled on the rugged, overgrown shore of Lough an Mhuillin, "the lake of the mill." Built in 1906, it was a 114-year-old mess: full of crumbling paint and peeling vinyl floors, a leaky roof, and a cinder block–lined backyard straight from the dank armpit of the seventies.

As I clicked through the photos, I felt myself start to light up—the place needed work, but the idea of putting in the effort to make it a real home was enticing. One picture showed a sun-drenched kitchen with a corner by some French doors I could imagine as a writing nook, another a bedroom I already felt sure was Robin's.

The Old Knitting Factory had first been built, the listing said, as a school to teach rural women knitting skills so they could support themselves financially.

A house built to foster women's independence. A place that had been centered on my favorite craft since its beginning, and that had been reincarnated several times already: as the world's first Irish-language cinema in the 1970s, and later as a jewelry-making studio.

For the last several years, it had been a little-used vacation home. It was one hell of a fixer-upper, but so was I: my broken marriage, my exhausted new-mom body, my hollowed and leaking heart. It was more of a witch's cottage than a castle, but this old knitting factory, imperfect as it was, might be a place where I could remake my own imperfect dreams.

Or at least, I might be able to write a book about it.

I wrote to the real estate agent from my bed. Moments later, as the clock blinked five, Robin woke up as usual. I made him his potato waffle breakfast with a sense of joyful presence, delighting in his sweet fat baby hands and cheeks, his cherub curls, his laughing brown eyes, for once able to match the happiness he always glowed with at five in the morning. We were together in that moment, that joy: I wasn't just trying to survive it, angry and brokenhearted that I didn't have the energy to enjoy it more. Something about having this wild dream to work toward once again made me a better mother.

With hours to go before his naíonra opened, I strapped him into his car seat and said we were going on an adventure. The sun rising behind us, we drove west, deeper into Connemara, to see the knitting factory for ourselves.

We passed huge mossy boulders that looked like the gods of all rocks, through valleys and past rivulet mountaintops that had made every friend I'd shown them to wonder out loud why humans had ever bothered with capitalism when we already had riches from the world like this. Each time we glide down into the valley that winds toward the Leenane fjord, I always think every white horse that lifts its head to watch us pass is secretly Macha, the Irish goddess of horses. In that gleaming early morning ride with Robin giggling to himself in the back seat, all the heather and gorse and mossy rock sparked pink with sunrise dew and possibility.

We drove over narrow stone bridges, past piles of low-tide seaweed strewn in glimmering humps on the exposed rocks like sleeping seals, the sky getting brighter behind us all the time.

As we neared the knitting factory, I realized we'd been there before. That autumn, when Natalia visited for Thanksgiving, she had gone online in search of a local Catholic Mass she could attend, and the closest one was in a village called Carraroe. On the way we drove past a low-slung house with a dilapidated black roof and a bright for sale sign sticking up from a small walled-off courtyard. I dreamed of it briefly, of course—ever since we had lost our home, I could never see a for sale sign without dreaming.

A minute later we had dropped Natalia off at a tidy and sweet-looking little church. She climbed the steep steps to the door by a rose-covered grotto in my rearview mirror while Robin and I continued on to a playground I'd seen on the map. The playground was tidy and sweet-looking, too, and I pushed Robin on the swings and cheered him down the slides, thinking about how nice it would be to live somewhere we could walk to a playground and still be so close to the sea. After an hour Natalia found us, laughing, and told us the whole service had been in Irish—she hadn't understood a word. We'd driven onward through that alien landscape to visit Leenane, home of Ireland's only fjord and the pub that serves my favorite

Irish coffee, and I hadn't given that one for sale sign among many another thought until Robin and I arrived there at dawn four months later.

The Old Knitting Factory didn't look like much from the road: most of what you could see before turning into the driveway was that worn-out roof. Just as in the pictures online, a single story of white stone and yellow brick peeked back at me through a row of oversized black windows under a gently gabled roof. It looked more run-down than the photos in the listing, but that didn't surprise me. It was tired and hadn't been much cared for in recent years. I looked worse than my pictures, too.

The road was higher than the base of the house, because the land it stood on sloped down steeply toward the lake. I'd seen in the listing that the garden behind the house had been built up to level, but that was decades ago, and the weed-ridden gravel grounds had started to sink and tilt toward the lake again, as if it was bowing to the water, the low bare walls surrounding the garden totally encrusted with ivy that pulled them down still farther.

But that was just the house. When I pulled into the driveway that dawn, Robin nodding off to sleep again behind me, what caught my heart was the lake. Bright and clear as a new mirror, pearly with the reflections of dawn clouds, stretching out farther than I could see to left and right. That water looked like it could wash anything clean.

I cracked a window so I would hear if Robin stirred, got out of the car, and stood watching the lake for a long time.

Down four concrete steps from the driveway to the garden proper, I looked through the double glass doors and the back of the house to see shadows of dusty furniture and a tall fireplace. At the same time, I saw the reflection of the pink morning sky and lake and the mountaintops beyond them, drifting in and out of soft billowing cloud banks, half heaven and half earth.

I was breathing dreams by then, imagining the factory's potential. I could see it with freshly painted sidings and a new roof, with the crumbling cinder blocks pulled up and the ground cradling beds of mint and rosemary, lavender and roses. I looked out at the vast expanse of lake behind the house and I could picture mothers and children kayaking, swimming, fishing, then coming inside for a warm dinner and long sleep. I imagined Robin playing with children from all over the world while I talked about writing and art and parenting with their mothers.

There was even a separate entrance for one of the bedrooms at the back of the house, so perfect for hosting the writing retreats and residencies I'd once imagined at the castle that it didn't quite feel real. If only we could live here, have our chance, I could make those retreats happen, I could sell enough paid residencies to pay for expenses and funded residencies and maybe even pay myself, too. Someday I could hire another single mom in crisis, like I had been, to manage the building, and give her and her children housing as part of her payment. The money that increased my bully land-lord's equity each month could go into this house instead, help Robin and me survive, and other families like ours, too.

A belief was taking hold of me—more than a belief, a conviction—that something beautiful could happen here at this lakeside cottage, if only I reached out with everything inside of me to grasp it.

The sun was well up, all the pinkness vanishing inside blue and white and gray, the lake beginning to ripple with ordinary daytime breeze. I got back in the car and drove away. I brought Robin to naíonra and myself to Galway City for class. I was so happy to see my students, who were more than halfway done with their spring semester and falling out of love with the novel drafts I was making them write, who were all wondering what the point was of continuing to hack away at stories they couldn't see the magic in anymore. They were each convinced that they were writing the worst book ever written, that nothing would ever come of the long slogging hours of work they were doing on a project they barely believed in anymore.

I told them about the castle, about the late nights I'd spent writing a memoir proposal for a story that had never ended up happening. The best writing I'd ever done, I told them, was for a book that would never be pub-lished. I told them how much the loss of that dream had crushed me. And yet, writing that proposal sustained me through a time when I didn't have much other hope. It didn't matter that the castle had vanished from my life, or that my book about it would never be. I had found creative work that kept me alive. That, I told them, these earnest twenty-year-olds deep in their first manuscripts and horrified to ever waste a word's effort, was the kind of writing I wanted them to do. Don't make the writing you think will get published. Make the writing that keeps you alive.

When class ended, I had a voicemail on my phone: the realtor, offering me a viewing at the Old Knitting Factory.

Fifteen

Come Around Again

SPRING 2020

for Abby

The next morning, I met the realtor at the Old Knitting Factory and tried to pretend I'd never seen it before. He turned the key in the French doors, and I thrilled to the sound.

Inside the dusty, airy space, the first thing I noticed was the sweeping scale of the combined kitchen/living room, its high ceilings and big, bright windows. The floors creaked underfoot, and horsehair poked out from the mortar in the old stone walls, but the strong rough stone and century-old buttery wood said this was a place that had stood safe for a long time. The view out to the gray expanse of Lough an Mhuillin and the distant Twelve Bens mountain range felt as dreamy and fairy-tale as a castle—so I told myself, and believed.

The realtor apologized for the strange wooden window blinds covered in burlap that I immediately, secretly adored, and fed me the standard line about how there was someone else who had just made an offer, but the owner was still open to hearing others.

I remembered what I'd learned from the castle. I wasn't going to lowball him. I wasn't going to say that it would take me years to make an offer. And

I for sure wasn't going to tell anyone else about this until I had the owner's agreement.

"I'm willing to offer the full asking price, dependent on a home inspection," I said—and I practically saw his startled jump, the euro signs in his eyes as he smiled—"if he will agree to let me rent to own for a year first."

The euro signs and smile vanished. "I don't think he'll like that, now," he said.

"Can I just ask?" I pressed on, the aggressively enthusiastic American. "If I write him a letter, will you send it on?"

He shook his head. "I don't know, now."

"I know the house has been on the market a long time," I said, hoping I was right that it was the same listing I'd seen in Irene's guest room in 2018.

He looked briefly at the floor and grimaced. I had him.

"Sure, write the letter and I'll send it on to him in the States," he said. "It'll do no harm, anyway."

I felt a glimmer: Americans, I'd learned, are known for our love of harebrained schemes. Besides, the knitting factory had been listed for years without a sale. Surely he'd rather take a year's rent than nothing?

The realtor must have seen my face change. He backed up a step. "I'm not making any promises, now. Don't get your hopes up."

My hopes, of course, were already through the knitting factory's worn-out roof.

When we got home, I saw a public service announcement message on my phone. I couldn't remember the last time I'd gotten one of those. I opened it, frowning.

All schools and daycare services were closing for two weeks due to COVID.

I stared at the message while Robin watched *Puffin Rock* and ate fish fingers, cheerfully oblivious. I was scared. The hours of childcare his naíonra gave me were the only way I was even half-managing to keep us afloat. I needed that time to have enough of my mind to myself to edit, to teach, to write. How was I going to do the work I needed to for us to survive?

But Shay: the last time he'd visited, he'd said that he loved me. He had turned to me in bed, when we were drifting off to sleep, and said it quietly. I had been a little startled, a little unmoored, and after a moment I had started to cry. I'd said I hoped he understood why I was afraid to say it back. He said he did understand, and he didn't mind, and he just held me.

We'd been dating nearly six months by then. I told myself I should have seen this coming.

There goes your "should" again, I heard Saoirse say in my head.

I had started thinking, more and more in those days, that you should only be allowed to say you love someone if you treat them well, if you act in a loving way toward them. I thought of my mother, telling everyone she still loved me and being pitied for it, praying for me every night but not doing an actual damned thing to prove her love through action. I thought of everything I turned myself inside out to do for Robin—I thought of everything Tommy, day in and wearying day out, had never done and I knew would never do—I thought of how scared I was, how much help I needed, how much love I needed, really, and what love should look like if it's real. And I picked up my phone.

Shay answered from his desk at the Evil Corporate Behemoth where he worked in Cork.

"I'm scared I won't be able to keep working with schools closed," I told him. "I need help." It used to embarrass me to say that—it still did—but it had become a simple fact, the way I'd learned to survive as a single parent: to admit I needed help and ask for it. They say every animal is born with its species' most crucial survival skill: newborn horses run, and newborn humans cry. Asking for help is how human animals survive. Every day, I remembered what Tommy had told me about lonely fields.

"I want you to come stay with us while schools are closed, and help take care of Robin so I can work," I told Shay.

It was a big ask: his company hadn't yet announced remote work, and we had no way of knowing that soon every company would be doing just that.

But: "All right," he said, looking at me through the video chat, the fluorescent lights of his open-plan office behind him. "Let me check the coach schedule. I'll come as soon as I can."

No "I'll need to check with my boss first," no "let me think about it," no "that's a lot to ask." As he hung up, I saw him reach behind his desktop monitor to unplug it. He was on the next bus up from Cork, with that monitor in a cardboard box, and as soon as he got to us—Robin squealed with glee and leapt into his arms while I hung back—he asked if I needed to work first, or take a nap.

I shook with gratitude. Maybe he really did love me.

I'd made two vows when I split up with Tommy, and I told Shay both of them early on. The first was that I would never, for the rest of my life, ever touch a grown man's dirty sock again. The second was that I would not move anywhere for a man, either.

The socks weren't a problem, Shay said, laughing. The other vow, he promised, was fine, too.

Still, I had my doubts that his stay with us would go well. I had basically nothing but doubts. But I had two safeguards from the idea of this becoming actual permanent cohabitation with Shay, which I was sure I didn't want. The first was that I was bound to Ireland with Robin until he grew up, and the second was that Shay was bound to the UK.

Shay's maternal grandmother had moved to England from Ireland when she was pregnant with his mother, and he'd spent his childhood summers on his cousins' farm in Sligo, but he'd only moved to Cork a few years previously, to support his then-girlfriend while she went to graduate school. He'd never planned to stay even as long as he had—but he'd stumbled into a good job, and since he'd never finished university he didn't think he'd find one so well-paid again, and he figured he'd keep it for a while. His mother's family had taught him to think of himself as Irish all his life, but he missed his family in the UK, especially his grandmother in Bristol. He was planning to move back within the next few years.

It was only the fact that it couldn't be forever that allowed me to ask him to come at all.

From Shay's first day with us he took on half the chores and childcare, as if it was obvious, as if it was a joy to him. Robin was delighted to have another grown-up there to lavish him with attention, to build sandcastles and throw rocks into the sea with for hours at An Trá Mhór.

The last day before the big travel restrictions came in, we drove through Connemara. I told Shay about the different colors every day, and he asked me about writing fairy tale retellings. I told him one of the things I love about all stories is how they're in conversation with each other, how every retelling is responding to the ones that came before. I rambled on long past when Tommy would have made some cutting remark. Shay listened happily and looked more at me than even the sacred landscape outside his window.

We drove to the Sky Road in Clifden, one of the most soaringly beautiful places in the world: a cliffside bay under the most wide-open sky you'll ever see, the freshest air, steep-sloping green fields studded with sleepy cows who surely don't appreciate the view, leading down to creamy sandbars and endless, achingly blue sea.

I told Shay the story of my friend Irene's grandfather, who swam across that crystal bay each morning to visit her young grandmother on its other side.

He sighed, holding Robin peacefully asleep on his shoulder: he was a romantic, like I used to be.

On our way home we stopped for lunch at an empty hotel, and we ate quickly and guiltily while the staff closed up shop for lockdown around us. And, because I couldn't bear the thought of leaving it unseen again for who knew how many weeks to come, we stopped at the knitting factory.

We clambered out of the car together, all three of us. Shay held Robin high above the weedy nettles and brambles as we waded through the cluttered, overgrown garden. The long white building still looked dusty and dark inside, but I pointed out its high ceilings and tall windows, so unusual in old Irish buildings, put there so the women would have light to knit by. Shay grinned as I showed him all the features I'd fallen in love with.

There was a gap in the crumbling border wall that led down to the lake. We explored a little, both of us keeping a careful hold on Robin despite his immense toddler confidence, and as we passed the wall I saw a big, pink, perfect scallop shell half-buried in the dirt. The sea was only half a mile away from us, and the lake behind the knitting factory stretched out wide and gentle into the west, rimmed with the glacial Twelve Bens mountain range. I thought about taking the shell home—it had been buried in the brush so long surely no one would miss it—but I didn't want to break the delicate spell of goodwill I could sense all around us in this place, to change the kind of relationship I wanted to believe I already felt with it. *You're falling for the castle all over again,* I warned myself. I watched the tall dark-haired man in front of me and wondered if I was just retelling one of my old stories with him, too.

But now I knew how to survive losing a dream, or losing a love. I wanted to search for them again, for both those kinds of home, and I knew how to make sure my baby and I would survive if they turned out not to be safe, or simply not to be meant for us.

I put the shell back, said goodbye to the golden lake and garden and tall windows, and drove Shay and Robin back home.

That night, Robin asked me to stay with him while he fell asleep. He lay on my chest while I sang him "The Daring Young Man on the Flying Trapeze," which had been his song since he was a newborn. Shay looked at us from the doorway with such tenderness that I was able, not only to know I loved him, but to tell him, too, and not to be afraid.

The next day I got a book in the mail called *The Feminist Architecture of Postmodern Anti-Tales: Space, Time, and Bodies*. The author, Dr. Kendra Reynolds, had written to me the previous year to tell me that she was analyzing my book *Tides* alongside the work of fairy-tale-retelling heroes of mine like Kate Bernheimer and my absolute favorite writer, Angela Carter, and to ask if I'd like her to send me a finished copy when it was ready.

I preened over that book like a megalomaniac. I don't know how Shay stood me reading it aloud, but, bless him, he did. He delighted in it right along with me, until I got to the chapter about the nature of time.

"Ooh, I love this," I said as I skimmed the opening page. "The violence of masculine clock time. Man, she's so right."

"Masculine what time?" Shay asked, laughing.

I read to him the book's argument—which I already considered a self-evident truth—that our modern conception of linear, measurable time was essentially patriarchal. I laughed along with Shay, but it was a laugh of delight in a newly articulated truth.

"The alarm clock has sounded: feminists have woken . . . the mechanical, chronological time of the clock created by dominant social forces (and therefore patriarchy) was established in order to regulate social life, maintain order, and provide a method of control . . . Chronological and clock time, despite being naturalized, are artificial."

"That's ridiculous," Shay said. "Time wasn't invented to control people. It wasn't invented at all. Time is time, and its arrow moves only one way. That's not *sexist*. Come on now." He was getting heated, I could tell: he was scrubbing the plates a bit faster. For him this was as much physical expression of anger as I saw. (I briefly remembered Tommy storming into our bedroom to smash plates against the wall and shout at me because I hadn't made him food to take to a horse show the next day.)

"But not even every human culture sees time as linear," I said, a bit frustrated with his frustration. "Or if they do, not in the same direction. Here she mentions a culture that conceives of the past as in front of you, because you can see it, and the future behind you, because you can't."

"That's cool," Shay said, "that's beautiful, but it doesn't affect what time *is*. It doesn't affect the nature of real time any more than our white western colonial bullshit whatever concept of time does. Our relative perception of it is always the same: one second per, well, second. Time exists out in the universe, it carries on from the big bang, bang bang bang, second second second. Time is what it is."

"But how can you know that? How can we know time exists outside of our perception of it?" I was getting too airy-fairy (bless you) for even my own taste by then, which takes some doing, but I had found my ground and I was going to defend it.

Shay shook his head, clearly outraged by this train of thought but still laughing, still looking at me with love and respect. "That's just what I mean. It doesn't matter. How could that matter to humans, if we can't even perceive it or conceive of it? Why bother talking about it, or trying to measure it in any way at all? The whole point of time is that it's a human construct, that we name it and use it so we can function as a society. If time weren't linear and constant and precise, it would be useless."

Robin, potty-training in front of the television, looked back at us from his plastic potty seat and cackled joyfully, which I felt was an excellent contribution to the debate.

(Tommy didn't speak to me at all for three days once because I said the protagonist of a TV show he liked was a misogynist. When I finally apologized just to get a word out of him, he made me grovel, then poked me so hard in the side I had a bruise and warned me not to criticize the things he loved like that again.)

"Don't you want to know that there are things you can't know, can't understand?" I asked.

"God no," Shay said. "Where's the romance in that?"

Maybe one of the key differences between us, I thought, was that Shay was science fiction and I was fantasy: not just in our reading preferences, but in our hearts. He loved the things he could understand, and I loved the things I couldn't. Science and magic.

And yet there we were, loving each other.

"Ah, here now," I said, a very Irish turn of phrase, as I turned to the next page. "Linear time is a phallic construct. Feminine storytellers can reject that linearity. There you go. Stop waving your big old linear time dick at me, Shay. I thought you were a feminist."

(I thought Tommy was a feminist. After Robin was born, I didn't keep the house clean enough for his taste—not that he ever cleaned it much himself—and he told me not to talk to him about anything but the baby's welfare until I completed a housekeeping course. He said it was only fair, since he had to go to this abuse perpetrators' group, that I take a course to stop abusing him through untidiness, too.)

Shay swiped a hand across his forehead. A sparkling trail of soap bubbles dripped from his glasses. "So what's the alternative, then? Genuinely?"

I smiled. "Isn't it obvious? Vagina time."

We both laughed again.

"In Ireland, actually—"

"Oh no—"

"No, in Ireland, the ancient Celts, they thought of time as a circle. A spiral, I mean, circles building on each other. The wheel of the year, you know? My ex's and my friend Diarmuid, every spring when he saw the new lambs in the fields for the first time he'd say: 'May we come around to see them again next year.' As if we'd be coming back to the same time, not just the same place. As if it would be the same lambs that we'd be seeing. He said that was a very old saying, and his grandmother used to say it every spring, too. He said saying it was like bringing her back for a second. I bet people have always been saying it here."

"And then the English came along with our clocks and our dick time and we ruined it."

"Pretty much."

The Celtic idea of time was something I'd always loved: not linear but spiralling, circular, a spinning wheel with eight spokes—the eight seasonal holidays, beginning with Samhain, the new year. In Celtic times, Dara Molloy had told me, a couple would be handfasted for a year and a day before their marriage. If, at the end of that year, they still wished to be wed, there was a second and more binding ceremony. If not, the cord that had once tied their hands together would be cut, and they would both be free. Any resulting children would be raised by the whole community, if need be, and neither bride nor groom was ostracized for their choice to end the union.

Tommy and I had been handfasted, six years earlier, on Inis Mór—a year and a day after our marriage, not before, so that we could have a little party with friends after our elopement. I could look out my window, right then, and see that same island, and I could see the spiral of all the other times I had been there, too: the ghost of myself seven and a half years before, stepping off the ferry with a heart unburdened by any of the years ahead;

returning with Tommy to be handfasted, and again for a babymoon when I was four months pregnant; returning with Robin and Johanna for the baptism; returning on a date with Shay just a few months before lockdown. Could I see the ghost of the next version of me who would be on the island, too? Who would she travel with?

I thought of how impossible it had been for me to leave my husband, how the only way I could walk out that door and stay out for my sake and my baby's was to believe that the good parts of our marriage still existed somewhere, were still real. I could not let him go until I gave myself permission to believe that we were still dancing to Leonard Cohen by candlelight in the freezing mobile home, warming each other, and that somewhere in space and time we always would be, and I could be there again whenever I needed to be. I couldn't set myself free until I knew I could return.

There were darker moments, too, of course, that would always be part of me, that would lurk in my body and heart as long as I lived. The most frightening moments with Tommy, with my father, moments that I will not hurt myself or a reader by detailing here. But—crucially—the versions of me that lived in those moments weren't alone. A little light filtered down from farther along the spiral and reached them, light from all the good things I'd found and done since, that helped heal them a little—and I started to see, and to trust, how things I hadn't even done yet were already helping to heal them, too.

I thought about texting with Claire in line at the bank while she wired the money for the castle. We'd spent that time talking about how we should totally co-write a story about a family of women who time-travel when they're carrying each other.

I looked at Robin by the TV, curls dancing as he bounced along to *Puffin Rock*, and I saw every version of him every day since his birth, saw my pregnant belly and felt his kicks from the inside again, the way his little feet kept pushing hard on my left ribs like he was lifting weights at a fetal gym, heard my own voice calling him *little pearl baby* as I looked for wild strawberries on the side of the road a few days before I knew for sure I was pregnant, reading him the Lucille Clifton poem "blessing the boats" on the day I did know for sure, before I'd even told Tommy.

I am remembering each of those moments here, now, writing this, from another point in the wheel of another year.

And now you are, too.

During lockdown, I felt far less isolated than I did in my first two years of single parenthood. I'd spent that time basically unable to leave the house, broke and alone with a toddler in the middle of nowhere. But suddenly I was getting invitations to virtual cocktail parties, book launches, and meet-ups of friend groups I hadn't seen in years. I had my tenth Smith reunion online and was even asked to give a talk about parenting and creativity, when I never would have been able to afford the time or money for a trip to Northampton if the reunion had been in person. Everyone else was suddenly as homebound as I was.

Besides, I was getting to sleep past five every other morning. I had someone to laugh with about potty-training mishaps and ridiculous toddler meltdowns, to witness my child's miraculous sweetness and wonder, someone else to see it and hold it and bear it all with me. Someone else who understood that it was precious. Shay doted on Robin—on both of us. He told me every day that he was amazed I could parent so well alone. Every Friday he put on a nice shirt and a different cologne from his collection and made a new cocktail recipe and we watched one of the plays that the Globe or National Theatre had made available for streaming. We cooked each other elaborate dinners and made space for each other to leave the house when we felt claustrophobic—my god, for the first time in my life I started *running* during lockdown while he stayed home with Robin, running along the Connemara Coast Road, *for fun*.

Aside from the creeping sense of COVID doom, inside the world of the cottage, I found myself hoping lockdown wouldn't end, because it meant Shay would be there longer. As much as I didn't think I ever wanted to give anyone a permanent key to my heart and home again, the partnership Shay gave me, and the loving-kindness he showed me and my child in those days, saved us.

Shay always said we saved him, too. That he would have been trapped alone in a tiny basement flat in the middle of a city otherwise, and instead he was playing on the beach every day with two people who loved him and whom he loved.

No, I don't think either of us wanted it to end.

And then the realtor called and told me the knitting factory's owner wanted to talk to me.

Sixteen

All Here Dwell Free

SPRING–SUMMER 2020

for Dara

The first time I saw the knitting factory, I thought of Avalon, of Brigadoon: magical havens that materialize out of the mist when you need them most. I thought of the little forest cottage that appears in fairy tales only after the heroine gets lost. It shows up maybe most famously in Snow White, but in quite a few others, too. One is in "The Maiden Without Hands." Like "The Selkie Bride," it is a story that has become both a mirror and a window in my life, a reflection and a frame through which I see the world.

Let's start where we are: in the middle of the story. A handless woman, once a maiden, later a queen, now an outcast, wanders lost in the woods. She uses the rags of her royal gown as a sling to carry her baby, since she has no hands to hold him. Near the end of her strength, the woman prays to anyone who might be listening for help in finding shelter for her child.

As her next footstep falls she sees an abandoned woodcutter's cottage, deep in the forest, where a moment ago she could have sworn there had been nothing. On the lintel of the door are the words *All Here Dwell Free*.

I remembered my dream of making tapestries embroidered with the names of crowdfunding supporters. I imagined long banners full of names on either side of the knitting factory's French doors, with those four words painted above them. All here dwell free.

In some versions of the story, the woman's hands grow back when her lost husband finds her again, or after she's been good for seven years.

But the version that rings most true for me is this one:

The woman and her baby live well and happily in their cottage in the forest. One day, the woman is doing laundry at a riverbank when the clothes twist out of her handless wrists' unsteady grip and start to drift away. As she lunges for them, the baby swaddled at her chest falls out of his sling and into the river, too, slipping quickly under, still far too small and weak to swim.

There is no prayer, this time. No request. Only the absolute knowledge of what must happen, and the absolute will of a mother to make it so.

Her flesh reaches out for her child with every iota of will and power in her, and her hands birth themselves from the ends of her scarred arms. She grabs her baby, lifts him into the air, and rolls with him onto the safety of the grassy riverbank. She hits the water out of his lungs with her new hands, her own hands. She holds him and shudders. And holds him.

And they live.

Fairy tales have always been survival guides as much as entertainment: they have given us, for so long, a code for the unspeakable. We may not meet dragons or ravening wolves in our real lives—except that we do, in other shapes, and stories teach us how to defeat them. Storytellers give us maps, escape routes, if only we can reach through the words themselves and grasp the truth behind them.

Here I am, reaching out my hands.

My friend Maeve had once told me, with great conviction in her voice, that my ancestors would speak to me through water. I'd started thinking about those ancestors a lot in the years since I came to Ireland, which were also the years since I'd left my parents. My father had been adopted, and his birth name was Irish—was, in fact, a Galway name. I didn't know anything about that whole half of my lineage, but I still felt sure, or told myself I felt sure,

I could see them in every shred of twilight mist over east Galway valleys, in the translucent lilac light of dusk and dawn. When I had a child, I understood with absolute certainty that my ancestors did love me, did look after me—because I knew with the same absolute certainty that I would love Robin for all his life, even after my own ended, and that Robin's children, grandchildren, great-grandchildren, no matter how many generations along, I would adore wholeheartedly, astoundingly, with devotion that no condition, not even death, could lessen.

I'm sure plenty of my ancestors were assholes. Among them were the Manifest Destiny colonizers I'd been raised to worship, not to mention the Scottish lord my maternal grandfather gleefully described torturing an abbot who didn't pay his taxes. Most of all, my ancestors had produced my parents: I didn't need more evidence than that.

But when I had a child, and loved him so much it reoriented every instant and iota of my life around keeping him safe, I started to understand. However many jerks stood between us, there were ancestors of mine out there who loved me that much, too.

I thought about them when the realtor called and told me the knitting factory's owner was willing to consider my offer. All the months of dreaming about the castle came rolling back over me, a rising tide hitting the high-water mark all at once. I could have that dream back again.

I spent another sleepless night adding more detailed notes to the proposal I'd sent to the owner, emphasizing my work as a writer and the "interest from publishers" which was in fact Friday Tea Smithies who worked in publishing and told me they thought my idea was cool.

I stayed up all night, Shay snoring beside me—so strange to have someone else in the bed while I was awake, and stranger still to realize I wasn't afraid, either of waking Shay up or of letting him sleep.

I told myself to stay calm when Patrick, the knitting factory's owner, appeared on the screen, the shadow of Key West palm trees flitting over his smiling eyes. He was friendly and kind and I liked him straightaway. He was very interested in my proposal, he said, but he wanted to be clear that the deadline for purchase was important to him: he'd already been trying to sell the house for years, and he had no interest in being a long-term landlord. He was willing to consider a one-year rent-to-own agreement, but not two.

I felt a lurch but quickly papered over it in both my own mind and my response. If I could do it at all, I could do it in a year.

"That's not a problem," I said, trying to believe in the confidence I heard in my voice.

"Okay, great," he said. "I'd like the year's rent up front. I'd feel better about it that way." The year's rent was €7500.

After two years of scraping by each month, I didn't have anything near that. There was the five grand—four, after the deposit on the Connemara cottage—from Claire, of course, but that was strictly for when I was actually going to buy. It seemed sacrilegious to use it before then. Besides, Claire was pregnant with her second child, and her husband was still relapsing several times a year. I wanted to hold on to that money for her, in case her husband became as suddenly dangerous as mine had—or in case she just as suddenly realized, as I had, his existing danger. I also cherished a secret hope that I could buy the knitting factory on my own and give her back her five grand and then some, to help her start her own new life without him.

I remembered all my crowdfunding plans for the castle. I'd considered trying to raise over thirty thousand for repairs at one point, and so many people had said they'd be in. Surely, I could ask for seven and a half.

"You have that, at least, right?" Patrick asked.

"It's not a problem," I repeated—and believed, almost, that it was true.

I stood up from the chair by the window in the living room and took a shaky breath. It was a bright afternoon, and light was starting to refract through the suncatcher I'd bought at the Knitting Show with Irene. Where the ceiling met the opposite wall, there were just the beginnings of rainbows.

Shay could see that I was shivering like a nervous dog. "You should book that building inspector today," he said, since the rent-to-own agreement was contingent on the house passing inspection and included the caveat that I would be responsible for any necessary repairs or renovations during my lease. That seemed dangerous to Shay, which was fair enough, but it was something Brigid and her husband had done with their chalet, and had suggested to me as a way to sweeten the rent-to-own deal with a prospective seller who didn't want to deal with keeping up their property anymore.

I waited three days for the inspector's report. Like so much time in lockdown, it felt like it stretched into eternity. But Connemara was always good at distracting me with its glory, fresh sunlight clinking off the landscape until every old rock looked like a new-cut gem, so sparsely populated and lushly beautiful that even when travel restrictions shrank all the way down to two kilometers, we could walk to An Tra Mhór, "The Big Beach," and find a ribbony stretch of silver-gray sand, embroidered with barnacled granite boulders. It was a perfect beach for children, the shore so gently inclined that at high tide there was no beach at all. Robin liked to stand at the edge of the concrete path by the lifeguard hut and laugh as brave waves splashed him. At low tide we could walk on damp, giving sand almost all the way, it seemed, to the horizon.

I filled up those three days of waiting by catching up with more old friends, having long conversations with people I hadn't spoken a word to in years. "You seemed so happy with him," so many of them said. "It's wild."

That would have felt like criticism not long before, but by then I was able just to shrug and say, "I thought I was."

On the evening of the third day, the home inspector called me. My heart was in my mouth before I picked up the phone.

"I have your report ready, but I wanted to call before I sent it," he said.

I could already tell it wasn't good news. I couldn't swallow.

"Hit me with it," I said. I get more American in times of stress.

"There's a lot to do in that house, now," he said. "You'll be needing a full rewire in the next five years, the roof's got a hole, pine roots are tearing up the border walls, the boiler's about to go if it's not gone already . . . jaysus, hardly anything is up to real modern standards, like."

That made me choke down a laugh. No house I'd lived in since I came here would pass that particular test—probably no house I'd lived in in my adult life would.

"But it's livable," I said. "You're not saying it's not safe."

He cleared his throat. "Sure, no, no, I'm not saying that. But it's an old, old house."

"Okay."

"You've lived in old houses before?"

"Oh yes. I grew up in one."

He sighed. "Sure, lookit. You're looking at at least fifty to seventy thousand euros to get it up to modern standards. It's not a project I'd take on. It's not worth the money. That's what I'm saying, like."

He wasn't being cruel. I'm not sure if he realized I wasn't someone who could just buy any house in a certain price range, that they weren't all alike to me. That for me, any house that was livable and would have me was a lifeline.

Suddenly it was all I could do not to cry. "Okay," I said again, hoping it sounded the same as the last time I'd said it, a few seconds before, when I'd had hope. "Thanks very much. I'll pay your invoice as soon as it's sent."

Shay had offered to get Robin ready for bed while I took the call, but they'd barely finished brushing teeth when I was done. Still, he saw my face when I came out of my room and said he'd do the rest of bedtime, too.

The report email arrived a moment later, and until Shay had Robin down, I scrolled obsessively through it, silently arguing with every point it made, even as the rising tide of all the things wrong with the house, the impossible-sounding figure of €70,000 to fix it, flooded my head.

Shay came out to the living room. "I'll make tea," was the first thing he said—the first response of any person on these small wet islands to any kind of trouble.

I curled my hands around the cup he brought me, and he sat down next to me on the little brown couch with wooden armrests that it seemed every old cottage in Ireland had. Only then did he ask me what the surveyor said.

"There are lots of issues," I said, "it's an old house. But he did say it's safe to live in."

Shay nodded. "Can I see the report?"

He read through it carefully, his brows knitting closer together with every page. "There's a lot of work to do," he said when he got to the end of it. He looked up at me, his brown eyes worried behind his thick glasses. "You don't have to take it, you know."

I shook my head. "I do."

"Why?" he asked. "I'm not saying—that this isn't a good idea, or that you shouldn't do it somewhere—but maybe—" I saw him searching for what to say. I knew he was trying to help me, and in turn I tried to force myself to listen, even though I was already scaling the walls of another castle in my mind and barricading myself and my baby inside, where nothing of our present reality could break through.

"Maybe this just means this isn't the place, and if you keep looking, you'll find something better."

"Better than an actual historic knitting factory and cinema with a private lakefront, close enough that Robin doesn't have to change schools?" I asked, and even I could hear the little crack of frantic longing in my voice. It wasn't unhinged, exactly, but the hinges were rusty and ready to go.

"Better than a place that needs fifty grand you don't have in repairs, on top of a purchase price—" *that you also don't have* hung too harsh to be spoken at the end of his sentence.

As did my answering, determined, utterly delusional *yet*.

When had we grown close enough, not to finish each other's sentences, but that the end of neither sentence had to be spoken? I felt a delicate lacing of fear wrap around me, reinforcing my refusal to stop dreaming myself away from where I was.

"You don't understand," I said, maybe because he did. I suddenly couldn't bear to sit next to him, and I jumped up to standing. "There is no other place, not that I've found in more than a year of looking. Rent everywhere is only getting worse. It's this or—or"—I couldn't say the word I hadn't let myself admit described my and Robin's situation when we'd lost our home—"or let myself be tossed around by the winds of fate."

I was being melodramatic, and we both knew it. But that, too, I thought, was my point: better to be ridiculous, to be pathetically bent on an impossible feat, than to rationally and defeatedly accept whatever life threw my way.

"I can't just have come to Ireland for no reason," I said more quietly. "I can't have given up everything else I had just to give my kid a shit dad and a shit life."

I didn't want to meet his eyes, but I could feel him looking at me sadly. "I know," he said, and I knew he did. "That's one of the things I love about you, you know. You keep doing everything you can for Robin. You never let anything beat you." He opened his arms.

I stood shivering a long moment before I went into them.

"This isn't the worst thing that's tried to," I said, my nose buried in his cream-colored Aran sweater, bought on a day trip to Inis Mór we'd taken in the other world before lockdown. He always smelled faintly of expensive cologne: he'd brought several bottles among the few necessary items he'd scraped together for his last-minute trek out to Connemara when the lockdown hit.

Tommy had bathed with Fairy Liquid dish soap (bless you), maybe once a week if I was lucky. I could close my eyes and know, just from a breath, how different things were now.

"No." He touched my thigh, where the day before lockdown I'd gotten a tattoo whose full meaning only he and I knew. "I know you've been through worse."

Journal: April 24, 2020

I woke up at 4:44 this morning & opened my phone & saw some internet thing with 444 comments. I am not big into repeating numbers meaning anything, but Brigid is—she always told me during the worst times to look out for repeating 1s, 1111, called them angel numbers. She said they meant my angels were looking after me & everything would be OK—& I just got bitter because I didn't see any repeating 1s at all, & the only numbers I did see were 4s. Not even third-place angels, bronze-medal angels, not even threes for me. Just fours, which obviously meant nothing.

But anyway all the fours when I woke up this morning made it occur to me to look up "repeating fours angel numbers," & it turns out all numbers can be angel numbers, which made me laugh, but then I read that four is the number of finding home & stability & I didn't feel like laughing anymore, I suddenly wanted to take it very seriously, wanted to believe even though I still didn't. I told Shay about it today & he told me about a study that showed that people who believe in lucky signs tend to look for them, & therefore to have better luck or better outcomes—not because the luck is real but because keeping a lookout for it is. I'm going to keep that idea in my pocket for sure.

It felt like a good sign. Maybe that's enough to mean it was.

Shay got up with Robin at 6 & then when I went back to sleep I had the most horrible dreams—first that Shay & I had an argument & he started yelling & throwing books & plates & telling me how many things were wrong with me, & then he rushed forward to attack me but I stabbed him in the ribs with a pen that I was holding & managed to uncap even though I felt slow & weak. Then I dreamed I took Robin to a doctor's appointment with my mom & I went outside to take a break because she said she could handle it & I picked some overripe strawberries but the seeds were the eggs of big clear spiders, & when I went back in Robin was gone. Mom said she had given him away because I was an unfit mother. I screamed & woke up & soothed myself but when I went back to sleep again years had gone by, & I'd been searching & searching for Robin but my mom was keeping him from me, & I was afraid she'd had him killed . . .

I had to cry & tell Shay about it when I woke up to feel better.

I am very psychologically transparent, I know.

I just found out we can start going ahead with the divorce now, & I am afraid about that, & the pandemic, & the future writ large, my ability to keep me & Robin together & safe. I am afraid of Tommy somehow getting custody. I am scared of the house not working out.

Shay said we've been living together six weeks with no blow-outs yet, & it made me realize six to eight weeks was the length of Tommy's blow-out cycle. I'm sure I'm afraid that's coming now I've lived with Shay that *long. By now Tommy would have yelled & told me how many things were wrong with me & thrown books & plates.*

But I must have faith in the future & move toward it. I must. Otherwise nothing . . . I don't know. Otherwise I won't feel in love with life anymore.

I know I should learn just to let things be. But I like to try, when it's something I care about, & it does make me feel safe even if that's pathological.

Robin update:

Shay asks "What's the magic word?" when Robin forgets to say please—so now Robin just says "Magic word!" instead of "Please!" & shouts it as a loud demand. It makes me laugh & laugh.

He has gotten very tan from going to the beach twice a day & is now as golden as an apricot. He gets more beautiful & sweeter every day.

The day after I got the survey report for the knitting factory, the time came for our weekly grocery run. Usually, Shay did it because he had less COVID anxiety than I did, but that day I told him I could use the time out of the house— which was certainly true—and that I'd prefer to do it myself if that was okay. (I was starting to notice how the training I'd gotten, to ask if every single thing I wanted to do was okay with the man I lived with, was still in place. I hated that.)

But I was lying a little bit. I didn't want to do the grocery run, to risk getting sick or bringing sickness home. I only did it because of something I couldn't quite admit I was going to do.

I drove back to the knitting factory.

A ribbon of open road across a yellow landscape tumbling with spring green, pollen glinting in the warm, bright air. Driving to the knitting factory in secret, even just to say goodbye, I thought must be the first time since Robin was born that no one, not even my baby, knew where I was. For that half hour, I existed only for myself.

The knitting factory had the gall to look sweeter than ever. Didn't it know I'd come to figure out how to say no, to break up with another building that didn't have my best interests at heart, that had only wanted to make me fall in love and not to make an honest woman of me at all?

I turned the car into the weedy gravel driveway, parked, and looked out at the lake: a blue mirror fading into more blueness in the mountains and sky, golden gorse all round its shore like a wedding ring.

I looked at the house, its tall windows and slumping roof, its sad, over-grown garden.

It was a dream I'd had for a while, too. Like the castle. Just a dream that had kept me going, that was all. Another dream I would have to let go.

I could find others. I was good at dreaming. I'd learned that much about myself, at least.

A lot of the weeds crowding into the driveway, I noticed, were deli-cate little bright-green ones down close to the ground. They had a three-leaf pattern and a curling, extending, elegant ballet-toed kind of tendril I knew well. Most importantly, they were jeweled here and there with pearly little five-petaled flowers, and a few tiny, perfect, ripening rubies.

I got out of the car and knelt into a sea of wild strawberries.

In east Galway, the summer I found out I was pregnant, I had found a patch a tenth of the size of this one and counted myself lucky to have stumbled on such a rarity. Here, though, were enough wild strawberries not just for a few precious, careful bites, but to eat all you could stand and do it again the next day, to make wild strawberry pavlova and shortcake and jam besides whole handfuls of them fresh.

They were both Robin's and my favorite wild food. Every summer I gave him almost all of the few I found and considered it one of my biggest motherly sacrifices. Here we could both have our fill.

Seventy thousand euros in repairs to bring it up to modern standards, the surveyor had said. On top of the two hundred grand it would take to buy it.

There is value in this place to me that there won't be to most buyers, I argued with the concerned, sweet-eyed surveyor in my head. There's value in the story I can tell about it, value that I can see, that I can bring, that no one else can.

Besides, what was worth a quarter million I didn't yet have—what more than all the wild strawberries my baby and I could eat?

I'm not here to say goodbye to you, my darling, I thought, and felt the house smile back at me. *I'm here to say hello.*

The next day, Shay took Robin out. He wanted me to have time to think, he said, to make sure the knitting factory was what I really wanted. "Remember how perfect you thought the castle was?" he said. "What if there's some other, better place waiting for you if you let this one go? What if there's a Selkie Cottage somewhere, with no repairs needed, waiting for you?"

I shook my head, but agreed with him that I should take the day to think.

"Take it to rest, too," he said.

I took my journal and headphones to An Trá Mhór and climbed in the hot rays of sun out past the low cliffs, farther than I let Robin climb or than I ever wandered when I was with him, to a part of the beach that was just deep-pocked black rocks filled with a hundred thousand tiny tide pools, where hardly anyone ever came. The sun crackled in every pool, reflecting back a hundred thousand tiny bright selves to the sky, as if Ireland wanted to prove it wouldn't be greedy when it got a good serving of sunshine like that, but would always offer it right back in fellowship.

I sat down on the least-stabby bit of rock I could find, opened my journal, and stared at the next blank page.

I pulled out my phone to text Shay and check on him and saw a photo and update from just a few minutes ago, a giggling kid, an *all is well*. I took a breath. I remembered my favorite line from a class I'd taken on medieval women mystics at Smith, from Julian of Norwich: *All shall be well, and all shall be well, and all manner of thing shall be well.* I tried to remind myself I'd miss this day sometime in an endless round of future drudgery, when lockdown was over and I no longer had Shay around to help me.

I thought of Shay, there to help just as soon as I asked him, to do more than I asked and to take joy in it, too. Of Claire, our endless looping conversations across the world, the money she'd sent me that had already saved my life and Robin's. Of the other single moms at COPE I so admired, of the chorus of Smithies in Friday Tea.

I hopped up and walked down to the water. As I waded, jeans scrunched tight around my knees and the water reflecting infinite little wave-sparks around me, standing by myself on the very edge of Ireland, I found the same faith I'd found the day before, sinking into a strawberry sea: that I was going to get the knitting factory the same way I'd gotten everything else I'd needed or dreamed of in the last two years. I was going to ask for help.

I needed to ask for six thousand euros to cover the rest of the up-front year's rent and a few initial repairs. It was a scary amount of money. I felt a sickly shame want to creep in—I had always felt ashamed asking for help, that was baked into the rugged individualism of my WASPy American heritage, and the fact that I *had* to ask for it to survive barely superseded that—but I was too desperate for this dream and I to have our chance, and too bereft of any other way into a stable home not to do it anyway.

I walked out of the ocean and started toward home.

On the way, I thought about Patrick's hard one-year deadline. Having just one year to buy the house, one year already ticking away, made me envy the two Brigid and her husband had to buy the chalet. They'd barely scraped it together in that much time—but then, I thought, maybe asking for two years was one of the reasons the castle fell through.

Still, one year was nothing: a thread already slipping through my hands. One year was the difference between birthing a child with the husband I loved and running away in fear on that child's first birthday. One year was the difference between meeting Tommy and marrying him. It felt like the most important parts of my life were measured along that too-short length.

I thought again of the Celtic wheel of the year, spiral time, circular time—vagina time, which always made me smile. I told myself this year would be a circle, a cycle, a ring: a commitment to this project, to spending all the little days that made up that big circle trying my best to do right by this dream.

Maybe next year would find me right here, safer because I had made this choice. I didn't know, after all, what our lives would look like at that time next year—the knitting factory or somewhere else, with Shay or single again—except that we'd be *here*, my baby and me, and I would hold hands with myself across that year. Memory and plans and needles and hands, knitting time together in the round.

Tea: wine in a mug.

Just one big, heart-lifting thing to tell you all this week, Smithies. I'm telling you first because you were all there for me when my marriage fell apart, when the castle dream fell apart, when pretty much everything fell apart. Now something good is building.

For the last few years, I've dreamt of creating a funded, childcare-inclusive arts residency for single moms (and other marginalized single parents) like me. In 2018 I thought I'd found the place for it, a small tower-house castle in east Galway. If you read my posts back then, you know how hard I tried to make it work. Unfortunately that dream didn't come true.

But I never quite managed to give it up. In March, while browsing real estate listings in a fit of insomnia, I came across a place that is less glamorous than a castle . . . but that I think might be even better fitted to the residency dream: an old knitting school in Connemara.

The Old Knitting Factory was built in 1906 as a place to teach rural women to knit so they could support themselves financially. In the 1970s it was converted into an Irish-language cinema, and later a jewelry studio. For the last five years it's been a little-used vacation home. It needs a lot of work, but I know I can make it beautiful again.

It has come at such a strange time, given COVID, but it's really happening. The Old Knitting Factory will be a stable home for my son and me (something that fills me with longing and hope and relief even to write) and a place where I can offer all the beauty and peace of Connemara, right on a lakefront and half a mile from the sea, to other single moms who need it as much as I did when I moved to the area last year.

I love the building's history, and I'm so excited to turn it into a place to empower women once again. I'm hoping to continue its use as a cinema space and offer screenings of films by Irish women directors, but that will have to come after the first step of this project: purchasing the building, making repairs, and funding the first residencies.

I'm asking to crowdfund the rent for the first year, as well as the purchase of some tools and supplies I'll need to make the place livable for myself and my son: a power drill, fencing rolls, etc. I am offering rewards for crowdfund supporters, and I hope you (or a mom you know) will love them! Funds will go toward the purchase deposit, repairs, and the childcare fund for the residency. Once The Old Knitting Factory is ready to open, I'll divide time in the private suite between paid residencies and funded ones, so that the former can help finance the latter.

Everyone who pledges any amount will have their name sewn into a handmade tapestry that I will eventually hang in the knitting factory. I would love for Smithie names to be the first ones there.

I know this is a difficult time for everyone, and if you can't pledge anything right now I more than understand. I'd be so grateful if you could sign up for the Old Knitting Factory's newsletter or follow us on social media.

I think I really kept believing in this dream because you all did, here in this Friday Tea group. Thank you from the bottom of my heart for your support, in all its forms.

I drafted that post, then made the social media profiles I'd realized I needed to make as I wrote. I remembered how the castle had slipped away right when I'd shared my hopes for it publicly. But Patrick and I had already agreed—he'd said he would drop the keys in the mail as soon as he had the year's rent—and it wasn't like I could hide this project from Tommy forever.

I looked at the darkness outside the cottage windows. I'd wait to post anywhere public until I felt safer, I decided. Tea was a good place to start.

I shared the post. I asked for help. I went to sleep. The asking itself took so much energy, as much excitement as I described feeling—and really did feel—about it, too. I had nothing left in me that night for watching the post and seeing how it would be received. Shay and I did Robin's bedtime together, and I crawled into bed right after my toddler did.

In the morning I found that the crowdfund was €2000 up already. There was even an eye-popping €500 donation from an older Smithie who said she had been a single mom, too. As I watched, the counter ticked up with more and more donations. It surpassed the €6000 I needed in two days.

In the days that followed, I started waking up before even Robin did, full of excitement. I shared my hopes for the knitting factory publicly, and nothing bad happened. I started posting to the project's social media account with photos from the real estate listings and ones I'd taken on my brief visits there. I took out a document I hadn't looked at in a long time: the book proposal about the castle.

I could do it again. I knew I could—I told myself I knew. The other part of the deal was already hounding me: to stay in the house, I'd have to buy it, which meant coming up with €195,000 by this time next year.

In June, the Black Lives Matter movement came to Ireland. I planned to take Robin to a protest in Galway City, but shortly beforehand, the organizers advised that we should stay home because of COVID and post on social media instead. So I did, sharing a photo of Robin and me and the BLACK LIVES MATTER cardboard sign we'd made together.

Burner accounts—such a *mystery* who was making them—immediately started accusing me of indoctrinating my child in political extremism and violence. Those comments were an unexpected gift: they were so absurd, so stupid, that instead of making me feel afraid, for the first time they made me laugh.

At the same time, the Smith online communities I'd come to rely on had a reckoning. Black Lives Matter started conversations that made it clear there were too many racists in our alumnae spaces, which is to say, of course, any racists at all. The parenting group I'd been invited into through Friday Tea, and which had become another precious source of support for me, went first: one of the group's administrators spent hours systematically deleting every one of the thousands of members so that she could then erase the group as a whole, as well as its years' worth of archived conversations, questions on everything from rash identification to co-parenting with an abuser: the collective wisdom of what I'd thought was a diverse group of thoughtful, empathetic, smart people.

I cried about its disappearance and then felt foolish for crying over an internet group—but besides the COPE moms, online Smithies had often been the only support networks I had.

When similar dynamics emerged on Tea, a group of alums of color started "Tea 2.0." Several thousand group members moved to this second incarnation of Friday Tea, and we began posting there instead.

Tea 2.0 became an even more beloved space for me than its predecessor had. The comments there were slightly fewer, because the group was a bit smaller, but they were also even more thoughtful and engaged than they had been before. The wreckage of something I'd loved was painful, but in its wake it brought me something even better.

That was a lesson I had learned before.

In June, too, *The Circus Rose* came out. I'd been dreading it. Even though I was proud of meeting my deadline, I was still sure it was the worst book I'd ever written. When I got an email from my editor saying the first big trade publication review was in, I felt lightheaded and nauseous as I clicked the link.

It was a starred review. Dazzling, they called it.

I screamed so loud Shay and Robin rushed into the room.

The Circus Rose taught me a very humbling lesson: that I truly was not the best judge of my own work, and moreover that I couldn't improve the quality of my writing through self-conscious caution or control. I'd left my bloody heart on the page, when I'd had nothing else to give. Maybe that was what I was supposed to be doing all along.

Now that the hope of writing a book to buy a house was turning real, I worried I didn't have enough to give to that dream, either. I was still overworked, overstretched, fearful, sleep-deprived.

But I longed to give myself fully to this dream. Even if all I had was more blood to leave on more pages, I had to believe that it would be enough.

Seventeen

Wild Strawberry Place

SUMMER 2020

for Margo

The keys to the knitting factory arrived on the summer solstice. I fished them out of the little padded envelope and held them in my hand like freshly de-oystered pearls. It was like the first time I held a real copy of my first book: I stood looking at this tiny life-changing miracle in my hands, smiling, but not quite able to move, not quite able to think, resting inside a private haven from my overactive inner monologue that I've only found a few times in my life.

That's what it was like the first time I held Robin, too.

Shay saw me smiling dumbly in the cottage's entryway and touched my shoulder. "Do you want to take the first night there by yourself?" he asked. "I can stay with Robin, so you'll get a good night's sleep in the new house. Just if you want."

I took a breath. The idea felt decadent, selfish. "Okay."

We explained the plan to Robin, who couldn't have cared less, and just asked Shay if he could sit on his back while he did push-ups again.

I had spent months walking in on Shay when he was with Robin and didn't know I was coming, or even nearby: this is a necessary step in learning to trust someone with your kid when you have the memories I have. I never told Shay I was doing that, of course. I do it still, with everyone, no matter how well I think I know them. People thought they knew my dad, too.

Shay and I loaded the car with a few boxes for me to bring along, I packed an overnight bag—it felt so strange that it was just for me, no toddler clothes or baby wipes included—and I left the boys and drove west into the pollinated summer sunlight.

Now ripe wild strawberries lined the border walls, the garden and glen, gleaming like pomegranate seeds in the summer sun. I posted a photo of them, miniature fruit on dollhouse vines, and a Swedish friend replied to tell me a word in her language that means a special secret place, a place where you feel at one with the world, a place you will only share with people you trust and love. Smultronställe: "wild strawberry place."

The berries were warmer than my mouth. I ate until my fingers and lips were stained ruby-red, the color of my birthstone.

I wanted to save the moment of unlocking the door, so I walked around the garden again, flamingo-stepping awkwardly over the rioting brambles. At the highest point of the crumbling cinder block wall, in the shadow of the overgrown pine trees the surveyor had told me were the first thing that needed to go, I found my perfect scallop shell again, right where I'd left it.

I picked it up and saw the mermaid-bra edges of two more shells underneath, nearly buried in the dirt. When I pried those out, they revealed still more: dozens of hand-size pink-and-white queen scallop shells, some still curved into cups, others pressed almost perfectly flat by time and tide long before they were gathered by whoever left them there. From the way the pine needles had turned to dirt on top of them, it must have been years ago.

I arranged them neatly at the end of the wall, a little cairn, a seashell prayer. Looking out at the lake, the skin of the waves gilded with sunset, I thought of how the Virgin Mary is called Star of the Sea, how I'd recently learned the word "virgin" used to mean a woman not tied to any man, a woman who was free, how free I had once felt stepping onto the silver shore of Inis Mór for the first time, and how this first moment of living at the knitting factory, looking out at the lake, felt a little bit like that, too. I thought of the Selkie Bride.

The wind went from cool to cold in a moment, as it so often does in Connemara. I went back to the house and unlocked the door with my own key for the first time.

The key stuck in the lock. I had to shove the door open. The air inside was dusty, but motes turned to fairy dust in the windows' light. What I remember from outside is golden light; what I remember inside is gray dust, so much that it seemed as if I had to dust not just each surface but the air itself. The couch and armchair in the living room were a matching set, brown and wooden-armed just like the ones in the cottage, and about as old and musty and ugly as possible. Cobwebs thick as curtains drooped across the high, vaulted ceiling.

I put on *The Best Little Whorehouse in Texas* soundtrack and had my own little moving-in montage: vacuuming the good-kind-of-old hardwood floors and the bad-kind-of-old colorless carpet, twirling cobwebs around my duster, soaking grimy old curtains in the bath and hanging them from tree branches, and opening every window to let in the summer air.

Standing in the evening light from the open windows, Dolly Parton blasting from the phone in my back pocket, I thought of how I used to try to have the house quiet when Tommy got home, so no noise would set him off. The home we shared, once so warm, had over time started to seem always silent, dark, and cold—and I had come to prefer it that way, because silence meant he wasn't shouting at me. I'd learned to think silence was the best I could hope for.

It was still hard for me to think that I deserved this house. But I knew my kid deserved it, and I could maybe give myself permission to think I deserved a *chance* at it, if not the thing itself. I had scraped out a chance to make this place ours, to make it beautiful, and looking up at the cobwebbed ceilings draped in sunset and dust I could see again what it might become, with love.

Some of the knitting factory's supporters had requested a tour of the house when we moved in—but now that I was really there, the idea scared me. I was scared that the people who had already donated would hate what it looked like inside, would realize it was just a house, and not a miracle.

I was also scared to show the interior layout online, in case Tommy saw it. I didn't want him to know which room Robin or I slept in. I worried that even doing this project, a central part of which involved talking about myself as a single mother, might anger him. I could see him thinking every photo I posted, every word I wrote, was meant to shame him.

Imagine how much worse he'd get, I thought, when he found out I was trying to write a book about it.

I decided to do the tour live, so it wouldn't stay up permanently on any of my social media. I felt scared, but I still wanted to share what these people had given me with them. I took a deep breath and pressed the red circle on my phone screen.

The knitting factory's social media pages only had a few followers so far, most of them from Friday Tea. Only they would get the alert, and I'd be able to see the usernames of anyone watching. If an account I didn't recognize, like one of the many burners I thought Tommy had made, showed up, I would just disconnect.

At first, no one was there at all. I walked around with the phone, talking only to myself, as if I'd become the real estate agent trying to sell the house: the cavernous factory space with its stone archways and big fireplace, the open kitchen with solid oak cabinets I loved so much lining one wall, the little hallway lined with more of those big airy windows, holding a built-in desk and bookshelf perfect for writing. Real stone fireplaces in two of the three bedrooms. The one I was already calling "the residency room" was dominated by a giant, moldy-edged picture window facing the explosion of wild cherry trees and lilac bushes, brambles and ivy in the overgrown garden and then the vast calm expanse of the lake, the tiny white houses dotting its opposite shore and the blue Twelve Bens beyond.

One room, however, was entirely devoid of romance: the bathroom. Its mold-spattered neutral colors and Jurassic grout looked dingy no matter how much I cleaned them. A sink with a wooden backsplash sat right in the middle of the room, and the toilet was built into the wall so you couldn't access its tank. What looked at first like a wooden bench in front of the tub was in fact a built-in step stool—to take a bath or shower, I had to clamber up its slick wood slats, sure I was going to twist an ankle every time. The bathroom had the most pointless twelve-foot ceiling, which I'd later learn sucks all the steamy warmth of a shower up into its leaking mouth, to be stored for mold production, and leaves you shivering in a sad little trickle. I was already dreaming of how I could renovate it into a wheelchair-accessible wet room for the residency space someday.

I took the handful of friends who had seen the live notification on their phones and signed on upstairs then, and showed them the one small room up there, the place that contained possibly the most spiders of all. There was a stained-glass window in the middle of an interior wall in this room, but its most interesting feature was a crawl space leading to a door that opened into nothing but air high up in the factory space at the far side of the house. I suspected this must have been the projector room when the knitting factory had been the first-ever Irish-language cinema in the 1970s. (I'd later learn that the filmmaker Bob Quinn's children used to sleep up there, lulled by the whirr and flickering light of the projector.) It still felt like a magical, child-size space: perfect for Robin, and for other children to play in once the residency opened.

"As soon as Robin saw this room, he asked if it could be his," I said, "and I would totally want it to be my room if I were a kid, too." A slanted, cavelike ceiling, long and cozily narrow dimensions, an exposed stone wall with a mysterious little hollow perfect for stashing a particularly beloved toy. Two more child-size doors in the walls that, when you pulled their old-fashioned handles, revealed only shadowy cobwebbed mystery. They were the kind of doors that definitely led to Narnia.

After that, I said goodbye to the three people who had logged on to watch—no great danger after all, I knew each of them well—and gave myself the gift that Shay had given me, of having the house to myself for this first night.

There was a little recessed nook in the exposed stone wall downstairs, by the French doors that looked out at the garden and lake. Two ancient candles sat there, once white and now so encrusted with cobwebs that they looked like a prop from a gothic film. I wiped them off and lit them, the flame crackling over the remaining dust and strands of spider-silk like miniature lightning. I posted one more quick video, just a small loop of the candles lit, with a line wishing my friends a happy midsummer, saying how grateful I was to everyone whose love had brought us here.

I sat on the dusty, cigarette-burn-pocked couch and stared at the flames for I don't know how long. Letting time pass was a luxury I'd forgotten. Shay had already texted me to say Robin was asleep, and I looked at the text history one more time, to remind my always-worried body that my baby was okay.

I'd put my sea-life-patterned oilcloth on the old wooden table. It was one of the first things I got for the bungalow, along with a TARDIS-shaped money box that I'd already put on the knitting factory mantel. I looked at them, looked at the candles, and just breathed. There was time and peace and space flowering inside of me, and it was mine alone. It was exactly what I wanted to give to other single moms.

I'd brought a carload of things to start moving in, and in the twinkly high femme sunset I started to do just that, walking out to my car up the sharp old concrete stairs, the driveway gravel stabbing at my toes. The next thing I unpacked was a corkboard covered with keepsakes that I'd had since I lived with Tommy in the mobile, before we even got married. I have carried it through all my Irish houses. There was a photo of Robin and me from his baptism there, a thank-you note from the students in one of my writing classes, a pin sent by the artist who made the first cover design for *The Forest Queen*, and a card I painted with Ram Dass's words, *We're all just walking each other home*.

I set it on the mantel and wondered if this would be the home that lasts.

When I brought Robin and Shay back with me the following day, we moved the books in first: bag after bagful, too many for even the big, rusty floor-to-ceiling metal bookshelves that came with the house. Near the bottom, where they would be accessible, I stacked Robin's board books and picture books, and higher up the books and journals I'd saved from my childhood home. I'd sacrificed a million keepsakes to bring them, filling just a couple suitcases because I didn't want my parents to know I was never coming back.

I'd run from two houses now: my father's and my husband's. I was still looking for Tommy's car in my rearview mirror as we made the many drives between the cottage and the knitting factory to move our things in. I still felt chased.

The only way to stop that grinding, exhausting fear, even for a little while, was to throw myself fully into what was happening around me, what Robin and I were doing together at the knitting factory.

So: What did it look like that day?

Golden light, so much golden light. Green blades of crocosmia not yet blooming, soft yellow coins of gorse petals among their evil spikes, blackberry brambles with blossoms so big and pink that I mistook them, at first, for wild roses. The white outer walls of the knitting factory as white as any old Irish house, which is to say a kind of moldy-gray. The pale-yellow bricks stacked at the house's corners and windowsills like blocks of butter. The windows big and opaque with reflected sun.

And when you turned away from the house: the lake, blinding-bright gleaming, out to the mysterious little houses across the way, the cursive horizon of the Twelve Bens not quite clear in the summer haze.

Tea: "Roses Are Red" black tea with almonds and rose petals from my favorite Galway tea house, Cupán Tae.

Best: We moved into The Old Knitting Factory. The first night we were all here mostly consisted of putting my kid to bed about twenty times: he was too excited to fall asleep for a long while. Finally, I sang him all the many verses of "The Daring Young Man on the Flying Trapeze" and he drifted off. I sat at the little table by the French doors and had a very late dinner and watched the sunset light drift gold across the kitchen cabinets. This morning we had to get going early, but had a breakfast of potato waffles and apples, and the move-in roses I bought myself yesterday had opened overnight in their Guinness pint glass and looked like they were glowing.

Worst: The heat and hot water aren't working. Thank goodness we moved in July, although in typical Irish summer fashion today is a cold

and rainy day. But the plumber is coming back with a small part that will
hopefully save me from having to spend most of the crowdfunding I've
raised so far on a new boiler. Keep your fingers crossed for me.

Robin and I found thousands more wild strawberries, tiny and sparking with
flavor, spilling over hidden corners of the neglected garden like a ransacked
candy store. Céad míle fáilte: a hundred thousand welcomes, the classic
Irish greeting. Céad míle sútha talún: a hundred thousand strawberries.

It smelled like growing green things, more wild meadow than garden,
left untended this long time. It smelled like earth. Bumblebees rumbled in
the bells of bright foxgloves, fairyland flowers (bless you), gorgeous but poisonous, too: digitalis. Eat them and they stop your heart.

Robin wanted to explore, to walk around the house's whole perimeter,
the almost impassable front path as well as the pine-needle-strewn, weed-
laden back garden with its ivied walls. We found one gigantic foxglove
growing in the strange little cinder block–lined courtyard by the driveway, a
huge bee mumbling in its biggest fuchsia bloom.

"See the flower, Mommy?" Robin asked.

"Don't touch it," I told him. "Foxgloves are poisonous. They are not for
eating." I'd started teaching him how to suck the nectar from the tiny purple
straws of blooming clover, the slim elfin goblets of honeysuckle. I loved to
teach him the foraging I'd always loved myself, but my worry was always
present, too: with everything I showed him, I wondered if I'd given him the
key to some future doom. Among the things I least expected about parenthood were the constant visions of death. Every time we ate a plant we found
outside, I told him: "Never eat a plant before I check it for you. Some plants
can really hurt you. Always check with Mommy."

"Don't eat anything unless you check with Mommy," he repeated
sternly, as if he was lecturing a still smaller and more vulnerable invisible
child next to him. My heart unclenched a little, for half a beat.

It felt so strange that when we moved into the knitting factory, Shay
moved with us. It was antithetical to the story I'd dreamed of telling

there, the home I was trying to make and share with single mothers. My identity as a single mom permeated every moment of my life, sleeping and waking.

And yet: Shay.

Another single mom from my survivors' group once told me over coffee that she was hoping to find someone who would want to be a good father to her kids. I recoiled from that at once. I said that if I lived with a partner again, it would mean admitting I couldn't do this alone. And I *could*. Other people saying it was hard just made my inner fuck-you voice louder. Oh, it's hard? Then I will see this hard thing through. I suffered through harder things for years. How dare you suggest *this* will beat me?

When Tommy first left the house, he asked me to meet a week later at a nearby bakery so we could talk. He sat down at the table and smiled at me, the eye-crinkling, sleepy, sexy smile that had uprooted me from my whole world five years before. His smile was inviting me to apologize—that was a pattern I knew well enough to recognize by then.

I don't know how I managed it, but I didn't smile back. I just blanked him.

His seductive openness vanished in an instant.

"So," he said.

"So."

"Have you noticed yet, all the things I did for you around the house, that don't get done anymore?"

I don't know where the strength came from to answer the way I did. Looking back now it feels like it came from my future self, from the detachment from him that I wouldn't really feel for years.

But maybe that doesn't give enough credit to the self I was then, still in love with him, still bleeding out. Besides, it was just the truth.

"Actually, I've realized I was already doing everything," I said. "It's been much easier to keep the house clean since you left."

His cheeks flushed.

"So that's it?" he said, his voice hard, full of derision. "You're going to be a single mother? You?"

· · ·

I've always read a lot of romance novels. My mother had a long row of them on a shelf in the guest room, and I flipped through them eagerly looking for sex scenes. They were never very explicit, and always very rape-y: the heroine would protest and cry out until it was obvious that the hero had overpowered her and she had no choice but to submit to his will, and then she would be swept away on the irresistible tide of their lust.

The accepted contemporary analysis of the "forced seduction" scenes in those books is that they were the only way women could access their sexuality without guilt. They weren't allowed to want sex outside of marriage, and they weren't even allowed to relate to a female character who wanted it: such a woman wouldn't be likable in the cultural context in which she was written. But if you were forced into it, then you could enjoy it. The romance novel rape is the fantasy of a sexuality that does not destroy your moral righteousness.

I have a friend who grew up in a strict church and who had an intense fantasy throughout her adolescence that a beautiful man would abduct her, tie her up, and then go down on her for hours. She wouldn't have any duties or obligations at home or school anymore: this guy would bring her food and plenty of books to read while he was away—kidnappers have to work, after all—and whenever he was home, it was a festival of oral sex. (I mean, I can't *not* see the appeal there.) And when she was eventually rescued, she would still be a (technical) virgin for her future husband.

My fantasy these days was far more perverse. I yearned, selfishly, evilly, for a world where lockdown restrictions never ended. I wanted COVID and its suffering to end, of course. But I kept catching myself in craven daydreams where this two-kilometer travel ban was in place forever, and Shay would have to stay with us. I wouldn't have chosen to give up single parenthood, wouldn't have had to admit I couldn't hack it on my own, or didn't want to. Shay wouldn't have to decide, either. It would be forced upon us, this happy home we'd accidentally made. Without having to deal with the weight of choosing it, we could just enjoy it.

Kinky.

Then, too, I wouldn't have to deal with all the reasons I might not want to choose Shay as a real, full-time life partner, or to have a partner ever again at all. If those decisions were taken away from me, I could just accept what had been given: a kind and supportive person.

One way he showed that support was taking seriously the need to make the knitting factory safe for Robin as quickly as possible. The estate listing breathlessly touted the house's eighty meters of private lakefront along Lough an Mhuillin, but failed to mention that said lakefront is impenetrably overgrown with stabby-needled gorse and brambles, the water utterly inaccessible. I was glad for that barrier. It made the house as mysterious as Sleeping Beauty's castle behind all those thorns—and it would keep Robin safe from drowning.

But I still couldn't help picturing my baby falling over the short, crumbling, ivy-encrusted walls. In my head he went straight into the lake, but the higher likelihood of falling a foot or two into brambles and stinging nettles, while less fatal, was also horrifying. What if he wandered out there in the middle of the night and I didn't find him 'til morning—or couldn't find him at all in the overgrowth?

It doesn't make sense. I reminded myself of the mom who told me her fear was that her toddler would go into the kitchen in the middle of the night, fill the kettle, boil it, and then pour boiling water all over herself.

The only place kids ever go at night is to their parents' beds. I knew that well. But every night was full of hypervigilance nonetheless.

So I dragged Shay and Robin with me to the hardware store, where we stood through a round-the-block COVID line and spent an hour belaboring the choice of which power drill and bit set to buy, then took several rolls of fencing home and attached them to the cinder blocks together.

Robin had a play drill, part of a gift set that Saoirse had chosen for him from COPE the previous Christmas. He stood next to Shay and pressed his drill button and made buzzing noises when it wasn't loud enough. It was exactly the kind of thing I would once have pictured him doing with his dad.

At the hazy height of Irish summer, the sun didn't set until after ten, and Shay and I received that after-bedtime light like a wondrous gift: the golden hour felt like freedom, and we headed outside to cut ivy or install hanging baskets of yet more strawberry plants by the front door. We used every bit of evening light the first week building that fence.

"When you write your book about this house," Shay said, as dusk finally settled in one evening and we traded our work gloves for cans of Guinness and a campfire in the garden, "say you built the fence alone. Don't give me any credit."

Shay knew that one of the reasons I was so desperate to find and keep a home in Ireland was because I wasn't allowed to take Robin with me anywhere else. And I knew that Shay had never wanted to stay in Ireland.

Still, sometimes we talked about the future. Shay wanted babies and a life partner, someone to grow old with. He had gotten out of a six-year relationship around the time Tommy and I split up, so he wasn't ready to plunge into that quite yet, but he was still enamored of the idea in a way that I just couldn't conjure up in myself anymore.

"You sure you want more kids?" I asked him that evening, as I often had, half-joking.

He smiled at me, a little sad, across the fire's glow. "Just one more. Yeah, I do."

I felt a little lurch as I realized we'd both said *more*, as if Robin was already his.

"I can't pretend the idea doesn't appeal to me sometimes," I said quietly. "I always thought I'd have three or four kids." I had mourned those never-to-be children, in fact, since I'd left Tommy. I always remembered it was children I'd felt waiting for me in that Inis Mór hotel room with him, not one child. "But I'm tired."

I always had to force my voice not to break when I mentioned that. It sounded self-pitying, which I hated. But it was also so deeply true that just voicing it was painful. It often felt like the truest thing about me: how tired I was. "And I need to make sure Robin is safe and okay before I can think about anything else. I really think—I often think—by the time he is, and then by the time I've recovered from getting him there, it will be too late, anyway."

It was almost dark by then, the air filled with the scents of smoke and lilac. The stars were coming out.

"I'm not asking anything of you," Shay said, "but what does that mean, for Robin to be safe? What does it mean that he doesn't have right now, that you haven't given him already?"

"The house." I took a breath. "Just . . . it scared me so much. Losing our home. Losing a home to give him. I need to get us somewhere stable. Somewhere no one can take away."

He nodded. "I know. It's amazing, what you're doing for him." He sighed. "I just, I have to say this. My parents didn't own a house when my sister and I were small. They were students. They were poor. It's why we lived with my nans so often. And I had a happy childhood. I always felt safe." He looked at the fire. "We were so happy."

Shay, I knew, had grown up in a working-class matriarchy, partly raised by both his grandmothers, and his parents had met as first-generation university students. The memory of that strong-hearted multigenerational stability called to him deeply—a feeling that, for all my own estranged family's wealth, I'd never come close to having.

Shay often talked about "the grandmother effect," a theory he'd read about that suggested humans had evolved to live so long because having grandmothers around significantly improves your offspring's likelihood of survival. I don't think he knew how sad it made me whenever he talked about that.

"Robin doesn't have a grandmother, Shay," I said. "Not like yours, anyway. She . . . " I trailed off. My mother was a sentence I could rarely bear to finish. "He just has me. I have to figure out a way to be enough for him, and this is what I've figured out."

He looked away. "I know."

Seventeen weeks after lockdown started, the travel restrictions lifted, and Shay went back to Cork. I didn't ask him to stay.

Eighteen

The Maiden Without Hands

SUMMER–AUTUMN 2020

for Anna

When Shay left, I felt the same initial panic I had when Natalia went home: that I didn't remember how to live alone with my child, that I couldn't. The idea of taking all the broken nights, every early morning, on my own again made my head ache with preemptive exhaustion. I'd slept twice as much when Shay was there, and not washed a single dish—and I was still tired most of the time. I had no one to witness all the hardship and sweetness of toddlerhood with me, no one else whose memories would help make it real. I found myself envying the other single mothers in the COPE group for the extended family they had nearby. It rarely helped them escape the housing insecurity that threatened all of us, but at least they had some family around who loved their kids.

I was better off without mine, I knew. But I was starting to understand, in a new way, what I had given up.

At the same time, as the days went by, I started to remember something I had forgotten or hadn't noticed before: that there were things I loved about being a single parent. My home was my own again, mine and my baby's, and I could feel us still *being* a family, just the two of us. We'd been thrust into it so suddenly and violently before, and I had felt only fear and lack. Now, for the first time in seventeen weeks, I felt the steady beauty of living only with the person I loved most in the whole world.

I felt the pleasures of singlehood again, too: a sweet space opening up in my home, in my heart, that was just for me. For the first time in seventeen weeks, I had my bed to myself, with no one keeping the light on later than I wanted, or coming back to bed in the middle of the night and frightening me out of dreaming with too-old memories of someone dangerous opening my bedroom door.

That feeling of safety, of peace, was something I wanted to nurture. I knew I needed to help myself learn how to keep it. I went back to therapy, something I had triaged out of my budget for years. As an at-home exercise, my therapist suggested I write a letter to my child self.

I chose a particularly calm afternoon to do it, nestled into a puddle of soft windowed light, the sky outside a blanket of haze.

As soon as I started writing *Dear Betsy*, I could feel it working, feel myself showing care and gentleness to a little kid who was so often scared.

I told myself not to worry or feel like I had to do anything or fix anything: grown-up me was taking care of it, and we were safe now. I had taken us away from the people who scared us. Things are better now, I said: you get to live in a house where only people who are kind to you can stay. You get to be safe.

When I saw my own hand had written *You get to sleep alone*, I stopped.

To sleep alone. Until I read it, I had no idea that meant so much to me, even though it seemed obvious as soon as I thought about it. I certainly wouldn't have imagined such a thing when I considered myself happily married. But as soon as I wrote it down, I knew it was something I needed. To get to sleep alone.

People often asked me, as I worked on the knitting factory crowdfund— they still ask me today—where my family was, why they hadn't helped me. I've learned to say no more than "We're not close," and let them infer what they like. It was my choice, after all, to leave my parents, and it is my choice to stay gone now. I'm sure they think of themselves, religious as they are, like the prodigal son's father, already congratulating themselves on the grace they'll show when they welcome my contrite future self back home.

Actually, that's not fair. I have no idea what story they tell about me. Since I left them, I think they can say whatever they want.

But I do know that the story I tell myself is different.

The fairy tale that makes me think of my parents now is "The Maiden Without Hands." I told part of that story before, starting in the middle. It begins like this:

One day a man met the Devil in the forest.

The Devil strolled up to the man, who was busy chopping wood, and said, "Why do you bother with hard labor like that, old man?"

The man laughed. "I am not so old that I cannot work. I was a miller once, but the water that pushed my mill has dried up. There is no work left to me but this: chopping wood so that my wife and daughter do not freeze in the coming winter."

"You might go home tonight and find firewood enough for every winter left to you, and every drawer in your kitchen filled with gold besides."

The man threw back his head and laughed still harder. "Sure, I suppose I might, you devil. And my wife grown young and beautiful again, too!"

"Yes, your wife, and yourself as well. All these things you will find, if you only promise me that which stands behind your house."

The man grew sober when he saw the Devil's expression. "That can only be my old mill," he said. "Why, you may have that, if you like."

After shaking hands, each man made his way home through the woods.

The miller's legs grew stronger as he walked, and his back straighter. By the time he arrived home he was a young man again, and two lovely young women waited for him at his cottage door. He could not tell who was his wife and who his daughter, and he embraced them both.

But one woman smiled, and one looked frightened. As the man's
wife showed him the gold that filled their drawers, their daughter looked
outside at the firewood that had appeared next to the mill—just behind
the house, where she had been out gardening all day.

As the three years passed, the miller grew so happy in his youth and
riches that he never noticed how quickly his pile of firewood dwindled.

And one day the Devil returned.

I do not know my father anymore. I knew him well, once. But I know
that you know him.

I don't mean you know him from my writing. The things I told you
about him first, because of what they are, define him here. They might be
all you ever see. But what I want you to see in him is other men. The men
you know and love.

My father is popular. He always has been. He is likable, affable, intelligent, funny. People enjoy his company. Many people love and respect him.
Think of a man you love and respect, a man who is your friend. Maybe your
brother. Maybe your husband. (My mother and my father are still married.)

When you imagine my father, I want you to picture a man you know
and love. I mean this very seriously. He is not a fairy-tale villain. He is not
the Devil. He is a normal man, with the same capacity to hurt and heal that
all human beings have. Sometimes I miss him.

You listen to me. He is not a monster.

My father sexually abused me. Much of it happened when I was so
young that I have no chance of remembering it all clearly. I was going to
write "no hope of remembering," but I do not hope to remember, not anymore. I believe my own mind is protecting me. Something deeper than my
mind.

What I have are body memories, heart-blood memories. When I get
flashbacks, bone-deep flashbacks that I can't articulate in images or words,
I ground myself by calling them a blessing, both for what they hide from
me and for what they affirm is true. I was taught for years to disbelieve my
own experience because my parents told me I was wrong, and the first few

people I told told me I was wrong, too. But my body memories prove that I am right, that it was real.

One memory I have for sure, one memory that's safe to remember, is lying in bed as a young child and listening to my father talking quietly in the next room with a friend who was staying for a sleepover. And wondering if he was touching her.

I was maybe seven. No seven-year-old would wonder that without a reason.

Except, my mother would say, for me.

You know my father. He is a man you love. He is a man you wouldn't believe could do something like that, because only monsters are molesters.

Listen: I am not a princess, and my father is not a dragon. We are human. This is what I most desperately need you to hear, and to believe. Because if in order to believe me, you turn my father into a monster, then you won't believe the child who tells you it was your beloved man who hurt them, because you know in your soul that *he* is not a monster.

If you tell yourself someone can't hurt you because of how much you love them, how good you know they can be, your love is as good a weapon as any they can use to keep you trapped. Ask me how I know.

"I'll take your daughter with me," the Devil said, "for it was she who stood behind the mill that day."

At first, the girl thought she would go. Anywhere was better than sharing this house with her too-young, laughing parents: her mother who used her face like a mirror, her father who liked to say that when they stood together it looked as though he had two pretty wives, and no child at all.

But she saw the Devil for what he was. A virtuous girl, she washed her body and made a circle of salt around herself for protection.

Neither her parents nor the Devil could reach inside the circle.

"I will come back in three days," said the Devil. "Give her no water, so she cannot wash, and then I will be able to take her."

The miller's wife would have reached for her daughter if she could, but at the edge of the circle of salt her hands stopped, and she felt only a cold, hard barrier in the air, like the surface of a mirror. When her father reached for her, he found his hands slid toward his wife instead.

They gave her no water. But when the Devil returned, the girl had wept into her hands so much and so often that they were still clean.

"You must cut off her hands," the Devil said, "or I cannot take her."

"Cut off my own daughter's hands!" the miller cried, but he was already reaching for his knife.

He grabbed his daughter by the arms, which had grown dirty enough to wear off their magic, and his wife helped hold her down. They cut off her hands on the kitchen table.

The girl wept so much that her tears flowed together with the blood from the stumps of her arms and washed over her whole body. Once she was cleansed with tears and blood, neither her parents nor the Devil could touch her again.

"To Hell with this," said the Devil. "I have no claim on her now." He left, taking the last stick of firewood with him.

"Oh, wonderful daughter!" the miller cried. "You have brought me a great fortune and released me from the Devil's bond. I will keep you in such splendor now that you will never miss your hands!"

The girl shook her head. "I cannot stay here with you," she said. "I must go out into the world, and have faith that compassionate people will give me all I need."

"But how will you survive without us to be your hands?" her mother asked.

The girl said nothing. She left that very hour.

Why was I as desperate to stay gone from my parents as I was to hide from my husband? They had money, resources that could have helped my baby and me, could have maybe kept our brush with homelessness from happening, if I groveled before them earnestly enough. But I knew that if I went back to them, all I'd find is a broken ring of salt, and blood on the kitchen table.

That's not quite true. I'd also find the other maiden, the one I left behind. My sister and I haven't spoken since I made the police report. She and my parents are still close.

I will keep you in such splendor that you'll never miss your hands.

There is an unbreachable gulf between us now. Even if we did speak, I don't know what either of us would say. I do not think our hands will touch again.

The only sisterly thing I can do for her now is not write about her further.

As for me, I have gone out into the world, and compassionate people have given me all I need.

You get to sleep alone.

I missed Shay. But a future of always sharing my bed, a space that felt safe to me for the first time in my life when I finally had it all to myself, felt claustrophobic.

I told myself I didn't have to decide anything right then. More important than Shay, or me, was something else the letter had shown me: that Robin was growing up without the fear I'd already lived through at his age. He was happy and carefree, and he was able to do things that were beyond me as a child, like introduce himself to his peers or older kids without being shy or frightened, enjoy spooky movies (*Nightmare Before Christmas*, which he called "Sally," was his favorite), and fling his body around the world and into the arms of everyone he knew, without an ounce of fear that they would do anything but hold him gently. Some of that, I knew, was down to personality—he was sunnier and more outgoing than I'd *ever* been, I was sure—but part of it, I was equally sure, came from living in a house with no one scary in it.

I did that, I wrote on Friday Tea that week. *I made us an abuse-free home. I am raising a kid who is going to be a lot different than I was. His naíonra teachers praise his ability to make friends with everyone and lead them in play, when I was afraid that speaking English at home and having an American single mom would make him an outsider. He seems afraid of nothing, sunny*

and loving and sweet. I am so proud of him, and so sad for my past self, and so
proud of the fact that I got us both here.

As the long evenings stretched on, I cut back the decades of ivy and brambles that covered the border walls like the thicket around Sleeping Beauty's
castle, put in a laundry line and compost bin, weeded the garden and driveway, grew tomatoes and chilies and herbs. I flung open the windows in every
room every moment I could, scrubbed and rescrubbed each moldy surface,
did battle with a hundred thousand spiders—céad míle damháin alla—vacuumed up legions of mummified woodlice, unspun long strings of cobweb
from each window.

Those windows were huge, at least for an old Irish house: they'd been
built to let in enough sunlight for women to knit by. I'd learn later they
were placed high up off the floor on purpose, so that when the women were
sitting and knitting in all that light, they wouldn't be able to see out the
windows and get distracted.

Ever since I learned that, I have made a point of looking out the windows and getting distracted from my work every single day.

Fixing up the knitting factory was what I did between my still-endless
gigs, teaching and editing and tutoring and writing, which I did between
childcare and housework, which came between sometimes managing to
sleep a little bit. I was still barely treading water—but unlike my time renting, my exhaustion wasn't going just to line the pockets of a landlord who
could decide to evict us at any time. It was going toward the hope, however
unlikely it still was, that I was building a life I could someday rest inside.

In the mornings, Robin and I walked along the shoreline or the winding country roads. We got to know Connemara through its plants: he had
learned his favorites and always rushed ahead of me, eager to be the first
to find treasure troves of sorrel or sea spaghetti. I kept an eye out for wild
rosehips to preserve as cordial in the fall, sloes for gin in winter, creamy elderflowers in spring, and bright, coconutty gorse petals any time of year at
all. One of my favorite Irish sayings is that the only time a girl can kiss a boy,
instead of waiting to be kissed, is when the gorse is in bloom—but its yellow

blossoms color the mountains all year long. It's an old, old Irish joke: a girl can kiss you, darlin', anytime.

As the summer slipped toward fall, the most pressing concerns about making the knitting factory livable again abated, and I shifted my focus toward writing my book proposal. Crowdfund donations were still trickling in—on advice from Friday Tea members, I'd raised the goal to cover more renovations and a general fund to help purchase the house—and I was hugely grateful for each one, but I was sure the kind of money I needed for a down payment could only come from selling a book bigger than my YA novels. I'd felt so sure, before I actually had to start writing it, that the story I could tell about the knitting factory had that much value.

But every time I tried to write I felt a hundred thousand tons of pressure bearing down on me. Even though I had five novels published, the stakes of writing a book to house myself and my kid were so high they paralyzed me.

Still, there were plenty of other writing-related projects I needed to do to keep us alive: finishing my sixth novel—*Reader, I Murdered Him* would bring me $8500 when I delivered the final version, something I was determined to do before the house's purchase deadline—teaching a new semester at the university, and making the crowdfunding rewards I had promised in the spring.

As one of those rewards, I researched and wrote a handmade zine about the building's history. The zine became a microcosm of the lessons I learn over and over again about writing books: that I always imagine a project as so wonderful that I end up putting too much pressure on myself even to start, because any start at all feels unworthy of what I had hoped to make. I started focusing on the zine because it felt less scary than the actual book proposal, but then immediately decided making the zine was scary, too. After all, it had to be good enough for the people who had given me money to get here in the first place, and I was already sure that nothing would be good enough to show the immensity of my gratitude.

I had been in this spot enough times that at least I could catch myself in self-sabotage and remember the ways I'd found to help myself before. I started with the part of the project I found least intimidating: instead of writing about my own hopes for the space, I started writing down its history, what already existed and didn't need to be changed.

The Old Knitting Factory had been described in the real estate listing as a place that "educated the local women in the art of knitting and provided much needed employment and income for the area," but in fact, its history is more complicated, less sweet, than that—as, of course, are so many of our own histories.

As often happens, the parts I'd found too scary to start with emerged on their own as I worked. The point, I learn over and over, is just to get started, on whatever tiny corner of ground I can manage to hold.

This is what I learned, and what I shared in the zine I mailed to the knitting factory's supporters:

The Old Knitting Factory was built in 1906 by the Congested Districts Board for Ireland, as part of an effort by the UK's Conservative Party to "kill Home Rule with kindness"—in other words, to quell Irish desire for independence from Britain by funding public works. The knitting factory taught skills that local women could ostensibly use to support themselves financially, but its name being "factory" rather than "school" (as I kept wanting to think of it) suggests that its true purpose was the product, not the students: commercial rather than educational or philanthropic. The Aran Islands knitwear industry that still exists today was created in the same context.

Irish nationalists criticized the CDB's reliance on the Church for management, the long-term nonviability of many of its projects, and its paternalism. Prominent nationalist Frank Hugh O'Donnell argued that the CDB was being used to fund Church-run projects like Industrial Schools, which already had a long history of underpaying and mistreating workers.

The rampant abuse that took place at Industrial Schools, Mother and Baby Homes, Magdalene Laundries, and so on has been amply recorded, but new evidence of old horror is also still emerging all the time.

Mother and Baby Homes: a sweet-sounding name for unspeakably brutal places. Beginning in the 1920s, over a hundred thousand people were
confined in these institutions, usually run by Catholic nuns—and that is
only the number included in the Irish government's official investigation
into their history, which itself was only begun in 2015.

Nothing I can write here will do justice to the horrors and abuses that
unwed mothers and their children experienced in the Mother and Baby
Homes, or in their sister institutions the Magdalene Laundries, where
women were worked to death in penance for bearing children out of wed-
lock—children who were forcibly taken from them, or who they were
manipulated into giving up; who were then adopted out, often to other
countries, and often at a financial profit to the Church.

My father's birth mother was a teenager, and she gave him an Irish
name. I don't know anything more about her than that.

I'm not saying that my birth grandmother came through one of those
places. I'm only saying that she might have.

The last Magdalene Laundry closed in 1996, twenty-one years before
Robin was born. If I had been a single mother just a few decades earlier, I
might have shared the possible fate of the grandmother I'll never know:
might have had Robin taken from me, might have lived out my days not
writing books, but washing dirty sheets with hands that ached to hold a
child I had borne but would never see again.

I'm only saying that I might have.

What was I fighting for, in working so hard to find a home for myself
and my child? What did home mean to me, if not a place where Robin and I
would be safe, where no one could separate us? I still felt under threat as a single mother, under constant scrutiny from my ex and the courts and TUSLA.
Plenty of the people who had run the Mother and Baby Homes, who donated money to them or to the Church that ran them, who sent their pregnant daughters there, who adopted babies who'd been placed there, probably
heard the word "home" and thought they were doing something good.

But a home where I could not protect my own child, could not keep us
together, would never be safe. Writing about the Mother and Baby Homes,

and thinking about my grandmothers—all of them—I knew what I really feared, and what I was fighting for.

In 2018 I took my baby to a walking vigil for those who died at the Tuam Mother & Baby Home, where the bones of hundreds of babies had recently been discovered in the building's sewers. I walked with Robin in his carrier. Someone a few steps ahead of us blew bubbles that floated in the sky above the vigil. I kept thinking that every baby who died of neglect and mistreatment there would have loved the bubbles as much as my own breathing, adored baby did.

A man at the vigil told the Irish Times *journalist Lorna Siggins a story of growing up there, and of only learning as an adult that his mother, Eileen, had walked to the home every day for five and a half years, begging every single day just to see him for a moment, and always being turned away.*

Over seven hundred babies died at the Tuam Mother and Baby Home and were put into sewers with no proper burial, in this building run by the Church. I was so angry I could have screamed all through the vigil, and gone on screaming, and still be screaming now.

When I first learned about the knitting factory, I imagined it as a space built to empower women, and most likely there were those involved in its creation who genuinely believed in that purpose. But I am almost certain that the first women under this roof were overworked and underpaid, that their need for help and hope for independence were manipulated by abusive power structures that wanted to kill that very independence, as they said themselves, with kindness: a sort of kindness that is really control.

I know that kindness well. I saw my father use it; I learned about it in training as a rape crisis counselor; I saw my husband use it, and I read about it over and over again in the history of Ireland and other colonized places. It is happening now in both the countries where I've lived. It is a classic aspect of the cycle of abuse.

The scariest threat my husband ever made was that he would have me deported and keep "his boy" in Ireland. He said that to me only weeks before news broke of the family separations at the US–Mexico border. The personal is political, the political is personal. I cannot write about myself without writing about history. When I think about Eileen walking to the baby home for five and a half years, when I think of babies taken from their parents in America, I cannot breathe until I am holding my own child, until I can smell his hair and feel his heartbeat.

My father was adopted, and all I know about his birth mother is that she was sixteen and had an Irish surname, a Galway name. What would I give her, if I could? What would I give to the women of the Tuam home, the Magdalene Laundries, the knitting factories and industrial schools?

A single mother I greatly admire, Violet Lea Devotion, once told me that when we heal ourselves, we heal our ancestors both backward and forward in time.

I would give them rest. I would give them time with their babies, and time to make things that are beautiful only to them, and only on their own terms. I know I can only do that by giving it to myself, here, now, here and now. I think the most radical thing The Old Knitting Factory can be is a place of rest.

What would I give to the women who have been here, to myself, to those who may come?

I would give us Home Rule.

Nineteen

May the Women Live Forever

AUTUMN 2020–WINTER 2021

for Chris and Liz

I had imagined myself going through the motions of a movie montage in my first months at the knitting factory. But the house was doing better than I'd hoped, at least for the purposes of one mother and toddler who weren't used to fancy living. It was old and run-down, yes, but in a way that was easy to see as charming rather than horrible—mostly.

The garden, for instance, was eager to assure me that it was at least as gorgeous as it was overgrown. The rioting brambles exploded with bigger blossoms, and a few months later, bigger and darker and more luscious blackberries than I'd ever seen. What I thought were tufts of oversized grass turned one morning into a blanket of soft orange flame, a flower I learned was called "crocosmia" and was in fact so tenacious it was practically invasive—once I knew what to look for, I saw its blades and bulbs in every inch of soil. Even the scraggly dark-leaved bushes by the road transformed to fuchsia, red-and-purple flowers with long-legged stamens dangling like thousands of earrings over the border walls, dropping their petals on my car.

Inside the house, too, we slipped little by little into routine without dramatic renovation—even the first battles with the spiders, plus a sprinkle of peppermint oil in every drawer and windowsill, seemed to have driven out the céad míle damhán alla. Sure, a plastered-over wall in the kitchen was crumbling, the keyholes dripped dew inside and out each morning, and the front entryway was so damp we always used the back door, but all those things faded quickly into the near-invisible background of living in any quirky old house. Every time I used those beautiful French doors with their west-facing view of the lake, I thought of the Discworld witches, who always use the back door. I thought I'd be happy to live in a tent, so long as it had that radiant, watery sunset view.

As autumn came, I felt for the first time like our little two-person family was finding something approaching a sustainable rhythm. I went back to teaching at the university, kept plunging through edits for my next novel and beginning to draft another—I knew I needed backup books in case the knitting factory proposal didn't sell in time—in addition to all my other jobs and keeping Robin and myself clean and clothed and fed. Robin was thriving back at naíonra, immersed in Irish and coming home with new words and songs each day: my favorite was féilacán, *butterfly*. It is always wrapped up in my mind with féilire, *calendar*, quick page-winged things fluttering by. I was trying to write, and trying to enjoy my toddler, as the last year of his toddlerhood and the remaining months before I had to buy the knitting factory wound their skeins onto the wheel of the year.

The flaming crocosmia that surrounded the house in summer faded to browning grass. The blackberry blossoms turned to hard green bumps, growing and reddening and slowly softening into sweet darkness, until September ended and, legend had it, the Devil spit mildew on them. Fat garden spiders began to spin their perfect cartoon webs between the brambles, the berries fuzzing white and dropping to the ground like a premonition of frost. Dew hung colder and later each morning on the leaves.

Halloween, Samhain, the witches' new year, passed. Winter started to take hold in Ireland again. The half of the year between Samhain and Bealtaine was ruled in old Irish legend by the Cailleach, the winter witch-goddess, who loosens her grip for the summer months but never feels far away.

Just as her cold fingers started to freeze the morning dew, the news arrived: another COVID lockdown.

Robin's school closed again. He was still only three. Even if I threw all our screen time rules out the window, there weren't enough *Puffin Rock* episodes in the world to cover the time I'd need to keep us treading water. The months before the purchase deadline were slipping away, and my book proposal still wasn't finished.

When Shay offered to come back up from Cork, I was relieved and conflicted: desperate for the support, and for the feeling of sharing time and space with a kindred spirit, a warm arm around me at the end of the day. But I was also still desperate to avoid the damage another long relationship could do, the way his presence seemed to urge me down a more conventional path than the one I was dreaming of now, the urge to trim and change my dreams for someone else. The way that same bed I loved sharing with him sometimes felt too small and hot when he was there, still sometimes reminded me of boxes of books shoved against my childhood bedroom's door.

I knew I had to tell him about the letter, how the first piece of good news I'd had for my child self was "I get to sleep alone." After working myself up to it on his first day back in Connemara, I managed to get out a whole two words before starting to cry.

"I have"—oh no, here they were, the tears and the stopped breath, as if my yearning to be loved was strangling me—"I have something to tell you."

Shay sat down next to me on the old pockmarked sofa and took my hand, his eyes so serious and worried behind his thick glasses that I saw he was afraid I was going to say something fatal. That made it just enough easier to plow ahead, even if it meant he wouldn't want me, wouldn't love me anymore.

"I'm so sorry," I told him, this man who had told me how he dreamed of having a partner he could grow old with, comfortable enough to clean each other up, to know every horrible intimate crevice of the other. "I'm sorry. You deserve someone who wants to sleep next to you every night."

Shay's eyes widened. "You're everything," he said. "I couldn't possibly deserve more than you."

He said he would sleep in the guest room, if that was what I needed.

Part of me, fickle heart, immediately wanted him with me once he said that, once the boundary had been both set and respected. But another part, the part I'd written the letter to, said that sounded good.

In the end, we slept apart about half the time. I still worried, looked for signs he was growing to hate me for it, but I found none. To my list of things I'd learned about Shay I added: he was the first man I knew whose love was not contingent on access to my body.

Robin's first Christmas, we'd gone to visit my friend Jacinta. Tommy had refused to come, being in one of his many moods. The second we spent at Irene and Cían's house, hiding from Tommy, afraid he would come to the bungalow. The third we had spent on a road trip—I still hadn't thought it was safe for us to stay in our own house, in case my ex found us there. We went on a pilgrimage to as many of Ireland's holy wells as I could find on the map instead. There are sacred wells everywhere here, little stone-ringed pools filled with disintegrating Mass cards and the rusty coins of old wishes, at the side of every road if you know where to look. Enough that you might start to think all the water in Ireland is holy.

But this Christmas, we did stay home, in a house of our own—not yet our own, but possibly our own, more so than any other house had been. I bought a Christmas tree at the local shop, an asymmetrical charmer that immediately shed piles of needles and gloopy beads of sap all over the floor. But it smelled good.

Winter in Ireland is not romantic, whatever Tommy had once told me. The Irish word for December is "Nollaig," which means "Christmas," but a clue as to its real nature can be found in the name for the same month in Scots Gaelic, its cousin language: An Dubhchlad. *The Blackness.* I had long ended my honeymoon phase with Ireland's winter, as I had with the man who had made me long for it with false promises: sometimes long cold nights are just long and cold, no matter how you try to warm them up.

When I first came to Ireland, I could barely light a match. It was Tommy who taught me the delicate skill of fire building, in the heady early days of our romance. I don't know how many winters it took for me to stop enjoying the painful tingle of warming my hands over iron stovetops so I could keep writing. The old Irish people say heat is all that keeps a building from collapsing in on itself with damp and cold.

At twenty-four, the dream Tommy painted for me of quiet reading in a small room, the smell of a turf fire around us, was heaven. By thirty my hands were freckled with tiny burns.

I did make sure to celebrate the solstice every year, just for myself: a little loaf cake with a triple moon piped in frosting on the top, or an offering of milk, bread, and honey left on the border wall outside for any birds or goddesses who'd be glad of it. This year, I took the last of the elderflower cordial we'd made at midsummer out of the fridge. We mixed it with water for Robin and sparkling wine for Shay and me.

"Sláinte!" Robin piped, as I had taught him, the standard Irish toast: like those in many other languages, it means simply "health."

But I was still trying to learn a little Irish whenever I could, and recently I'd come across another toast that I had instantly adored. That night I taught it to Robin and Shay as we drank down the sunshine cordial I'd made six months before, our mouths and bellies full of summer flowers.

"Sláinte chuig na fír, agus go maire na mná go deo!"
Cheers to the men, and may the women live forever!

The darkest night of the year, I always tried to remind myself, meant that a brighter day was already coming.

On Christmas, I dressed Robin up in a little navy blazer, a red sweater, and khakis. He presided over the duck I roasted with all the dignity of a sixty-year-old paterfamilias, even if the only part of Christmas dinner he deigned to eat were the peas. But we all looked nice, and Shay urged us toward the tree while he set up the delay timer on his phone to take a picture. He hefted up Robin, who squealed with delight, and I tried to smile without looking like I was trying.

I looked at Robin in the photo, wrapping his arms around Shay's neck and grinning in adoration. A loving partner and father figure had appeared in our lives like magic, and with him the chance for a full-time family, a Christmas-card-ready life. I knew that was what Shay wanted.

And there he was, being a better father to Robin than Tommy had ever been. I felt as if I could summon the other 1.5 children, the dog and the picket fence, in one word if I wanted. The idea both tempted me and made me want to scratch my own skin off.

When I was a teenager, I used to explain my mother by saying that it didn't matter what was going on behind the scenes, as long as the family Christmas card looked good. One year we'd posed for pictures by the pond behind our house for hours, until my mom finally dragged one smiling photo out of my grimacing toddler sister—whom it later turned out had broken her collarbone falling out of bed the night before. My mother had spent hours angry at my sister for struggling to smile, telling her to stop whining, not bothering to find out what was wrong. The year after I left my family and married Tommy, I got an email from a surprised relative after Christmas: *I thought you weren't talking to your parents anymore?*

I'm not, I replied. *Why do you ask?*

You're in the family Christmas card. In a gallery, she said: several photos of my sister, me, mom, and dad—none of us together, so it didn't look strange that I wasn't in a group photo.

At the time, that made me howl with laughter. Now it just seems bizarre. I hadn't heard a word from my parents since the year I left them, the year I made the report. I don't think I was in the Christmas card that year—but presumably she added me back the next year after getting questions about my absence. That year, I received a single line from her through the contact form on my author website: "Today and every day, I wish you a joyful life." I was sure she'd put more thought into choosing which Facebook photo to steal for the Christmas card than she had into that one generic line.

I was writing *Venturess*, the sequel to my Cinderella retelling, that year. I had the wicked stepmother say the same thing verbatim in that book. It made me feel a little better.

I looked at Robin laughing in Shay's arms. Did I want this now? No one obviously missing in the Christmas pictures: man, woman, baby, and myself not first on that list?

I wasn't even divorced yet, I told myself. There was no need to think about that stuff until I was.

The specter of the divorce loomed more horribly all the time. It reminded me of the danger of ever giving a partner so much power over us again. I still wondered if Tommy would bring something to court that could tear Robin and me apart permanently. A tiny, secret part of me I never wanted to listen to wondered if this would be my last Christmas with him.

Looking at the photos Shay had taken, I couldn't stop wondering if bringing another man into our lives was just careening us toward the same old disasters. Every time the two of them did something sweet together, I was scared.

I stopped journaling during that time. I think I didn't want to know what I would say. The notebook that covers that month is just lists of Christmas groceries and brainstorming for the knitting factory book proposal. I didn't want to admit how happy Shay made me, made Robin.

Did I owe it to Robin to want to be with Shay, to give him a good man to grow up with? Did I owe it to the world to be with someone? Or to myself?

The day after Christmas, I woke up to find a pile of black trash bags left outside in the knitting factory's driveway.

I knew who they were from even before I saw the pedal-powered play car behind them. Even before I opened them and found a child's jacket and hat, far too small for Robin, clearly chosen by someone who hadn't been around enough to know what a gentle giant of a child he was, who thought he was a three-year-old who wore three-year-old-size clothes.

I was sure they were from Tommy. They weren't really presents for Robin—I knew that right away, too.

I started to feel lightheaded. I wanted to put my head below my heart until my blood came back but couldn't bear the thought of not being able to see the road, to see around me.

Instead I went inside, locked the doors, and asked Shay to watch a movie with Robin—the upstairs room, the cavelike gate to Narnia, had become our TV den. You couldn't see into it from outside the house.

Then I called COPE's hotline. Saoirse wasn't there, but the woman who answered said she was certain this, at last, would be enough to pin Tommy for breaching the safety order. Maybe, I dared to think, he'd given us a Christmas present after all.

That was more fairy-tale thinking, though. The guards said I had no evidence that he was the one who'd given us those bags. Even if I did, what was wrong with a dad giving his son presents, when he wasn't even allowed to see the poor child?

I put the too-small clothes in the duffel bag I was always gradually filling with Robin's other outgrown things. When it was full, I would bring it to Aisling, who always knew another single mom whose kid needed clothes that size.

I left a SAOR IN AISCE / FREE sign on the pedal car, which was also far too small for my off-the-growth-charts-tall child to use, and put it at the end of the driveway. When I looked again ten minutes later, it was already gone. I hoped it had made someone else's Christmas better.

I felt the eyes on me that I'd managed not to feel since we moved to Connemara. I'd look at the driveway again in another ten minutes, I knew, and much more often going forward than I had until today. I'd start closing the blinds at dusk again.

The shape of the bags was still outlined in frost on my driveway. They weren't presents, I reminded myself. They were Tommy's reminder that he could still get to us, still mark his territory, still be the wolf at the door. They were meant to let me know that no matter how far away I went, he could still show up at my house in the middle of the night.

They were my ring of salt, broken.

Just after the New Year, I got an email with a large attachment: Tommy's defense statement for the divorce. It was a document so full of vitriol that it still makes me feel dread now, as I write these words some years removed from the one and only time I read it, even to think of what he said.

It is a sealed document in Irish law, so I can't detail the things he said here. I can only say that by a few pages in, I was hyperventilating. I had spots in my vision. My eyes hurt, but I couldn't tell if I was crying.

I went to Shay where he was playing with Robin in the residency room. He took one look at me and gave Robin a game to play on his phone and brought him to my room.

He came back and asked me what had happened. I found I couldn't even speak, just like in my old nightmares when my dad was hurting me and my voice was lost.

He sank down on the bed and held me while I gasped and wept. Part of me wanted the support, needed it, but part of me was already starting to fear it, fear the connection my body had made before, more than once before, between being held like this and being hurt. I felt like I was going to break apart, all the way down to my bones.

"Tommy said some—bad things about me," I said, between gasps. "He's going to say them in court when we get divorced. Horrible things."

"I'm so sorry," Shay said, but I barely heard him, already retreating into a space deep inside myself I hadn't visited since the last time Tommy screamed at me, a place I had practically lived in as a child, when my dad used to scream like that all the time.

Shay reached out to hold my hand. I wanted to flinch away, but I let him hold it for a moment, because letting someone do what they wanted with my body in spite of what I wanted was an old, deep training in me too, especially when I was scared.

Then I remembered, thank god, that Shay was kind enough not to mind if I pulled my hand away.

As soon as I did, I felt sure I never wanted another man to touch me, ever again.

That night, after Robin was in bed, I walked into the guest room, feeling like I was crawling. Shay was watching something on his laptop, but he closed it when he saw my face.

"I—" I immediately started crying. I couldn't make it stop.

"What is it, darling?" he asked. I think he already knew.

"I think, when you go back to Cork this time, that we should just be friends." A million hitches between each of those words, a million ways I didn't want to say them, even as I felt sure I needed to.

I had spent an hour journaling about the decision, listing reasons why I should break up with Shay: he was more outgoing than I was, needed more social time, needed to live in a city, drank more than I did, continued to forget to put knives away even when I had told him many times that it wasn't safe to leave them out where Robin could find them—had told him so many times that he'd told me a few days ago, his own voice shaky, too, that he thought maybe he wasn't fit to have the children he'd always wanted, if he couldn't remember to do such a simple thing to keep them safe.

It was the knives I was thinking about, not Tommy's defense, as I entered the room, as I spoke those words. Sharp things left out where they could hurt my kid. How I needed to make our home absolutely safe, at any cost to me.

"All right," he said. "Okay, if that's what you want." He said he could see how much I was hurting, that he still loved me and Robin, but that he understood.

"You probably want to leave now," I said, sitting down because I felt too ashamed to stand up, my voice quiet and hoarse. I expected he'd want to, whatever he said about still loving me while he slept in the guest room.

"Do you want me to leave?" he asked.

I had no words for that. My body answered for me, shaking my head, more tears. My arms opened a little for a hug I couldn't bear even to ask for, and he opened his on instinct, welcoming me in.

An hour ago, I'd thought I never wanted another man to touch me again. I didn't understand myself at all.

But when I admitted that I wanted him to stay if he wanted to stay, he did. He still took on half the childcare, and slept in the guest room.

A recent referendum had ended Ireland's four-year separation requirement before divorce, reducing it to two, but another issue arose: family courts were closed due to COVID lockdowns for at least six more months. I'd have to stay married a while longer.

That presented another problem: I couldn't buy the house until I was legally divorced, or Tommy would have a claim to it.

I wrote to Patrick and asked for a six-month extension. He kindly, reluctantly, granted it. We agreed that November 1, 2021, would be the hard deadline to make a formal purchase offer. If I couldn't do it by then, he would put the house back on the market, and Robin and I would need to move out by the end of the year, December 31. I promised that we would.

I was grateful for the extension, but I still didn't know how I was going to afford the house. I was still struggling to figure out how to write the proposal for the book about the knitting factory, and thought the friends who had crowdfunded my rent must be tapped out.

I buried my fears in the ground around the house. I planted little hazelnut-looking anemone bulbs an inch or so down, on a patch of ground where I'd dismantled a decrepit hazard of a shed, and sometimes still found bits of broken glass.

Anemones are perennials, and Claire's favorite flower. I told myself it was good to plant them, even if we would only see them once: a springtime symbol of someone who loved us. When my son and I were gone, our flowers would still bloom.

When that winter's lockdown ended, I drove Shay back to Cork.

We sped over the rolling countryside and hillscapes of west Ireland, through rain showers and sun that played musical chairs with each other every twenty minutes. Through innumerable rainbows. There was no awkward silence—there never was with us. We talked about books and movies and science and storytelling and God. We talked about what the future held.

"I just want you in my life, always," Shay said. "You and Robin. I love you both. Really love you, not just—it's not just that I'll be in love with you for a while." He took a deep breath. "I didn't want you to break up with me, of course. But the thing is—I think it's because of my parents' divorce, but every long-term couple I know, no matter how happy they seem—I always wonder when they're going to break up. I always assume they *will* break up someday."

Rain and sun spattered the windshield as we drove, the fields rising in impossible greens around us, like a jeweled cup.

"That's funny," I said. "Whenever I see a long-term couple, no matter how happy they seem, I always assume there's something messed-up going on behind the scenes." I laughed grimly. "I think it's because my parents are still married."

We both agreed that, for our own opposite reasons, we thought friendships were more likely to last a lifetime than romance. And we were friends, family really, after the lockdowns.

We rolled out Robin's sleeping bag in Shay's bedroom and took turns reading him picture books: Shay's favorite, *Whatever Next?* and mine, *Owl Babies*. We settled him to sleep and told him we loved him. And then we curled together on the black leather couch of his small, moldy basement flat and wished for impossible things.

I thought about how important Shay had become in our family, the love and care he had offered to Robin and me, that he continued to offer, whatever shape my own love and care for him took. I thought about how Tommy had coerced and convinced me to change my whole life for him— and about how loving someone has to mean the opposite of wanting to control them, of wanting to shape their life to suit your needs.

Even if I could want the kind of life Shay wanted, I knew I couldn't keep him in Ireland when he longed to go home. I wouldn't want to change his dreams for him.

"Well, at least now that we're friends, we know we'll love each other always," I said, thinking of our conversation in the car, trying to laugh again.

"We will," he said, taking my hand carefully in his. "That I promise."

I met his gaze. "I promise, too."

There are no ceremonies to honor friendship the way we do romance: no engagement parties, weddings, anniversaries. But I wanted some way to express how important Shay had become in our family, no matter what happened between us.

I remembered that day on Inis Mór when my heart had broken yet again waiting for Tommy to come to Robin's baptism. He was supposed to bring a godfather for Robin that day, but he never did.

Shay had spent more days and hours taking care of Robin than Tommy ever had, and likely ever would. He'd been his godfather for a long time already, I thought, so that night I asked him to take the role officially.

Shay, a staunch atheist, was more moved than I had ever seen him. He agreed.

Twenty

A Mermaid's Purse

SPRING 2021

for Vanessa

Journal: February 23, 2021

Last night I showed Robin "The Court Jester," one of my favorite films, &
when we got to the lullaby scene Robin said "The daddy is singing to the
baby." I didn't think it would be useful to point out that Danny Kaye isn't
that baby's daddy (although maybe I should have) so I just said "yes, he's
singing to him because he loves him." Robin started cradling and cooing
to the plastic T. rex he got from Brigid, & then he gently carried the
dinosaur to his play tent & tucked him under his blanket & kissed him &
said "have sweet dreams."

I said "You're a nice daddy to the T. rex." & he said "Yes, I am" &
smiled proudly. It made me sad but also so proud of his resilient sweetness.
He still calls every grown man he meets Dad & I don't want to give him a
complex by acting like it's not a word we can use.

This morning he put on his toy unicorn's seat belt & said "I'm a nice
daddy" & I said "Yes, you are a very nice daddy to your toys." All those

things, singing & rocking to sleep & tucking in & keeping safe, are things I
do. So at least he is acting out parenting as care & gentleness.

    I am afraid he will hate me for leaving his daddy someday. But I
cannot, cannot be sorry I did. He only knows gentleness now. Not for
always, I know. But for as many of his first years as I can make it so, I
swear.

One of the strangest-feeling echoes of lockdown was that I still liked to go
running a few times a week, while Robin was at naíonra. I'd spent my childhood making coaches late for their next class while I walked the required
mile in gym. I used to say I'd rather get eaten by a bear than run away from
one. But claustrophobic lockdown restrictions had combined with years
of frustration at being stuck in the house with my child, and with all my
conflicting feelings about needing desperately to stay in Ireland while also
mourning my inability to leave without Tommy's permission—the way he
managed to control, and to make me fear, both staying and leaving. I'd always left my body, lived in my head alone, when I was afraid. Running gave
my body, and my ability to move, back to me.

    I am probably the world's slowest runner. But once I gave myself permis-
sion to be no more than that, I enjoyed it. I let myself stop to take pictures
when I wanted to. I breathed fresh air. I felt warm on the coldest days, without turning on heat that the knitting factory just leaked out again like a sieve.

    I was running over the hill from the knitting factory to the sea one
day when Saoirse called. She did that every now and then since lockdown
started, to check in on me.

    I stopped running and sat down on a rock by a little pier to talk to
her, looking out at curlicued low-tide mounds of wet brown seaweed, still
breathing hard from running, the air salty in my mouth and nose. It was a
gray day, not quite wet enough to call it raining, water just floating in the air
and tingling onto my skin in small, cold, sparkling drops.

    "I just got back from my holidays and saw your email," she said—I'd
written to her about the trash bags left in the driveway after Christmas.

"We'll be starting the group Zoom sessions again next week, but I wanted to call you right away. I'm so sorry. What a prick."

I snorted. "Yeah." Her word choice was so blunt, so un-therapy-speak. I loved it. "What a prick!"

We talked for the next hour, while I sat on the rock and looked out at the sea. Her voice in my ear, the salt water in front of me and the white rime it left along the rocks where I sat—even the sweat cooling on my face, the slowing pulse that thrummed through me, my run warming me even now that I was sitting still: all those things helped me voice what I hadn't felt able to acknowledge, to understand, while it was still happening. I spoke aloud, for the first time ever, about what I'd forced myself to write down only once I'd left Tommy—what I'm not allowed to write about, even here.

"What kills me," I told Saoirse at the end of it, "is that I'll never fucking know for sure what happened."

"That must have been terrifying." Saoirse gave me one of her strong, thoughtful silences. "Are you sure you don't know?"

I shivered. "If I ever say what I think it was at this point, I'll sound crazy."

"Mm." Another beat. "There was a woman who came into COPE once, and her baby cried all the time whenever her husband was watching him and she left the room. She could never figure out why. But when they visited her brother's house, he had security cameras her husband didn't know about, and it turned out that whenever she left, he'd pinch the baby until he cried and she came back. Just hard enough so he'd cry but wouldn't bruise."

"Oh my god."

"Yes. When a father doesn't want to care for his child, but he knows it would look bad for him to say that, in my experience he'll find other ways to get out of it."

I started remembering, and telling Saoirse, a thousand things I can't write about here. I felt so ashamed that any one of them hadn't made me run with Robin as soon as they happened. "It's like I'm only seeing it clearly now," I said, "the farther away I get."

"I hear that from survivors frequently," Saoirse said.

I could barely get the next words out. "I think Tommy was a lot more dangerous to Robin than I ever realized at the time."

"I know," Saoirse said. "I know."

"Last night I kept waking up scared about the divorce. I kept dreaming about Tommy putting Robin in situations where he'd get hurt, on purpose, if he gets unsupervised access."

"He still hasn't come to a single one of the supervised visits you've offered, right?"

"No. He keeps saying he won't see him there, won't let his son grow up thinking he's the kind of monster who has to use a place like that."

"So instead he's choosing not to see him at all?"

I sighed. "Tell him that. I hear he's at the pub every Sunday while we're waiting for him, telling sob stories to anyone who'll listen about how I'm keeping them apart."

"You'd be surprised how common that is. You know, I was in a pub watching a gig a few months back, and this lad was singing sad songs all about how his wife was keeping his children from him. She and the kids are staying at COPE right now, hiding from him."

"Seriously?"

"He must have shown Tommy his manual."

We both laughed. Saoirse's laughter was always so healing, so magical in its ability to casually turn an abuser from a threat into an object of contempt.

"I just want to remind you, Betsy," she said, "that Tommy has already escaped his duty of care. He's avoided seeing Robin for over two years now. He doesn't have to hurt him to do that. I don't think he wants a relationship with him at all."

"That's not what he's going to say in court." We had both heard too many horror stories about family court from the other moms in the survivors' group to imagine that Robin was safe from unsupervised visits with Tommy.

"I know." Saoirse gave me another moment of quiet acknowledgment. "I know there are things to fear in the future. But you are safe right now.

You did get Robin out before any real harm came to him. When you start thinking about these things, I want you to remember that you got him out, and got yourself out, and that you did it early."

I closed my eyes briefly. "I did."

"You did. And right now, you are safe. Your child is safe. Maybe that can be your mantra." Saoirse was training as a meditation teacher, and she often led us through chants and breathing exercises in the group. "Breathe in: I am safe. Breathe out: my child is safe."

"It hurts so much, Saoirse," I said. "Just processing all of this. It takes so much time and energy just to grieve. And there is so much still to come."

"I know. It takes so much time." Her voice sounded older when she said that. I knew she'd come to this work through her own experience, although I didn't have any more details than that.

"All right," I said. I breathed in, long and slow. "I am safe." I breathed out. "My child is safe."

I wondered how many repetitions it would take to start sounding true.

Being alone with Robin at the knitting factory again gave me a space I hadn't fully understood I still needed: to grieve, on my own, to think over and feel through the things that had happened that led me to where I was, on the edge of a new, old continent with my baby. Nightmares about Tommy, and about my father, came thick and fast again for a while, so that it was even more impossible than usual to focus on anything.

But I also knew I needed that time, like combing through a mess of wool for burrs before I could wash and spin it. If I was going to turn the things that had happened to me into a story, a crafted piece that I could make with my hands and then hold in them, too, I had to keep working through my own life, carding and combing and soaking it, so that the dirt rose to the surface, in order to spin the yarn.

And I did. The grieving that I still needed to do had been blocking me all autumn and through winter, keeping me from really writing. Maybe the way things changed with Shay helped shift it. Maybe the cruelty of Tommy's divorce defense, as violent and awful as it was, gave me more clarity about his character than I'd had before.

Whatever it was, at last, I was writing the knitting factory proposal, and I was liking what I wrote.

Every night after Robin fell asleep, I wrote in the old stone cavern of the factory space itself, now the living room. It was as if I could feel all those generations of people working side by side, the women knitting stitch by stitch, Bob Quinn stitching together film strips and his wife Helen writing scripts in the upstairs room, the jewelers who had lived there in the 1990s, Jackie and Ed Keilthy, silversmithing their custom necklaces to the pattern of a wedding dress's lace, a baby's christening gown.

One word at a time, one stitch, one cell of film, I added the thin layer of my own work, my own craft, as methodically as they had, over theirs.

Journal: March 5, 2021

I just received a handknit shawl in the mail from a Smithie in Maryland named Laura. I started to cry when I got the package and realized what it was. So many things went through my head at once: I could suddenly feel why doing work can matter just to one person and still be important, why it doesn't have to be this big earth-shattering thing, and I felt free to write in a way I haven't in months: if it means as much to one person as this shawl means to me, then that is enough, and that is good. And if all the book means is that Robin and I get to have a house, and other parent-artists get to make things here, then that is all it needs to be, and that is wonderful.

I want writing to be a warm and open, gentle thing, like knitting a shawl. One ordinary word-stitch at a time. I can work on it a little or a lot. I can do it while I'm doing other things. While I am mothering.

I want to read and see art by people who don't always have a room of their own.

All the things good writing is not supposed to be—loose, open, warm, soft, gentle, sentimental, personal, intimate, domestic, minor, incidental,

broken, small, fat, familiar, comfortable, not-brave, shy, vulnerable,
boundary-having—all the things non-male writers are not supposed to be
if we want to be taken seriously.

    The shawl says someone cares enough to send a stranger a gentle
touch. God that is all I want my art to be.

I worked almost dreamlike on the memoir for two months, and I was finally left with a finished proposal that made me proud. It had a looping, circular structure, partly because the story I wanted to tell wasn't finished yet: I hoped that the happy ending would be selling the proposal itself, of course, so that I could buy the house. I presented the ending as a kind of magic trick: the book allows me to buy the house, and the house allows me to write the book.

I just had to hope it was a kind of magic someone else would believe in.

I sent the proposal off to my first trusted readers, and then to my agent, who said she loved it. Everything started to seem full and round with possibility, where the winter had felt thin and dark as a sickle moon. My heart beat fast and happy when I thought about the future again. I felt once more like I was taking the right steps, steps that had been laid out for me like a dance I had forgotten in my exhaustion and pain, but that I was finally starting to remember.

Journal: April 4, 2021

Today is Robin's fourth birthday. On this day, at this time, four years ago,
I was in the hospital, waiting for the time to push. Tommy took smoking
breaks during my labor. He later told me I'd imagined that, but I don't
think I did.

    Three years ago, I left the cottage we shared for the last time,
although I didn't know it yet. It was about this time of day when we were
in the art gallery & Tommy made his first threat to take Robin from me.

This time two years ago I was getting ready to take Robin to his first long access visit with Tommy. I was so afraid that Tommy would take him & not bring him back, as he claimed I'd done on the first birthday, but instead he didn't show up at all.

The last time he saw Robin was a week before his second birthday. More than half his life ago now.

This time last year it was the beginning of lockdown, & Shay & I had Robin at the beach most of the day. I remember freaking out because Robin didn't want his cake & I felt like I'd never given him a good birthday.

Today I am sitting in the knitting factory garden, the sun is shining & the air is gloriously warm. I'm going to go pick up Robin from naíonra soon.

There are still so many things I worry about, but let this be a moment that lasts forever, a moment when everything is safe and good.

I've adopted the idea that for each holiday a kid should get "something to wear, something to read, something they want and something they need." This is what I got Robin for his birthday this year:

Something to wear: gold dress-up wings

Something to read: picture book about the pirate queen Gráinne Mhaol

Something he wants: a purple cat (I knitted it!)

Something he needs: a godfather

The knitting factory proposal went out to publishers one late April day as I picked up Robin from naíonra. I was too excited to bear the twenty-minute drive home, so I whisked him down the road to An Trá Mhór, where the rising tide had reduced the beach to a tiny strip: we clambered over rocks and along the scrawls of seaweed flung across them.

As we walked, I noticed a little golden-brown translucent rectangle, strung at each corner with delicate cursive curls. I actually gasped, because as much as I'd searched, I'd never found one in the wild before.

A mermaid's purse. The color of beer-bottle sea glass, and as translucent: if the baby shark were still inside, I'd have been able to see its tail lash back and forth to the beat of the waves, its heartbeat pulse, just like the ones that had entranced me at the aquarium.

This mermaid's purse was empty, dried and perfectly preserved, just a neat slice at one edge to indicate where its inhabitant had slipped out to sea. It was perched on top of a clump of seaweed as if it had been left as a gift, just for me.

I imagined a seal out there in the dark water, watching. A selkie who had longed for home and safety and her own skin, who knew what the mermaid's purse and I knew about becoming a tough and transparent protector of a precious being. What it meant to nurture and adore something with your whole self, and then to set it free.

I was sure the mermaid's purse was a sign. It was a sign that the proposal was going to sell for enough money to buy the knitting factory, and for Robin and me to be protected. A sign we were protected already.

I breathed. I am safe. My child is safe.

But the book didn't sell.

The editors who read it said the same thing over and over—it's too risky to buy a memoir of a story that isn't finished yet. It was a complete catch-22: I needed to sell the book to buy the building, but I needed to buy the building to sell the book.

I wanted to scream. I could do it, I knew I could. Only one editor needed to understand the magic spell I was trying to make real. I just needed someone to save me, to have faith in me.

Sometimes, in my darkest moments, when I thought about my husband and my dad, it felt like no one ever had.

But then I would talk about it: with Claire, with Friday Tea, with Shay, with the COPE moms. They showed me, over and over, the faith and love I'd longed for all my life.

And whenever I made a new post, a few donations would trickle in. The project's followers had told me over and over to increase the crowdfunding goal, and I started to wonder if I might get to a down payment on the house that way.

I started to think maybe that was the kind of faith I needed: not one big commitment, but a gathering of small ones. I'd been looking for one outstretched hand that could pull me into a new life, but there were already many hands helping me hold on to the life I was already building. Not marriage, but community: not a book, but a story I told a little bit at a time, over and over, to whoever was listening that day.

That was a lesson I was already learning, turning the focus of my life away from the marriage that had hurt my baby and me, and toward the many people who were healing us. When enough people love you, no single one of them has to save you.

The proposal didn't sell, and neither did the backup book I'd written, an early reader story about scientist mermaids. In a way, that scared me more. The divorce proceedings were finally moving forward, albeit slowly, and along with that progress came more legal bills as well as more acrimony from my ex.

The idea of divorce court also brought the looming knowledge that not only would I have to spend the day in the same room with the man I had a safety order against, the man I was so afraid of I had moved multiple times just to get away from him—but also, because he was now legally representing himself, he would have the opportunity to question me on the stand.

I thought of all the times he'd most intimidated and confused me, how he could summon my worst fears with just his words.

Saoirse and the survivors' group moms had said so many times that one of the worst things a mother can do in family court is get emotional on the stand: don't get angry or shout, and especially don't cry. A man shouting or weeping about his children in court is often viewed sympathetically, they said. For a woman, it can lose her the case.

I've always been an easy crier. My mom referred to herself as having "a low dew point" and insisted her tears meant nothing. When I was crying every day for months on end during my marriage I told myself the same thing, because I didn't want to acknowledge the feelings my tears expressed.

Like most women I know, I find it easier to express any emotion through tears than a raised voice—I have been taught that one is more acceptable than the other all my life.

I could barely talk *about* Tommy without crying, let alone *to* him. How was I supposed to face him, let him ask me whatever insidious questions he wanted to ask, laced with words that might sound normal to someone who didn't have our history, but that he'd crafted over years with the intimate, exacting knowledge of how best to hurt me?

The survivors' group moms had tools for this. Never look at your cross-examiner, only at the judge, and remember the answers are for them. Take a deep breath and count to five before responding. Remember that you're doing this for your children. Imagine a suit of armor, like a medieval knight's, and one by one put all the invisible pieces of metal on before you step onto the stand. Let the group chat know when you're in court, and let us text you back *good luck* over and over through the day. Then keep your phone on silent in your pocket, so that while his voice washes over you, you will feel all the vibrations of our prayers.

One spring morning, my friend Aisling called me sobbing.

"I'm so sorry to call you like this, Betsy, I—I just need help, I don't know what to do," she said.

Aisling was the one who helped everyone else: I brought her Robin's too-small clothes every few months when he outgrew them, because I knew she'd always know families who needed them. In exchange, I received shopping bags stuffed full of hand-me-down clothes in the next size up for Robin. Aisling *was* the circular economy for single moms in Connemara. Whatever you needed, she knew how to help: a handyman who'd do the work for a steep discount, which social service to talk to (and at what hour you should call to get the social worker who was least judgmental), just the right dirty joke to tell when you were at your lowest.

I'd become friends with Aisling because she saw that I needed a friend and informed me that she was it. I'd called into the survivors' group video chat a few months after moving to the knitting factory, upset because the one Carraroe woman I'd managed to become friendly with had started icing me out. It happened right when she found out I wrote queer-themed books, but I still thought it must have been my fault. "It makes me feel like I'm just bad at making friends," I said.

Aisling scowled into her phone ferociously. "Come see me," she said, "drop into me anytime, sure Jaysus knows I'm always at home with my demon children. I'll be your friend."

And she was: that first visit she gave me a mug printed with "Love is Love," and before long we were visiting almost weekly. She became one of my closest friends, in fact.

While it's never a competition, I can easily say Aisling's ex was worse, to both her and her children, than mine. She had less, too, getting by on welfare and waiting nine years and counting for a council house. But she never, I mean never, asked for anything: only, it seemed, endlessly gave and gave, to every other mom around her.

So when she called me, crying, asking for something for the first time ever—whatever it was, I was going to give it to her if I could.

It turned out that she was really looking for help for someone else.

"It's Róisín. She took her. She's gone."

Róisín was a friend of Aisling's thirteen-year-old daughter who had been staying with them for a few weeks because her mother, Ina, also a single mom, was in hospital. In hospital, unconscious, and likely dying. Róisín had three older sisters, a seventeen-year-old and sixteen-year-old twins, who could look after themselves pretty well, but Aisling had taken in the youngest kid to give them a break.

Aisling was calling me because Ina's estranged mother, against Ina's express wishes, had taken Róisín out of school and away to her farm in another county, and had confiscated her phone so that she couldn't contact her friends or her siblings.

Aisling, one of the most stubbornly independent people I knew, who never asked for help with anything, asked me to come be with her because she was so distraught. Róisín's oldest sister was coming over, and Aisling needed to be able to be there for her, to be the mothering presence that Ina couldn't be in that moment. In turn, she needed a friend, to give her the strength to support that young girl.

I was sitting at my desk in the knitting factory's bright little hallway alcove when she called me, writing another post about the crowdfund for my social media pages. I was so lucky, I knew, to have even the chance I had at this home. It was a chance I only had because of the people I knew. I couldn't stop picturing Ina, alone in her hospital bed and unable to help her children.

Well, Ina knew Aisling, and Aisling knew me. "Robin, put on your shoes!" I hollered.

"We're leaving now," I told Aisling. "Give me twenty minutes and we'll be there." I picked up a shepherd's pie on the way because I was certain Aisling wouldn't have eaten, and got there in record time.

Aisling and her kids lived in a dilapidated housing estate even farther out in Connemara than we were, every house looking the same, or almost the same, from the outside. Discarded toys filled Aisling's yard—a lot of the estate kids, as well as her own, played there every day—and the rest of it was dominated by a vivid hydrangea taller than I was. I'd taken a cutting from it once, but even though it flowered prolifically blue and pink like Sleeping Beauty's gown for Aisling with, she always said, no interference from her at all, I couldn't get that cutting to take for me. I always think of it as tied to her particular magic.

Her neighbor's yard, in contrast, was always immaculately tidy, with a border full of the most spectacular eye-poppingly-bright yellow roses I'd ever seen. It was gorgeous, but every time I passed it on my way to Aisling's cluttered yard, that I knew her neighbors judged her for, it made me think about who gets the gift of time to tend their gardens.

When I got inside Aisling's house three other women were already there. One I knew from the survivors' group, and two others introduced themselves as single moms who knew Ina, too. Then there was Ina's seventeen-and-a-half-year-old daughter, Máire. Aisling had told me on the phone that this girl had just been fired from her waitressing job, and that the manager of the restaurant just happened to be one of Ina's mother's best friends. Ina's mom had told her she didn't want her working, wanted her to move to the farm in Offaly instead. Máire stared at the steaming mug of tea in her hands, red hair falling into her eyes, silver pentagrams painted on her nails.

Even if everyone else hadn't happened to be wearing black—a heavy metal T-shirt, yoga pants, an old Aran sweater—they still would have looked like a coven.

"We are going to help," one of the moms I didn't know said, leaning over Ina's daughter. "Ina is strong. You're strong, too. I know you are. We are going to help, and it's going to be okay."

One mother would wait at Róisín's school the next day, in hopes that the grandmother would at least let her keep attending school, to make sure she was all right. Another would look after the twins. Still another would help the oldest daughter find a new job.

Aisling had told me fond stories of Ina now and then, but I'd never managed to meet her. Still, the idea of any single mother dying in the hospital while her estranged mother used the opportunity to take her child away left me breathless. It was one of my own worst fears playing out. Every time I stumbled on a step or swallowed a piece of food the wrong way, a life would flash in front of my eyes: not my own, but Robin's. What would happen to my child without my constant guarding? Would my ex get him, would my parents? Which was more frightening?

I had two good godparents for Robin, I knew, who would not let that happen. I had Claire and Brigid and Irene. And I had the growing knitting factory community, who had come to care about me and my child. Every time I wrote online about why I wanted to make a space for myself and other single mothers, I was also asking people to see me and my child, to care about our welfare. My friends would not just let him be taken in my absence, I knew.

But what could I do here? I didn't know this family, this frightened girl. There was no reason for her to trust me.

"What can I do?" Máire's words echoed my thoughts. "Telling me to be strong, or whatever, is fine, but I'm still a minor for six more months. I can't be my sister's guardian. And it's not like I can afford a lawyer. I can't even afford to meet with one."

But I did have something that I could offer this girl—that I could offer, really, to her mother. I had connections to people with extra money, and those connections were what meant Robin and I had never had to be truly homeless, and that we still had our chance now at a more stable home than any of the other women at that table. I had the people who supported the knitting factory.

"I've been learning how to fundraise," I said. "And I know people who'll donate. I'll keep it anonymous, I won't mention your name. But I can get you money for a legal consult if that's what you need."

The girl looked at Aisling, who nodded, and then she looked at me. "Okay."

I started writing. The fundraiser I made and shared to the knitting factory's social media pages got money for a lawyer, and emergency funds on top of that, within hours.

And standing with those women around that little oilcloth-covered kitchen table, ushering a young girl into the strength she would need for a caretaking role she didn't ask for, I felt and knew the strength of what single mothers will do for each other.

That spring, the knitting factory's ancient boiler finally broke. I boiled water for Robin's baths and alternated between plunging myself in the freezing Connemara sea and begging showers at friends' houses. But after a few months of cold water and cold rooms, with small donations to the knitting factory's crowdfund still drifting in and my promise to upkeep the property to Patrick on my mind, I decided that it was time.

I made that decision, unfortunately, when I still thought the proposal would sell.

I learned it hadn't just after the new boiler was installed. That same week I was hit with more legal bills. The teaching semester was over, which meant I wouldn't be paid by the university again until classes started for the new school year in September. My publisher was overdue with notes for *Reader, I Murdered Him*, and I wouldn't get the next payment I was counting on until those notes arrived and I completed revisions.

One night I looked at my bank account and saw a single digit. I was out of money.

Twenty-One

Brigadoon

SUMMER 2021

for Kim

I was done. I had eight euros to my name. The whole project was finished, had failed.

I started to hyperventilate, sitting on the ragged brown couch by the knitting factory's French doors, staring out at the nighttime garden. I could smell incense in the air as I tried to breathe and I hated myself for buying it. I despised myself for every time I ate anything but oatmeal, every small, unnecessary pleasure of the past year. Had I really needed tea? Those anemone bulbs for the garden?

I called Shay. I hated myself for still leaning on him, too, after I'd let him go: one more lash in the litany of things I was punishing myself for.

"How much do you need?" he said immediately.

"No. No. That's not why I'm calling. I just—" I could barely catch my breath. "I just needed to tell someone. I just needed you to be the first person I told, because I knew you would—you wouldn't—it's over. It's over. It's all my fault. I thought I needed—if I hadn't been so stupid—"

"You thought you needed what? Food you like to eat? Warm clothes? Things that make you happy, that make your child happy? Betsy." His brown eyes on the video call were warm and loving behind his glasses, and I made myself look at them, even though I felt sure I wasn't worthy of meeting anyone's gaze right then.

"Betsy," he said, "you're being far too American right now."

That startled me out of my self-flagellation for a moment. "What?"

"You're being a Protestant." (Have I mentioned that every serious relationship I've had has been with a lapsed Catholic? How pathological is that?) "You're listening to all your Calvinist ancestors, all those Puritan pilgrims who left England because life wasn't miserable enough for them back home. Listen to me. You are allowed to not want to suffer. You are allowed to keep yourself from suffering." He was getting worked up: his accent was a little more Bristol than London, which was one of the ways to tell with him. "No matter what our relationship looks like, you're my family now," he said. "That means I am not willing to let you suffer if I can prevent it. Now. Tell me how much money you need to stop panicking, and I'll loan it to you. And then you'll drive down to Cork, and I'll help you with Robin, and you will rest."

"All right," I whispered. I was still stuck on the definition of family he'd just given me. I'd never known that family could mean that, not until I'd become a parent and felt it for my kid. I'd never had family that said to me: loving you means I keep you from suffering.

That conversation gave me the strength, at least, to confess my failure to the project's supporters. It was about one a.m. by then. I wrote an update, a newsletter in which I acknowledged, for the first time, the idea that the project might not work. I'd always spoken of it with a kind of religious faith before.

Old Knitting Factory newsletter

Part of me has thought all along that the knitting factory and I were meant to be. Like I was drawn here by the universe or something. All the pain I've been through bringing me here. It's foolish and melodramatic, I know. Trauma has no deeper meaning, as I have known since I was very small.

But I have had this horrible Faith That It Will Work Out all along. The knitting factory has been one of the things that's kept me going. Like, given me a will to live, you know, through the pandemic and the detritus of my marriage and everything. I can't leave Ireland until my kid is grown up because of international custody laws, and I can't even leave County Galway for at least a few years because I have to prove to the court that I'm not trying to alienate my kid from the dad who refuses to see him. I have kept writing, and I have chased this beautiful place that I could give to myself and other single moms, because it felt like refusing to be bullied by the winds of fate—like I was still getting to tell my own story, instead of having it told for me. I thought, if I could do this magical and wonderful thing, it would mean that none of this has beaten me. I can make a good story out of these bad circumstances. I can win.

Then, a few months ago, the boiler broke at the knitting factory. I have been taking cold showers and boiling water in the kettle for my kid's baths because I wanted to save the money I'd need to replace it for the down payment on the building. I had been hoping that between the crowdfund, my own savings, the advance on delivery I have coming for my next novel, and the advance for the book proposal I wrote about the knitting factory, I would have enough to cover a down payment for a mortgage. The remaining purchase price, since the rent has been taken out of the asking price, is €179,200, so that doesn't seem like a total pipe dream. At least I thought not. I was OK with spending the crowdfund on what we needed to make the house safe and livable for our first year, since that was part of the rent-to-own agreement I made with the current owner.

But after talking with some friends recently, I reluctantly admitted that we need warm water, so I ordered the boiler replacement and sent a deposit. I figured I had just about enough to cover the rest of the boiler payment and my usual budget for the month, until I was hit by some big personal expenses—legal bills far higher than I expected, and taxes much higher, too. Those things together were enough to knock out my own savings completely. Completely. I looked at my account tonight and saw a single digit. I need to buy the knitting factory by November, five months from now, or the owner will put it back on the market. I haven't felt so sick in years.

The crowdfund money was spent on rent and a boiler, new mattresses and bed frames, because rusty springs were poking out of the mold-ridden mattresses that came with the house, but couldn't we have sucked that up? Couldn't I have been more thoughtful and responsible and rational? Spent on a drill set so I could fix the broken curtain rods and install fencing, which I also bought with crowdfund money, so my kid wouldn't fall into the lake. Spent on a driveway gate so he wouldn't run into the road. I can't hate myself for these expenses because they kept him safe. But I want to. And I want to hate myself for the boiler. I could have dealt with cold water for a few more months.

I look back at this past year at the knitting factory, this past year of lockdowns, and I don't see a single day when I wasn't working at, or beyond, my capacity. I am, goddammit, proud of the effort I've put into this project, regardless of the outcome. I'm just so sad and ashamed that it still might not be enough.

The book about the knitting factory could still sell, I suppose. All the rejections I've gotten have come with nice things to say about the proposal. I could try again with other publishers. I could, I don't know, try to crowdfund the whole darn purchase price. It's not an expensive building, as far as buildings go.

But looking at my account balance and seeing a single digit really scared me. It brought me back to when I had just left my marriage and had nothing, nothing. Not even a home. It was that fear, that nothingness, that brief experience of homelessness which is nothing to what so many people have suffered, that scared me enough to imagine any way I could into a stable home.

I remember ringing the doorbell at the domestic abuse center with my baby on my chest in his carrier, knowing we couldn't go back to our house that night, knowing we didn't have anywhere else to go. I remember the nights in a hotel in another town where my ex wouldn't find us. I remember staying in the guest room of my only Irish friend who hadn't sided with him, while I looked for a place we could afford. I remember the Smith alum network helping me pay my rent when it turned out I couldn't afford even that tiny bungalow for one month. And then I think, how dare I have thought I could buy a house. How fucking dare I.

But I couldn't not have tried. I guess that's the thing I keep coming back to right now. I remember how scared I was, how scared I've been the last three years since we left our home and were threatened with separation, my baby and I. I couldn't not have tried.

I have also been thinking that what would make me the most sad if this project didn't work would be giving up the space for other single moms—and that means that the central goal is not actually me owning a home, as much as that was the driving force behind the idea all along. So I am thinking of proposing to grant organizations or individual investors that if they bought the knitting factory as an investment property, I could pay them rent until it's set up and then they'd get a share of the profit from the paying-residency side of the operation.

I once dreamed of being able to hand this place on someday to another single mom who needs it, to hire her

*as an on-site manager so she could have flexible work
with housing included for herself and her kids. The knitting factory felt like it appeared out of the mists to save
me, like Avalon, like Brigadoon. I'd thought maybe it
could be a place that keeps on saving people. Maybe it can
be that still, just in a different way than I had thought.*

*There are options, I know. It could still work. But it
doesn't feel like a story I'm telling any more, one that has
to work out somehow in the end. It just feels hard. And I
feel tired, and defeated, and ashamed.*

I hate feeling so scared again.

*I want to forgive myself for trying, because I couldn't
not have tried.*

*I think I just need someone to tell me they think I've
done as well as I could.*

I pressed send on the newsletter. Without even changing my clothes, I crawled into bed and went mournfully, frightfully to sleep.

When I woke up, there were thousands of euros in new donations.

That newsletter kicked off a surge that saw at least a thousand more euros coming in each day for more than a week. It turned out that confessing my failure and despair rallied everyone who cared about me around the project. Friends from childhood, high school, summer camps, college, graduate school, the group of help-exchange girls I worked with on Inis Mór, all sent new donations, as did friends of friends I'd never met.

Most jarringly, people from my old east Galway village, the place and people I thought had banished me completely, donated, too. Several of them sent me private messages saying they'd always known about Tommy's anger, and for all the stories he told in the village pub these days, they didn't blame me one bit for running away.

I don't know if I'll ever feel safe going back to the village in east Galway where I first brought my baby home. But if you can, go there and have a drink at the local pub, and dinner in the adjoining restaurant. And if you meet some particularly kind waitresses while you're there, tell them thank-you from me.

Shay loaned me enough money to see out the month, and then we drove down to Cork to see him.

He brought Robin to his local playground, fed him takeaway from his favorite Indian place, and let him push all the buttons on his PlayStation for hours while I slept—more deeply than I ever slept alone at the knitting factory with Robin, knowing that he might need me at any moment, and no one else would be there.

Shay was there. I could sleep.

Journal: June 6, 2021

Family over here, a supportive friend, a man who is good to Robin. Despite my best efforts in my own frantic directions, the universe gave me instead, as gently as possible, exactly what I need.

Six months previously, when I'd thought I had the money to do it, I had booked ferry tickets and a discounted night at a little B&B on Inis Mór for Robin and me, on my birthday.

So two weeks from my scheduled day in divorce court, I found myself back on the island that had first made me love Ireland, on the day I turned the age my husband had been when I met him.

I watched the early-twentysomethings holler and laugh as they coasted their rented bikes down the islands' roads, chased each other like children across the sealskin-colored strand, and ordered their beers in voices they hoped sounded nonchalant.

I felt so tender toward them, but also so separate from them that I might as well have been another species.

Fuck you, Tommy, I thought. The wistful, longing feelings for him that had plagued me for so long were depleted. The many things he had done to me, the many things he had failed to do for Robin, had beaten them out of me by then.

That was a kind of freedom, too.

Robin ambled up to me from his own beach wanderings, his eyebrows quirked just like Tommy's, to give me one of his wonderfully squishy toddler hugs.

I scooted him onto my lap. "You exist because of this island, you know," I said. "Nine years ago, this island started making you."

He giggled, without a notion of what I meant, and hugged me tighter.

Journal: July 13, 2021

The crowdfund hit a 10% down payment last night. Even when I set that as the goal part of me thought it wasn't possible. I immediately started worrying about next steps: will I be approved, will Tommy say something horrible in court on Monday that will undermine all of this. . . . but no. I can worry about those things another day. Another day.

So much of my life I have felt so obligated to "accomplish things" & "live up to my potential" that my only options for emotional response have been failure or neutral. But I can see that I will spend my whole life that way if I'm not careful, so I am going to be proud of myself right now, right now & all day long. & forever, too.

I was stunned to be able to apply for a mortgage like a regular person. Now that I had a down payment, and I was already paying in rent the same amount that I'd owe in repayments each month, I told myself there couldn't possibly be a problem. I called the credit union and told them I wanted to buy a house.

"What's the sale price of the property in question? How much are you putting down?" the brusque voice on the phone asked.

When I told him, he harrumphed like a cartoon character. "What's your monthly income?"

I told him, with as much confidence as I could wedge into my voice, that it varied—I was a bestselling author and writing teacher at the university, among other jobs, and that I'd made a little under €30,000 the previous year.

"Absolutely not," he said. "That level of income won't reliably support repayments."

"I'm paying that much in rent right now," I said, "and I've paid more in the past. I've always paid my rent on time, I can send you the records, you can speak to my landlords—"

"It's against policy," he said.

"But—"

"Stop. It's not possible." He must have heard my shaky breath. He sighed. "Now, if you had a co-signer with their own income—predictable income, mind you—you could come back to us. But not 'til then."

I could feel myself about to cry. "All right," I said, and ended the call.

Shay offered to co-sign the mortgage with me. Our combined incomes met the minimum requirement, and he had that steady office job besides.

I agonized over it for a while. I can't do this, I texted Claire.

Girl, why not? This is the dream!

Claire's favorite movie is *Gentlemen Prefer Blondes*. She always took beneficent joy in spending her own and her husband's money on her friends. It was because of her that I had the five thousand euros that had let me try to get in escrow for the castle, and that in the meantime had made the credit union trust me enough to give me a loan for the car I needed to survive. Claire had saved my life and Robin's with that money, and she had opened up the possibility for me that people would offer support, real concrete financial support, out of the kindness of their hearts.

This is love beyond romance, she told me. *It's a forty-year commitment. This is real.*

Her husband had relapsed yet again. She was parenting her own children, and even though our material circumstances and securities looked very different, she was often emotionally as alone in parenting as I was. And we both still had enough broken nights to need a friend, eight hours ahead or behind, who could talk to us from the land of daylight when it was night-time where we were.

But what if it messes things up with him? What if I poisoned this strange new family I'd found by tying our finances together? Hadn't both my other families been poisoned too? What was the common denominator there but me?

Girl. You already broke up with him. And he's still there. You're not gonna mess things up.

Thank you, I told Claire for talking it over with me, and then, a hundred thousand times, I thanked Shay, too.

The person who filed our application at the credit union smiled at us and said we'd be a shoo-in. I started to think I could breathe a little easier.

At least once I was through with my divorce.

Twenty-Two

The Boathouse

SUMMER 2021

for Alex

My milk came back in the night before the hearing. Robin had weaned a year and a half before, but there it was, dripping out of me as I got out of the shower, like all the tears I knew I wouldn't be allowed to shed on the stand. My stomach was cramped up tight, thinking about having to face my husband. Every muscle and gland in my body ached. And now I was leaking milk. I thought of how hard it had been on me when Robin had decided to wean, the vivid nightmares I'd had of him dying, my body convinced he was starving no matter how many of his toasted-marshmallow baby rolls I squeezed during the day. It felt like I started making more milk at first, not less, when he decided he was done with it. What is it about stress and fear that make our bodies decide it's time to feed people?

But there is something primally soothing about taking care of someone else when you're afraid. I'd known that long before I became a mother. I thought of how at Smith we'd bake cookies for each other during finals week, how that was often the only kind of study break we permitted ourselves—the kind where you were helping someone else. I thought of how much comfort food Shay and I had made during the lockdowns, how

Brigid's first response to seeing me holding back tears was to make tea. And I knew it, of course, when caring for Robin was the only thing keeping me functional in all those winter months when my marriage was collapsing, when I could only make myself eat so that I'd be able to keep nursing. When knowing I needed to save him was what made me save myself.

The reckoning about whether I would be able to stay with him had come. My body knew how afraid I was. I think it wanted to provide for him while it still could.

I chose my court outfit with agonizing care and slept with a tea towel shoved in my nightgown, because I didn't have any nursing pads left.

I dropped off Robin at naíonra a bit late, because he'd slept almost as badly as I had—I felt sure he was detecting my anxiety like sonar and amplifying it into his own. I drove the hour into town terrified, parked my car in the most expensive parking garage because I thought it was the one I'd be least likely to see Tommy in. I locked the car with trembling hands, telling myself that at least when I unlocked it again I'd be divorced.

Walking through Galway's cobblestone streets as quickly as I could, wobbling in my clearance-tag heels, I heard my phone ping in my purse. I figured it was from my lawyer: I knew call-in was in just a few minutes, the time when everyone who will be heard in court for the day has to basically take attendance. I opened the email, already planning my apology and promise that I'd be there before call-in.

Instead I saw an email from Tommy, received just one minute previously. All it said was "see attached." My belly clenched.

The attachment was a doctor's note. It said Tommy had severe stomach pains and was excused from any obligations for the next three days. It was dated two days earlier.

I lurched to a stop. My first thought was: of course he waited to send the note until just before call-in. He wanted me to feel all the anxiety and pain of getting ready for the date, knowing he wouldn't be there. And most of all he wanted me to have to pay for the day in court. Since he represented himself, canceling didn't cost him a damn thing.

He canceled, I texted Claire and Shay as I hurried into court—I knew I'd still have to go through call-in and officially tell the judge he wasn't coming. The fucker canceled.

Asshole, came their almost-synchronized replies. I'm so sorry.

Afterward, I trod back to my car and unlocked it, still married after all, and drove back to Connemara to pick up Robin and go home.

Thursday, he was there.

I was just as scared walking up to the courthouse that day, in the sweltering heat this time, one of the hottest days I'd seen in Ireland—or maybe it just felt that way because of the control-top black tights sticking to my legs. I felt about a thousand times less polished wearing my second-best dress than I had in my first, but I had very little presentable clothing after my years of motherhood and lockdown and working from home and I hadn't wanted to wear the same outfit again, worried that it would look to the judge as if I couldn't provide well for my kid and myself.

It turned out that there were so many cases being heard that day, with COVID restrictions still in place, that they were using the boathouse across the way from the courthouse for family court. To abide by social distancing rules, everyone waiting for their case to be heard was asked to stay outside.

I was intensely aware that Tommy would be nearby. No matter how many other people were there, I didn't feel safe.

I scanned the growing crowd that milled around the boathouse for his face.

My eyes found Saoirse first. Her gray punk-rock pixie cut, the sharp and sympathetic gaze behind her glasses, the layered clothes and cool boots that I thought of as her uniform.

"Betsy." She walked over to me, radiating calm and confidence, and took my hand. "Here we are. I'm so proud of you. How are you feeling?"

I'd written to her after the no-show on Tuesday, asking if COPE could send one of their court-accompaniment volunteers, since Tommy would have several hours of access to me before the hearing.

She'd come herself.

Tommy showed up a few minutes later, his white dress shirt unbuttoned halfway down his chest in the heat, an effect which would have devastated me five years before. But he'd grown older, too—he looked much older, in fact, and at once thinner and more swollen, like he'd been drinking a lot. It was just enough of a change that his romance-hero posturing looked embarrassingly try-hard now, instead of dreamy. Or maybe my gaze had matured a little, too.

He saw me, glared, and started forward, shoulders squared.

Saoirse stepped between us. She took my arm and helped me turn away.

"Remember, you don't have to look at him all day," she said quietly. "He wants you to, he wants the drama, but you don't have to make eye contact with him at all. You only have to look at the judge."

I took a breath and managed to smile at her. "Thank you, Saoirse."

She stood in the sun for hours, blocking him from me every moment, until it was our turn to go inside.

Family court records in Ireland are sealed. Not being able to talk about what happens in those courtrooms, I truly believe, protects abusers far more than it protects children.

I can't tell you what happened. But I can tell you how I felt.

When I took the stand—actually a folding table in the boathouse's makeshift setup—milk did start to leak through my second-nicest dress, but it was dark enough that I hoped no one could tell. I've always had low blood pressure, and I could feel my ears ringing and my head buzzing with it, the years of dreading this moment tangling up my blood.

I kept my gaze on the judge as I answered questions, just as Saoirse had reminded me to. I followed the COPE group's advice: put on my invisible armor piece by piece, take a breath and think for a moment before each answer, no matter how obvious the question—I could feel that riling Tommy.

Just think of Robin, I told myself. Every breath and every word is to protect him. Make it strong and calm and steady.

My head still buzzed and swam, but I also felt the buzzing over and over again of my phone in my pocket: well-wishers from the COPE group,

Friday Tea, all over the world. Each one of them made me stronger and calmer. I remembered Saoirse, standing right outside, waiting for me.

And I got through the day with my immigration visa and my custody of Robin intact.

When it was over, I walked out into the sunshine and Saoirse's waiting hands.

"It's done," I said. "It's done. I'm divorced now."

Saoirse laughed with joy and hugged me.

It was surreal. I took a deep breath, the light spangling in my eyes. "You know, my mom always thought divorce was one of the worst things someone could do. She's always been so Christian. She's still married to my dad."

Saoirse took my shoulders and looked sternly up at me. "I imagine she needs to think that, to stay married to someone like him," she said, brooking as little nonsense as ever.

"Oh," I said. "Oh, right."

"Personally," she said, "I've always thought *divorcée* to be a very glamorous word. I nearly wish I'd married my lad, just so I could divorce him."

We smiled at each other. My phone was still vibrating, and I took it out and showed Saoirse all the kind messages I'd gotten.

She nodded. "You know, Betsy, you have a really big family."

On my drive into the city to get divorced, I'd kept thinking about myself when I was a bride: how hopeful and trusting and in love she was, how sad she would be to know this day would come.

But then I thought: if I talked to her, if I told her about everything that had happened, I knew she would be standing right there with me in the courthouse—or, as it turned out, the boathouse. I could nearly feel her hand on my shoulder.

For the last three years, at least, some part of me had lived inside divorce court every day, imagining it, dreading the experience and its results. Part of me had felt like I'd be trapped in that courtroom, in that marriage, forever.

As I drove home, I wondered if my older self had been there with me that day, too. It pleased me to imagine the triptych of us standing together, strong: at twenty-five in the cream-colored floral dress I'd eloped in, stained with frightened milk at thirty-three, and older—seventy, maybe—with all my current fears long gone, and Robin safely grown.

But I knew immediately that she wasn't there. I'd been thinking about and connecting with my future self a lot lately, so that surprised me, but then I realized: it was because I hadn't needed her. I'd leaned on my future self so much in my past, believing that she would find the strength to leave my parents, to become a writer, to find a safer life. For the first time, driving home from the boathouse to the knitting factory, I started to have faith that I could lean on my past, too, on all the selves that had gotten me to where I was.

My future self was not in that room because she was not in that marriage. She didn't need to be. I had set her free.

Journal: August 5, 2021

Yesterday I gave Robin a bath with extra bubbles. He pointed out some bubbles in the shape of a heart & said "That's your heart, Mommy. That's for you because you are the winner."

I pointed to another group of bubbles & said they looked like a T. rex, & the T. rex was for him, because he was the winner.

Then he moved my heart into a bigger pile of bubbles & said "Look, Mommy, your heart is a brachiosaurus."

Twenty-Three

The Home That Lasts

AUTUMN 2021

for Mary

The Irish word for "deadline" is spriocdháta, which translates to "target date." I have a deadline: Tá spriocdháta orm. There is a target on me.

I was in the vet parking lot, covered in cat diarrhea from a tiny, starving kitten Robin had found in the knitting factory garden, when I got the news. My mortgage application was denied.

The man who called me seemed annoyed that I'd even applied. "You both have a recent history of low balances in your accounts," he said. "Keep them up for at least six months and you can apply again. Not before then."

I had just over a month until the deadline. In six months there would be no point in applying again. My chance would be gone.

I brought the kitten into the vet, feeling numb, and looked through rental listings on my phone while we waited for the appointment. There were three in all of Connemara, and even the cheapest one was out of my price range. I widened my search to everything in County Galway, hoping there was somewhere I could afford that wouldn't bring me closer to my ex-husband.

There was nothing. Nothing we could afford anywhere in the county. That had been true the last time I'd been looking, when we'd moved to Connemara two years before, and the housing crisis had only gotten worse. Dublin had become the most expensive city in the EU—which seemed a particular cruelty given all the European cities Ireland can't begin to compete with in, say, the sunshine and vineyard championships. Ireland was becoming hard for anyone to afford, and many people my age were emigrating. But I was as tied to this country as ever. I would have died before leaving my child here, and I couldn't legally leave with him. But over and over again, I faced the threat of being unable to find us a place to stay. And as soon as I failed to, I was sure, those anonymous reports to TUSLA and accusations from Tommy of my unfit motherhood would reappear.

I couldn't ask Patrick for another extension. I had given him my word we'd be moved out by the new year if this didn't work.

I just didn't know where we were going to go.

Tea: chamomile.

Worst: I thought I was so close to being done. I actually felt so at peace this weekend because I thought it was happening. I feel like I should be able to write something compelling here, to give you, since you've all given me so much. I am going to apply to other banks, of course, but it seems like their answer will be the same. The knitting factory was on the market for at least two years before we made this agreement, so even though the current owner seems to think it will sell as soon as he puts it back up, I know that's not necessarily true. Who knows, maybe someone who's been following the project would be interested in buying the building in their name and my paying for everything, or giving them profit from the residency & retreat business once it gets off the ground. (And hey, on the off chance this is you, the sale price of the building is €179,200, I have the down payment and ongoing monthly mortgage repayments covered, and I'd love to talk to you.)

I cried for a long time after getting the phone call, talked with my co-signer and got angry together that it feels like we were denied on a technicality after being told we'd be fine, and cried some more.

So, worst case scenario, we have to move again at the end of the year and I give people back their money. I know that's not the end of the world. I know everyone has dreams that don't work out. And I know for sure that I have tried my hardest. There isn't any more I could have given to this project.

But then I think of how my kid pronounces it "the living factory" and how he tells the other kids he meets "I live with my mommy at the living factory," and every time we drive back here he says "Look, mommy, it's our home!" and my heart feels like it's cracked, like it's stopped beating, every time. I really thought I was almost done.

Best: Today, at least, my kid and I are safe. Whatever way this all goes is very minor in comparison, of course.

In the days that followed I careened between numb panic and desperate mania. I kept teaching at the university, editing and doing customer service and website administration for *Parabola*, teaching online, and working toward finishing *Reader, I Murdered Him*. I also taught myself how to apply for a business loan. Maybe that was a better answer than a mortgage all along, I thought. It was the business's potential, rather than my own past income, that mattered most, and I could use the building as collateral.

I kept posting every day on the knitting factory's social media sites, kept sending newsletters, talking about my dream and how close it was to the knife's edge. I got up to a 20% down payment, almost €40,000. A sum so big was almost abstract to me, and it should have felt like a fortune—but now it just seemed like it probably wasn't enough.

Then, three miracles: three people each offered to loan me 10% of the house's purchase price. The first was Kimberly Brubaker Bradley.

If you're in the children's book world, you know her name. Two of her books are Newbery honorees. All of them are incandescent.

There's a beautiful tradition of children's book authors who have come from Smith: Sylvia Plath, of course (yes, she wrote a children's book), as well as Madeleine L'Engle, Jane Yolen, Ann M. Martin, Theanne Griffith, Lisa Anchin, Barbara Cooney, and Kimberly Brubaker Bradley.

Kim casually mentioned in my Friday Tea comments in 2018 that she wrote books, too, and we'd been friends ever since. Then when I posted a couple years later about my parents and why I cut them off, she declared herself my and Robin's adopted aunt. She requested our birthdays for the purpose of sending gifts (impeccably chosen picture books for Robin, a beautiful hand-knit lace cowl for me), and she told me to talk to her if I ever needed an aunt.

She'd been one of the crowdfund's biggest supporters all along. *I wish I could buy it for you*, she wrote. *My husband and I can loan you 10%. I keep thinking of what you said Shay told you, that family means I'm not willing to let you suffer.*

Oh Kim, I replied, *I don't know how to thank you enough. I ran out of the right thank-you words long before the project got this far.*

I hope whatever happens, she said, *you're proud of yourself.*

That was too tall an order, I thought. But I was grateful to have someone like her want it for me.

Christina, a prior housemate at Smith who had been a year ahead of me, a beautiful butch woman with snapping blue eyes who had been on the crew team at Smith and had gone into public health, wrote to say she had been thinking of getting into real estate, and she was wondering if we could have a video chat.

I was nervous taking that call: I'd always thought she was way too cool for me when we were in college. We'd been friendly, but not close, for just that reason.

But: "Betsy!" she cried warmly when our faces appeared on each other's screens. "It's been way too long!"

Somehow I was instantly at ease. "Thank you so much for writing to me about this, Christina. I can't tell you how much it means."

Her wide smile softened. "Did I ever tell you I have a single mom?"

She went on to say she'd already looked into buying the knitting factory herself and leasing it to me. She hadn't been able to find a mortgage broker that would agree to it, but she wanted to loan me another 10%.

"Christina," I whispered. "I don't know what to say. Thank you."

Shay's offer to co-sign the mortgage with me had been astoundingly generous, but at least I'd had a context for it: this was a man who loved me, who wanted to buy a house with me, to provide for a woman and child he loved. As Claire said, that's what men who are in love with you are for.

The crowdfund—asking a little bit from a lot of people—had gradually become something I had context for, too. Crowdfunds were common enough, after all. I understood what they were and how to go about them.

But a friend from college, someone I hadn't spoken to in years, showing me this kind of love? It was something my imagination didn't have vocabulary for.

I saw her watch me trying to come up with the right words. "I wish more people had helped my mom," she said. "I know about family court, and housing, and ... " she trailed off. "A conversation for another time. Anyway, I really believe in your idea. And I want you and your kiddo to be safe."

We just looked at each other.

"Thank you, Christina," I said.

"And maybe," she added hesitantly, "I could come visit you sometime?"

"Of course! Anytime you want. My house is yours. Truly."

"Great. You know, I wish we'd been better friends at Smith," she went on. "I always thought you were too cool for me, though."

I felt an actual little shock run through my body. "Um. I thought the same thing."

She laughed and waved her hand. "Seriously?"

"Christina. I thought I was a bridge troll when I was eighteen. I thought I was Gollum."

She laughed more. "Me too. Oh man, me too."

One more person loaned me 10%: Sharon, someone I had never met at all, a single mom in California who had signed up for the knitting factory's newsletter because she was interested in creating a similar space where she lived. She asked if I had a business plan, I shared it, and we agreed quickly to the loan's terms. It made me feel professional, like someone who could be taken seriously.

The support I was getting astounded me, even as I kept wondering if it could be enough.

I wish I could do more, Claire wrote after making yet another donation, but Drew is getting worse again. I don't have much money that's actually just mine, and I might have to use it to move me & the kids.

Honey, you have done too much already, I told her, and meant it with every cell in my body. Stop. Think about yourself and your babies. Besides, maybe it can be my turn to help you soon. No matter where you are, you'll always have a place here. With me, in Ireland, whether it's in this house or not.

Yeah, if I can get a visa, she replied with lots of laughing emojis. I know how hard it's been just for you to keep getting yours renewed each year. How many generations back do they accept Irish ancestry for citizenship, again?

I'll marry you, I said, not kidding at all. You saved Robin and me before any-one else. If you need it, you can always, always come here.

I know, my love, she said. We have each other's backs. Lorelai and Dorothy.

Damn straight.

I love you.

I love you.

Good night, my love.

Good morning.

As the deadline approached, I kept getting sick. I stayed up late every night finishing *Reader, I Murdered Him*, and I finally turned it in at the last possible moment of my deadline day, on October 15. I caught every single one of the colds Robin brought home from naíonra. I felt sick all the time, and I was sleeping maybe four hours a night, like the newborn stage all over again. I'd be woken up, not by a baby's cries, but by my own anxiety. I was determined to give back all the crowdfund money, including what I'd already spent, if the project didn't work out. But I kept waking up wondering how long it would take to pay back what was already gone, on top of what I'd need to earn and spend just to keep Robin and me housed.

A thick snow of pain and fear, of the weight of failure, piled up against the old walls of my heart. In October I lost my voice from a cold, and didn't get it back for nearly a week. It felt far too pat, as metaphors went. As the weather darkened, I thought of the last solstice and Christmas and new year we'd had at the knitting factory. Would the darkest day of this year find us packing to leave? Where would we go?

Tea: masala chai.

The absolute final deadline to be able to buy the knitting factory is November 15. I am still speaking with any mortgage broker who will talk to me, and I've increased the crowdfunding goal to the full purchase price of the building, because you never know. I also wrote an essay about the project that's coming out in the fall issue of the alumni magazine of my grad school alma mater, Notre Dame, next week, and I'm hoping it will attract notice from their "Fighting Irish" readers. So I am not surrendering yet!

Thank you to everyone who has reached out in the last weeks. It's been a big, painful emotional rollercoaster, and I am still catching up on messages, but I am unspeakably grateful for your support. I had this narrative in my head of writing a book to buy a house, of being able to do this project all Independent and Strong, and I think I am those things, but it absolutely would not work at all without the community support I've had and that I continue to receive. A good lesson for a single mom.

Journal: November 1, 2021

*Two weeks left. I thought I'd know by the time I wrote the last entry in
this journal, but I don't. This is the last page. I keep dissociating ... it's
taken me almost an hour just to write these few sentences. My hands &
head & heart feel stiff.*

*Maybe I'll go for a walk. I hope the sun holds so I can take Robin to
the beach after school. I know he's all that matters.*

When I brought my business plan to the bank, the loan officer told me
he couldn't imagine I wouldn't get approved. I was asking for a loan of
€100,000 and providing the rest of the building's purchase price myself, between the crowdfund and my private loans, and I had the building as proposed collateral and my platform as a bestselling author and experienced
writing teacher to offer as a guarantee of attendance at the writing retreats I
wanted to offer on-site.

Walking out of the bank, I felt excited and powerful. This could really,
finally work. Maybe it was always coming to this, after all. Maybe this was
the way it was always meant to be.

I don't know a more addictive, or insidious, thought than that.

The next day I got a follow-up call from the bank, from someone who
told me in a condescending voice that I needed to apply for a personal mortgage instead of a business loan.

I wanted to scream.

Instead, I used the unemotional voice I'd practiced for family court to
say I was planning to use the premises for business purposes, besides which I
had already pursued a personal mortgage and been very clearly redirected to
a business loan instead (the most positive spin I could put on rejection—a
skill every writer has to learn at some point).

Then he miscalculated the repayments and quoted me €8000 a month.
He didn't seem to have even looked at the business plan, or any of the fig-
ures, at all.

Finally, he told me there would be a decision within twenty-four to forty-eight hours—but after he hung up, I got an email from the bank that said it would be up to fifteen business days.

I didn't have fifteen days of any kind. I had no idea what to think.

Journal: November 11, 2021

No word from the business loan yet.

　　—later—

　　I just got a "confirmation of decision not to proceed" from the bank &
about had a heart attack, but it was for the personal mortgage application
I'd already made.

　　At least I know I won't immediately collapse if my business loan is
rejected.

　　For fuck's sake.

On November 12, three days before the deadline, my business loan was denied. I got the call as I was pulling into the driveway after bringing Robin to naíonra.

I sat in the car, staring out at the lake, with my head buzzing, struggling to feel worthy of taking a deep breath. I knew it was the end. I had been checking all the online real estate listings every day, looking for any newly listed rentals. There was still nothing that we could remotely afford.

But I knew that was how it was for most single parents—for most people, now, in Ireland's housing crisis. Skipping meals to make rent and knowing that a single illness or complication could take even that much away. That was how it would have to be. We would go back to scraping by.

I'd overcome nothing. Not my broken marriage, not leaving my parents. I could offer my child, and my community, nothing. My hands and heart were empty.

· · ·

One of my donors, an English writer living in Orkney named Sara Bailey, had asked me to do some one-on-one writing sessions with her as she worked through her latest novel. We had a video appointment that morning.

I hoped I looked presentable enough for the meeting, not like the void of despair I felt, but "My dear, what happened?" she asked, as soon as the session started.

I explained that what felt like my last reasonable option had failed. That I'd tried so many things, and I didn't know what else to do.

"It will work out," she said, with the easy faith of someone for whom it already had: after her own brush with housing insecurity and single motherhood, she'd found both a tenured professorship and an adoring new husband. "It has to. It's meant to be."

"I used to think that," I said. "But it's been so hard. Not only that—more than that—how dare I think this is meant to work out for me? I know so many other single moms who need it more, deserve it more. Nothing's been *meant to work out* for them, trust me." I thought of Aisling, on the waiting list for a council house for nine years, getting constant harassing calls and visits from her ex but still never granted a safety order, dealing with children who believed she was stealing their child support. I thought of Mairéad, whom the courts had ordered to let her abusive ex sleep in her bed every other weekend. I thought of all the women at the COPE shelter, the women around the world in straits so dire I couldn't even imagine them. There was no innate sense of justice in the world, I knew. Children died every day, leaving mothers who loved them just as much as I loved Robin. There could be no justice, no kind fate, in a world like that.

"Sometimes things just don't work out," I told her, trying not to let her hear my voice catch. "This isn't a fairy tale with a happy ending." I thought of the Selkie Bride, the Maiden Without Hands: stories of women who lost parts of their bodies, their first homes, to men, and found them again in motherhood. I had tried so hard to make every part of myself a magic home to give my child, but I couldn't grow new hands by force of will, couldn't find a skin to bring us safely to the sea. I still was not enough to save us.

"I wish it was. I tried to make our lives, our need for home, into a story. I tried so hard. But it isn't."

She frowned at me. "What if it was?"

I looked away, out the French doors to the gray sky over the lake. "What do you mean?"

"If this were a book. If it were one of your novels, and you were the main character, and it had gotten to this point. What would happen next?"

I took a breath. "If everything that's happened so far had happened?"

"Yes. Exactly."

"Oh." The strange thing was, I knew the answer right away. "I think I'd have the project fail."

It might not have been the answer Sara wanted to hear—I imagined she wanted me to say there would be some miracle ending, a deus ex machina— but as I spoke, a sense of peace washed over me.

"I don't think it would be realistic to have it work out now, not at this point." A little of the pain inside me ebbed away, just a little bit, but enough that I could feel it, even so. "I'd have the fictional me move on, in hope, with my son. Still together. Safer than we were before, because of all the love and support around us. Alive. Still finding hope."

If I could forgive a fictional version of myself for failing so profoundly, maybe I could forgive myself a little, too.

A fairy tale is not the only kind of story worth telling.

I walked through the house and garden like I was mourning them already. Like we were already gone, and I was wandering them only in memory. Every day I remembered looking at the old candles in the wall the night I'd moved in, setting my corkboard on the mantel and wondering if this would be the home that lasts.

I thought of the anemones I'd planted sleeping underground, waiting for a bloom we might never see. Robin and I had repainted the border wall and left whitewash handprints there: his hands were already bigger than the print he'd left last spring, but the marks remained.

What kind of home does any parent make for their child, except for one that vanishes with childhood? Even the haunted house of my own first years was gone: that the New Hampshire farmhouse itself still stood didn't matter. The kind of home Robin would have had if I'd stayed with Tommy, though it still haunted me too, was a ghost that had never lived.

I had made us this home, if only for this one and a half years. That would endure, I told myself over and over, longing with all my heart to believe it. Could that be true of a marriage, too? The love people give to each other, make into a home in their hearts: is it still there, somewhere in time, after the marriage ends? I thought of the memories I could step back into and make real whenever I wanted to: dancing with Tommy to Leonard Cohen, talking to Robin as I looked for strawberries before I knew for sure I was pregnant. I had built homes in memory from those moments, even as they passed away.

At some point in the past decade, I'd stopped hating my parents. I had hated them when I was under their power. But after I left, at some point, that just . . . stopped. There were days, more and more days, when I didn't think about them at all. And from that freedom, I could look back with kinder eyes. I could start to tell Robin stories from my childhood when he asked for them. Leaving had, at some point, given me the gift of seeing the better times I hadn't been able to stand looking at before I left.

I'd given my future self the gift of leaving Tommy. Now, already, I was that older woman, free from the fear of divorce court. I had the freedom to look back on my marriage with love again, with the love I'd had to push away in order to be able to leave.

I often thought the best parts of Tommy, the parts I'd always love, were there in Robin; and I had the chance to save them, to keep them from getting overwhelmed by the pain and violence that had hurt Tommy past bearing, so that he pushed them onto his wife and child to bear instead. Can a child be the wonderful parts of a marriage, living on after that marriage dies?

We're all just walking each other home, the Ram Dass line I'd painted on my corkboard said.

Can a home last forever, even if you leave it?

•   •   •

My daily prayer became: if I fail, let it not be because I stopped trying. I kept sharing the crowdfund, sending the newsletter, writing to everyone I knew. My plan was to offer everything I had to Patrick and try to make some kind of compromise. Offer to pay him back month by month for the rest, or something that had yet to occur to me. I knew I'd already strung him along, and I was sure he'd say no. But if I had to walk away, I needed to know that I hadn't given up while I still had time, even if that time was only a day. In stories, you never know which beggar at the side of your path will turn out to be the sorceress in disguise. You keep trying, even in the face of certain failure.

On the night of November 14, I sat on my bedroom floor, playing dinosaurs with Robin.

I got an email from the mother of a friend I only knew a little bit, asking if she could call me to talk about helping with the knitting factory. I could barely string words together at that point, but I wrote back as professionally as I could, thanking her and giving her my number. Some delusional part of me dared to wonder if I might convince her to offer another 10%, so I could give Patrick €130,000 in the morning.

Mostly I was trying not to think about anything but dinosaurs.

The phone rang. A number I didn't know.

I picked it up.

"Hi, honey," the warm, no-nonsense voice said. "This is Mary's mom. She told me you need some help getting to your goal for the knitting factory. How much do you need?"

My head had been full of nothing but that number all day. It was unfathomably big. "Ninety thousand euros."

"And what is that in US dollars?"

I'd just looked it up. There was a bleak little laugh in my voice when I said, "A hundred and three thousand US dollars."

"Okay." A brief pause. "I can wire it to you tomorrow."

Twenty-Four

This Stranger's Heart

WINTER 2021

for Terry

Robin was making his dinosaurs screech on the floor. I could hear my blood rushing in its tracks in my head.

"Oh my god," I said. I couldn't think of anything else to say. "Oh my god."

"I know you're probably shocked," the voice on the other end of the line said, this American voice, this mother of a friend I'd only met a few times.

"Yeah," I managed to squeak. "Um. Thank you so much. Thank you so much."

"Mary told me about this project, and she is rooting for you so hard. She has such a good heart. I want you to know that I am doing this because I love my daughter."

What do you say to someone who has just saved you? I still don't know.

"I know what you mean. I mean, I love my son. This is going to be . . . I wanted to do this for him."

"I know, honey." Robin was still shrieking dinosaur noises in the background. "Okay. You can send me your details by email."

And the call was over.

I got back down on the floor to hug Robin. I couldn't stop shaking.

"We get to stay," I said into his curls, over and over. "We get to stay."

He roared, oblivious. Just a kid playing dinosaurs in his mom's bedroom. In his house.

I still couldn't stop shaking, but I picked up the phone again. The first person I told—well, the first person who wasn't more interested in dinosaurs—was Claire, who had been the first knitting factory donor, way back when we thought it was a castle.

> Claire:
> OH MY GOD

Me:
That's what I said! I still don't know what to say!

> Claire:
> OH MY GOD
> A HUNDRED THOUSAND DOLLARS
> BETSY DO YOU KNOW WHAT THIS MEANS

Me:
Haha, I don't. I'm still astounded. I think my brain is broken.

> Claire:
> IT MEANS, BETSY, THAT YOU
> ARE AMERICA'S NEXT TOP MODEL

A cacophony of celebratory GIFs started pouring in.

I texted Shay, who was visiting family in England. His response, while happy and amazed like Claire's, felt a little more subdued. I think we both had wondered what the future might hold for the family we'd made if Robin and I left this house.

We'd never talked about it, not explicitly. But I think we both had wondered.

It didn't matter now. My dream had come true.

I set down my phone, still trembling. I could feel myself breathe, feel all the air in all the hundred thousand open spaces in my lungs, like it was clean, like I had space inside myself again. It was a little like the first breath I took when Robin was born: when suddenly my belly was soft and empty and pressureless, and I remembered for the first time in months what an easy, full breath felt like as he was placed, still bloody, on my chest, over my heart.

I had my skin and hands back, after all.

There were so many people to tell. Hundreds of people.

But it was Robin's bedtime. My kid still needed me most, and the news would keep. It would keep forever.

Once he was tucked in, there was nothing I wanted more than to go to bed, too. In my own bed. In my own house.

So I did. I put on my warmest New England flannel nightgown and snuggled under the duvet, warm from my electric blanket. I looked around at the four walls of my room.

I picked up *I Capture the Castle*, which always lives on my bedside table, to read a little bit, to clear my head, but tiredness flooded me.

I put the book down and went to sleep.

Old Knitting Factory newsletter

Hello. I am a writer who does not know what to say.

Last night I got a phone call from someone who gave me the remainder of the knitting factory's purchase price. The call lasted maybe three minutes, and I was apologizing for R's play-yelling half the time and pretty much incoherent with shock for the rest.

I've been writing this post for an hour and this is all I have, because I still don't know what to say. I keep having thoughts like: I'll be able to see the anemones I planted bloom this spring. I can renovate the terrible bathroom. I can fix the leaky windows. I can get goats. I can sleep so much more deeply than I did Saturday night.

One thing I do want to say is: I don't think this happened because it was meant to be. Every week I go to the single mothers' group at my local domestic violence center and I listen to those women's stories and I think, I don't work any harder, I am not any more deserving, than any of them. Many of them have so much less than I did even before this project, and they deserve so much more. Most single mothers deal with financial or housing insecurity, and very few get the surreally miraculous happy ending that has blossomed into this house. So I ask you not to believe that this was always going to work out, because that's not true. Maybe it's because I'm a child abuse survivor that I rebel so viscerally against the idea that everything happens for a reason. There is so much tragedy and injustice in the world, and to say that I get to rest easy now because that's how this story was meant to turn out feels really facile. There are many single mothers who never get to rest easy, ever.

This journey to find a home has been so hard, and that's with all the privileges and connections I have that made it possible for me to try this in the first place.

I have a house now, or I will when the papers are signed. I wish I could give every single mom in my support group a house, too. Every single mom in the world, every person in the world, deserves a home that is their own. This process has made me think so much about housing insecurity, and now that I am starting to have the freedom and the platform to work toward good changes, that's what I want to do. Everyone should have a safe home.

I am so shocked. I sincerely would not have written an ending like this in my fiction, because it's too pat, too neat. But this is not the only time something has happened in real life that would be unbelievable in stories.

I thought the only way I'd get to buy a house would be to tell a story about it. That turned out to be true, if in a different way than I thought. I am stunned to be writing this particular ending for you right now (which, like most endings, is of course also, and even more so, a beginning). I'll write more soon.

Thank you so much for being here to listen to this story. It would not be coming true without you.

I had never had so many people tell me they were crying with me, in their homes, their offices, on buses, waiting in cars to pick up their kids from school; in America, in Ireland, in Germany, in Kenya, in Iran. I thought of the wild strawberry place the knitting factory had been when we'd arrived a year and a half before: a place where you feel at one with the world. A place to share with people you love and trust. Everyone was there with me that day.

I took Robin to the playground after naíonra that afternoon. "I live with my mommy at the living factory," he told a kid the next swing over, and my heart just kept on beating.

In 2015, when my second book came out, I received a message from a reader that changed the way I thought about my work forever. I'd written about something she'd thought was unique to her, something that embarrassed her so deeply she'd never spoken of it, let alone imagined seeing it in print. *Thank you, from the bottom of this stranger's heart*, she wrote, for expressing something that made her feel less alone.

I kept that line on a sticky note by my desk for years, reminding me of why I write: not for wealth or accolades, as much as I might wish for them, but to make the kind of life-saving connection with a stranger that books had made for me all through my life. From the bottom of this stranger's heart. It's now tattooed on my right arm.

That week at the university, I was scheduled to lecture on classical story structure. I helped my students choose fairy tales or myths to retell, and showed them how to make Vonnegut's story charts. We talked about the hero's journey.

But then, as always, I told them that I don't believe in it anymore. Not like I used to. I always made sure to talk about how limited it was, how even though Joseph Campbell argued for his own theory's universality, it was, of course, based on very white and very male stories. I felt the spirit of my own fairy tale teacher at Smith, Betsey Harries, with me, when I read Barre Toelken to my students:

"The same plot, clearly, does not always mean the same thing; without the implied meanings and shared connotations supplied by cultural context, we may very well have a coherent text whose meanings are totally misapprehended. This is one of several points missed by those who believe 'archetypes' are universal in their meaning . . . an assertion that can be maintained only by suppressing thousands of stories . . . "

Neither our lives, nor the books we write, have to look like the hero's journey, I told them. It's been a very influential idea, and it's useful to understand, to be able to see how many of our most popular stories use it, but that doesn't mean it's the only way, or the only kind of story there is.

I showed my students the chart for the hero's journey. It's a circle— something I found moving from the first time I saw it, as someone who struggled to accept linear time long before I argued about it with Shay over the dishes. It begins at the top, with the hero's call to adventure. The hero refuses the call at first, but then some cataclysm happens that forces them to set off on their journey anyway, and they enter the Unknown, the land where they learn their lessons, fight their battles, pursue their quest. They have to overcome threshold guardians, find mentors, meet harder and harder challenges as they descend the curve of the circle, until they come to the Abyss: the moment in the story when all seems lost, when hope is gone, when they are forced to confront the fact that both their quest, and they themselves, have failed.

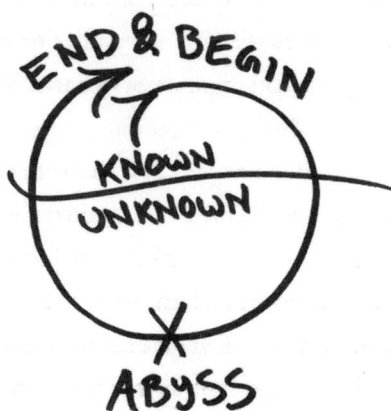

But the Abyss is also the moment when the hero proves their heroism, I always told my students. Because, even in the face of certain failure, they keep trying anyway. And that exact determination, that persistence, is what gives them the tools they need to triumph, the things they never would have found if they'd given up.

The hero moves up the arc of the circle then, atones for what they've done wrong, receives a gift from a goddess, and passes the threshold back into the Known, the place where their story began. They return triumphant and wise. The story comes full circle, and they can begin again.

When I first read about the hero's journey, I didn't see that chart, and I assumed it was a line: masculine clock time personified, beginnings leading down roads you could never retread, to endings that couldn't be changed. (Even a clock, of course, is a circle, too.) I do believe that the insistence on the universality of the hero's journey has done a lot of harm, has limited our understanding of both story and hero, and kept many people's heroic journeys unseen, dismissed. I try never to follow it completely in my fiction.

But as I looked at that circle, all I could see was the story I'd just lived.

I thought of the Celtic wheel of the year. I thought of maps: how you can only see the shape of something when you look at it from a distance, when you describe it to someone else.

I knew I would not have my home if I had not believed I could tell a story about it, could tell a story to get there.

Maybe I would not even have left that other home, holding nothing but my baby, and flung us into the Unknown, if I had not read and listened enough to know that others had done the same, and lived.

Maybe I would not have left my first home, either, if I hadn't read books that told me stories of a kinder world and made me believe in it. Those books built a home for me in my future long before I had ever heard of the knitting factory.

My mother, before she had children, volunteered as a literacy coach. I got my love of books from her. For all she'd never been able to do, she had given me one kind of key, one kind of magic spell, that got me out, even if it never did the same for her. Books had always been magic spells, lifelines, to me. That was part of what had drawn me to writing for young adults: I wanted to offer that sense of connection and hope to other people who were going through the times that I'd found hardest. From the bottom of this stranger's heart.

I wanted to do that still. When I had first looked ahead at a life of single motherhood, a life stuck in a foreign country without family support or even a roof to put over my baby's head, all the stories I could imagine of what that looked like were bleak—until I started telling myself a story that was better. A story I believed in so much that other people started to believe in it, too. And together we made it true.

My story of single motherhood, of life after divorce and domestic abuse, wasn't going to be one of scarcity and brokenness and horror—or, it wasn't going to be just about those things. I had drawn a map of a life for myself and my child that was beautiful, bountiful, full of more hope than fear. And as of November 14, I couldn't honestly call my story anything but magical.

It was a map I wanted to share with other single moms, with other people who found themselves in the mire of a frightening family and needed to see a path out.

In the end, I'd bought the house without the book I thought I needed to write to get it. But I knew, talking with my students that day, that I was still going to write this book.

Twenty-Five

Goddess of Thresholds

SPRING 2022

for Allegra

It took until spring to finalize the sale. Paperwork made its slow way back and forth across the ocean. Solicitors drummed up their fees by talking to each other.

I slept a lot.

December, January, February passed. I marked Imbolc, my favorite Irish holiday, by ordering some tiny charms shaped like house keys and engraved with TOKF, for some of the dearest friends who had supported the project, and for me. They felt like friendship bracelets, and I wear mine every day.

Imbolc is my favorite day for many reasons. The first of February, it marks the midpoint between winter solstice and spring equinox. Snowdrops peek through the dead leaves of last autumn, and you can sense, new and wonderful every year, the "grand stretch" of the evenings getting longer. It is the balancing point before winter tips toward spring. The word comes from an Irish term that means "in the belly," and it is a time, in nature and on farms, of pregnancy: animals coming into their milk, Imbolc marked by sheep's udders swelling a month before the lambs are born. (May we come around again to see them next year.)

Despite my love of warmth, I've spent my life moving to cold places: from coastal New Hampshire, to the Pioneer Valley, to the snowed-in Midwestern winters of Indiana, and finally to Irish wind and rain. Imbolc feels like a lifeline thrown out to me across the cold: a reminder that through all the dark, when it still feels like winter, you know that warmth is coming.

Imbolc is also the day sacred to the goddess Brigid, later the Catholic St. Bridget. Among other things she is the goddess or the patron saint of thresholds, meaning both literal doorways and threshold moments: dawn and dusk, birth and death. She presides over childbirth, and if you leave a cloth out overnight on Imbolc eve to catch the dew, you'll make a brat bhride, a Brigid's cloak, which will have the power to heal your pains all year—any kind of pain at all, but especially the pain of childbirth.

The morning of Imbolc in 2022, I went out into the knitting factory's garden in the misty, lavender-silk dawn to wrap myself in my still dewy brat bhride: a flower-stitched scarf I'd bought at the Knitting & Stitching Show four years earlier, on the day I had first dreamed of writing a book to buy a house.

The day I finally signed the deed, I came home to floors that felt more solid under my feet. I kept running my hands along the walls of the hallway. There were still so many steps to take, but I wanted to try to appreciate how far I'd come (something, to be honest, that I still struggle with). I'd subscribed to Violet Lea Devotion's Patreon—someone I had quoted, in fact, in my zine about the knitting factory—and won a drawing for a free tarot reading that they offered to their supporters. So shortly after the purchase closed, I found myself checking in again with one of the people whose wisdom had helped, however unknown to them, to set me on the path that had led me home.

It was a long reading, with many cards, over video chat. There are some things they told me that I will treasure and keep private. I am learning to do that, too.

But I will share one thing they said. We were talking about taking time to notice how far you've come rather than immediately looking ahead to the next problem or challenge, and the next after that, and the next.

"Your ancestors want you to be proud of yourself *now*," they said. "It's not about what you still need to do. It's about taking a breath. It's about rest."

I shuddered and laughed at the same time. "It's been so long since I felt like I could really rest," I said. "I've stopped even dreaming, you know. I've been too tired. I used to have great dreams. Now I just pass out, and when my kid wakes me up in the morning, it's like no time has passed."

They nodded. They were a single mom, too, although their kid was a young adult by then.

They turned over another card, an image of white feathers on a clear blue background.

And they said: "Someday you will have dreams that are not about survival."

I couldn't even imagine, in that moment, what those dreams would be; but I longed to dream them. It was what I wanted for all the moms in my survivors' group, all the moms I wanted to bring to the knitting factory. That our most daring dreams would not be only that we and our children would live.

On St. Patrick's Day I baked three loaves of bread with Robin, each of them braided with three colors of dough: green from spinach, golden from sweet potato, and plain, so they managed a decent Irish tricolor. I tucked them into paper bags and wrote on the outsides "Lá Fhéile Padraig Shona Duit, from Betsy and Robin at the Old Knitting Factory."

I had been so shy about introducing myself to my neighbors. I didn't want to seem like an overly loud and bombastic American, not sure what they'd think of me moving into one of their village's historic buildings—especially when I hadn't known for sure if we'd be able to stay. COVID's social distancing had also meant that it was almost unheard of even to run into neighbors accidentally in the time I'd been there.

But that had also been an excuse to avoid my own nervousness. It had been far easier, in its way, to introduce myself and "build community" online. No one was looking at me while I did it. I've always been more of a writer than a talker.

Now the time had come. My heart was pounding, ridiculous as that was, as I walked Robin across the road to give our neighbors the bread, as I let Robin, always far more extroverted than I, skip forward to knock on doors, while I hung back clutching the loaves.

No one, it turned out, was home. It was a dry day, so we left the bread on doorsteps. Robin was devastated not to have met new friends, but I was deeply relieved. I had made my gesture and hadn't had to watch myself fail at making conversation with anyone.

The next day, I was out gardening when I saw an auburn-haired older woman step out of the house across the street and walk toward me, waving. I scolded myself not to be afraid of talking to people, for goodness' sake, and I waved back.

"Máidin mhaith!" she said, and I said it back, *good morning*, then rattled off the first Irish phrase I'd memorized when I moved to Connemara:

"Tá brón orm, níl mór an Gaeilge agam." *I'm sorry, I don't speak much Irish.*

"Oh, goodness, that's all right. Bless you for trying." She smiled, and I smiled back. "My name's Hilaraí. I've thought of introducing myself to you so many times, you and your lovely ladeen there, but I wasn't sure how to do it. I can be a bit shy sometimes, you see."

Ah. Now that was the best way to override my own shyness—my sympathy for the other person's makes me forget my own. "I felt the same way!" I said, and we both laughed.

"I'm so glad someone's living in the knitting factory again," she said, "especially someone with a child. There aren't enough children out here in rural areas anymore."

Here I knew I had my in. "I know. I'm really glad I can send him to a Gaelscoil—he's starting in the fall, and he's in naíonra now. I love that he will grow up just knowing the language."

Hilaraí's smile grew. "It's my first language," she said. "If he ever needs any practice, you'll know where to find me."

I smiled back. "I will."

A man with a trim white goatee joined us at the fence and introduced himself as Hilaraí's partner, Noel. "You should sell that bread," he told me. "My goodness."

Robin, who had been busy making mud pies, came to the fence then, and it turned out he and Noel had dispositions as similar as Hilaraí's and mine: they were cracking each other up in seconds, pulling faces, doing funny voices. Hilaraí and I could just smile at them and, shyly, at each other.

Noel and Hilaraí's house stood right across the street from the knitting factory and farther uphill, so they could look down on us and across the lake. I asked them if they'd lived there long. It turned out it was Hilaraí's family home, and she told me that as a little girl she'd watched the knitters and the knitting machines through the big windows I loved.

"I've heard a lot of different things about this place's history," I said. "Do you know what it was like for the women who worked here?"

"Well, they were girls, really, more than women," Hilaraí said. "A rare one of them would have been over twenty, I think."

"That makes sense," I said, adjusting my mental image. I thought of Smith, and the girls' halls at summer camp. "Do you think they liked their time here? Do you think they were treated fairly?"

Noel smiled, a little sadly. "Ah, now, those are two very different questions."

"Well, the real estate listing said it was a school, basically a charity, but when I read up about the Congested Districts Board, it started to sound more like a workhouse."

He shook his head. "I'd say it was mostly a warm place to gather. You know, those young girls, living way out in Connemara, they didn't have a place to meet and talk with each other. If they weren't in school, they were stuck in their homes all the time. And their cottages would have been very cold. The knitting factory was warm, and it was a place they could make friends."

My breath had vanished at what he said. "A warm place to gather." I thought of all the supporters who had gathered around the knitting factory, around my child and me, who were the reason we were there, and safe. The project had become that gathering place for them, too, I knew, which in turn had been one of the greatest gifts it had given me: I pursued the deepest dream of my heart, and that dreaming drew the right people around me to help make it come true. I thought once again of the other mothers I hoped to bring here.

"It still is," I said.

After the purchase came through, it turned out there were still a million things I needed to do to start the single mother residencies I'd dreamed of: register the business, for one. Despite all my crowdfunding work, the idea of being a Business Owner intimidated me to the point of near-terror. Both my father and my ex had, in their own special ways, made me feel stupid about and terrible with money, and even in light of all the evidence otherwise, it was hard to rid myself of those beliefs.

I also worried about sharing the space before it was renovated: the leaky old bathroom, the drafty old windows, the garden with its crumbling walls. I'd started asking around about renovation quotes, and the numbers I heard made me see it was going to take years before I could turn the space into everything I dreamed it could be. As much as I'd learned, as much as this project had healed and grown my heart, I was still insecure, still convinced that when people met either me or the knitting factory in person, they'd be disappointed.

Still, impatience rode my back every day. I hadn't asked for this house, this miracle, just for myself and my kid. Now that we had it, every day we didn't share it was a shame.

But another thing I'd learned from the project is that you don't wait to do things until you feel ready. You show up as you are, with all your pain and fear, and you have faith. The knitting factory had offered me so much rest and healing, and I was trying to learn to give it to myself, too: knowing that other people bore witness to my single motherhood and thought it worthy of respect, of celebration, of loving-kindness and care.

It wasn't about a new bathroom or a manicured garden, I knew. It was about time, and space, and peace.

I wanted to offer the house, and myself, just as we were. I didn't want to wait for any more perfection than I'd already found.

With Connemara swimming through spring and into summer besides, everything was turning beautiful again: gorse petals shining like golden coins along the roadside, strawberry and blackberry blossoms kissing the sides of all the knitting factory's pathways, concealing the sins of the old cinder blocks. A drafty window is a gift in an Irish summer by the lake, letting you breathe the freshest air in the world even as you sleep.

After the purchase came through, I texted the survivors' group and told them that as far as I was concerned, any of them could come for a residency anytime they liked. The first one to take me up on that was Aisling. She brought her kids for a weekend and they slept in the guest room, and we piled into the car to go to the beach together and they screamed and ran around with Robin until they were all exhausted. I made them roast chicken and potatoes with a wild sorrel salad, picked by Robin, for dinner, and caramel-apple cinnamon rolls for breakfast. We ate with the same gusto as the children, and with caramel in my mouth I remembered the winter months after Tommy had left when I could hardly bear to eat dry toast. I could feel the weight I'd gained in the years since then, soft on my hips and arms and chin and belly. I was glad.

Aisling looked at me across the table cluttered with crayons and crumbs. "Any mother would be glad to come here," she said, "just as it is."

So just as we were, the house and me, I announced the knitting factory's first official residency. Inspired by activist and theologian Tricia Hersey's Nap Ministry, and by my own profound need for rest, I decided I wanted this one to not be the arts residency I'd first imagined, but a *rest* residency. I wanted to give another single mother the time and space to rest that I'd been craving for years. The rest that filled the exhausted survivalist dreams of every single mother I knew.

I asked people not to include their names when they wrote their applications because I assumed I'd mostly be hearing from people I already knew, who already followed the project, and I didn't want to be swayed by any of those friendships.

But the call for applications went viral. It was shared thousands of times. People from all over the world told me how much this idea meant to them, as single parents, as children of single parents, as people who love a single parent.

I got so many applications that names didn't matter.

I read every one with care. So many broke my heart. Every single parent who applied deserved to rest. And, of course, they deserved so much more. There were no best applications, none most deserving—I felt and still feel a horror at the idea of ranking them.

In the end I offered the residency to a woman named Tawasul. She had brought her two young children from Sudan to Belfast, where she started a women's support group and community garden for refugees, and where she now works for a human rights organization. I was in awe of her strength and kindness.

So many people told me that just writing to me, telling the story of their single parenthood and their children, and why they struggled to get the rest they needed, helped them affirm for themselves that they deserved that rest, even if they'd never been able to ask for it before.

When we don't write our own stories, too often they get written for us: by a controlling ex or a cruel parent, by overwhelming cultural stereotypes that insist they know how our lives will play out better than we do—even just by our own worst critics, the parts of ourselves that believe what other people say is true.

When we tell our own stories, we choose how they're told, how they end, how they begin again.

The knitting factory had become a way for me to tell my story. But reading those applications, I thought: What kind of story was the house going to be? I'd hoped, back in the castle days, maybe even when we moved here, that it would be a happily ever after.

But even with the miraculous happy-ending moment of the purchase coming through, a magic ending I wouldn't even have believed in a novel, I didn't see it as a happily-ever-after story anymore. Happy endings still haunted me sometimes; sometimes they haunted me so much they nearly broke my heart—the happy ending I thought I'd found when I was younger: a lasting marriage, lasting love, more children in the farmhouse I'd dreamed

Tommy and I would share. In my ugliest, tenderest heart, sometimes I still longed for those other homes. Sometimes I still longed for my husband.

But, like every person who wrote to me, I had mended those longings into something stronger. Mine was a secondhand, darned dream: the dream of a divorcée, a single mom, a woman who fled my parents and my country before I was really done growing up, and who'd had to start over several times since then.

The Old Knitting Factory wasn't a happy ending. It was a chance. I had the chance to mend this house, this old factory where a hundred years ago women had worked to remake their lives. I'd hoped I could remake my own story here, too.

And I had. Writing about the Old Knitting Factory, sharing my story and the story of this house, brought my son and me home—largely through small crowdfunding donations from people who recognized some part of their stories in mine. My words and their faith made my home, my dream, come true. That's the realest magic spell I know.

I take my life in my hands. I feel for the holes, I find them, and I mend them where I can.

That is the story I am telling now.

The next day, June 4, was the anniversary I always dreaded most: the day I'd asked Tommy to marry me, the day, in spite of everything, when I felt the pull back around the spiral of time to all the happiness we'd shared on that day in other years.

It was also the day, nine years before, when my first book, *Tides*, came out.

After I put Robin to bed, I went out into the wild, unkempt garden, planning to hack away at the weeds and tidy Robin's toys. The garden nagged me every day to do more with it. Around the little space I'd made that Robin and I could play and relax in, it was still rioting with brambles and gorse, still an impenetrable wall down to the lake. The gravel from decades-old landscaping was veined with ivy and dusted with the brown remains of wild cherry blossoms.

I brought my gardening gloves and pruning shears inside and swapped them for my folding chair. I boiled the kettle and made tea from my lemon balm plant, grown from the seeds I received on Robin's first birthday. I left Robin's toys, many of them hand-me-downs from Aisling, scattered on the gravel, sat quietly and watched the sun go down behind the mountains and the clouds.

The ghosts of the knitting factory girls were always there for me, working by windows built high so they wouldn't look outside. I wished I could reach back in time and give them something. I imagined them in the garden with me too, warming their tired hands on their own cups of tea, laughing and talking quietly with each other in Irish, going home barefoot in the sunset light, this time of year at least, instead of darkness.

"Ghost" wasn't the right word, I thought, for how real they felt. They were just people from this same point in the year's circle, a hundred and sixteen circles back.

There in the garden, unbidden, were suddenly my other selves meeting me at the same point in other circles, too: embracing Tommy in the mobile home when we decided to get married, breaking with longing in my lonely bed my first summer away from him, returning to the knitting factory to say goodbye and falling in love with its wild strawberries instead, standing in this same place and wondering, frantically, how I had managed to lose all my money. Further-back selves, too, at the ends of many school years, looking out across summers at a home where I never felt safe. And here, again, this late spring evening, with the dream of a safe home for myself and my child at last come true. I could mother and love all the past selves there with me in that moment, partly because of the love that had been shown to me, and partly because I'd been able, in the tiniest way, to begin to pass that love on: to Tawasul, who would arrive in August; to the moms from the survivors' group who came to stay in the guest space; to Aisling's friend Ina and her children.

Ever since the knitting factory dream came true, it felt like that love opened up a way back to my child self, my abused-wife self, and let me take their hands and lead them here. Every time I brought a mother to the knitting factory, that's what I would be doing. What we, all the people who helped me make this project happen, could do together.

Come here. Take our hands. We will care for each other now.

Twenty-Six

How Great Is Ireland

SUMMER 2022

for Tawasul

On June 11, I got a brown-paper government envelope in the mail. Immediately I thought I must be in trouble. From my undocumented days when Tommy was trying to get me out of Ireland, to the parental visa letter that warned me not to rely on the supports I'd been hoping for, to its renewal every year that I could never really afford and was never guaranteed, to all of Tommy's endless, varied threats—part of me was still always waiting for something bad to happen, for Ireland and Robin to be taken from me somehow, despite all that I had achieved.

I stood in the sunny driveway for a moment, putting on the survivors' group's imaginary armor so I could read whatever had come.

I opened the envelope. The paper inside was a pale leaf green.

It was an invitation, in ten days' time, to become an Irish citizen at a ceremony in Killarney.

I closed my eyes.

It had been four years and two months since we'd run, since Tommy had made the threat that had changed the course of our lives. It had been four years since I'd had any real faith that the place I was standing one day would be safe to call home the next. That was the fear that had underpinned my desperation to find a home for myself and Robin that was *ours*, that no one could take away. The many miracles of the knitting factory—I was so grateful for them, but that underlying fear had remained, that somehow it could all be taken from me, and then my baby would be, too.

I opened my eyes and saw Ireland all around me. The sun was almost right overhead, just before noon in the open, bright blue, skewbald sky, and everything was bright yellow and green with it, one of the Irish spring-into-summer days that make you think it's impossible it could be anything but warm here, the kind of day that must have been what possessed Nora Roberts to name a romance novel set on this rainy rock *Jewels of the Sun*. All that gem-bright air smelled sweet with honeysuckle, coconutty with gorse, a hint of the seaside that lay around the corner and the fresh lake water that cupped the edge of the knitting factory's wild garden like a gentle hand. It was June, and the wild strawberries were blooming.

I saw it all, and it's not that it was mine—more that I belonged to it now, and I always would.

I saw my neighbor Noel walking across the street to say hello. I tried to smile a normal-person, not-shaky smile at him in greeting, but it definitely didn't work: "Looks like you've got good news there," he said, brows raised, eyes twinkling.

I showed him. "I've been here for a decade, and I'm going to be a citizen now."

"Just like your little boy!"

There was no chance of not shaking then. "Yeah."

"Well, fáilte. And it's in County Kerry, too," he said, glancing over the invitation. "The most beautiful part of Ireland, you know, now, that's for sure."

"Really?" I asked. "Better than Connemara?"

He scoffed. "Oh, yes. You'll see."

On the summer solstice, I became an Irish citizen.

I drove Robin down to the ceremony in Killarney and we made a weekend of it, doing things in Ireland we'd never done before. I booked us one night at a B&B in Dingle and one in a tiny village that had remade itself in a *Star Wars* theme after a few scenes from the sequels were made on a site forty minutes away—it is a very Irish thing, of course, to milk American money for all it's worth. The sculptures of Yoda and Darth Vader made from old tractor tires filled Robin with delight. The pub on the village's main road advertised *craic agus ceol*, fun and music, but also *Star Wars Viewing Point.* It was the most traveling I'd ever gotten to do with him, but now that we would both have Irish passports, I hoped I could petition the courts to let us go on short trips outside the country someday soon. Robin's love of dinosaurs was expanding, as his fifth birthday passed, into an adoration of all reptiles, and he talked daily about wanting to swim with marine iguanas in the Galápagos, see crocodiles in Australia, rattlesnakes in the US. I was starting to believe that one day I'd be able to bring him to those places I had never been, as well as to the country of my birth that he had never seen.

For this first trip, though, a galaxy far, far away and two counties to the south was plenty.

In Dingle we ate brown-bread ice cream on the pier and went dolphin-watching with other tourists on a sleek little boat that slipped through the water of the bay as clean as a wish. I kept thinking of a fragment of an old story I'd heard from the Irish-language poet Nuala Ní Dhomhnaill a decade earlier. It has become one of my favorite moments from Irish folklore, and it goes like this:

A young boy has spent his whole life in the same small valley, never climbing the mountains around him. When he (in classic hero's journey fashion) is called on his great adventure, and for the first time ascends those peaks with his mentor, he is awed by the grand vista that surrounds them and spreads out to the horizon. "O, how great is Ireland!" he cries. But it's a joke: the mentor, the storyteller, and the listeners all know that what the boy can now see is still only a tiny fraction of Ireland's true expanse.

In the decade since, whenever I felt trapped here—when I learned that I would not be able to move out of Ireland until my child grew up; when I spent that dark, cold winter in the bungalow—I remembered that story. I could live here all my life and still find endless new things to see.

• • •

The citizenship ceremony was held in an arena in Killarney town. My friend Mindy came up from Cork to look after Robin during the ceremony. I took them both on another boat tour, glass-topped in a lake this time instead of open to the ocean air, and we marveled together at the glorious, saturated greenness of Kerry.

It was spectacular, that was true: dramatic rolling hills and cliffs, clear water sparking sunlight, deep drenched greens that the poorer soil in Connemara could never match. But I knew I was really a Galway girl then, because I thought none of it could hold a candle to the craggy mountains and shores back home.

After the tour, we moved through an eye-watering amount of traffic toward the conference center, and finally some harried-looking traffic workers directed us to a huge sea of a car park. There would be nine hundred and fifty new Irish citizens that day, from ninety-two countries, including me.

Mindy took Robin off to play in a nearby park, and I walked in alone. Shay hadn't been able to come, and I'd been afraid even to tell other people it was happening. I was still afraid, although I didn't want to admit it, that somehow my ex would find a way to stop it. This was the last thing, the very last thing, that he could hold over me, that he could use to keep me from Robin. If he knew I was becoming a citizen that day, I was sure he'd try his best to find a way to ruin it.

But as I walked toward the hall, I was swallowed at once by the crowd, a crowd of people from more than half the countries in the whole world, many of them in beautiful traditional dress. None of them looked afraid at all. Only joyful.

And Tommy couldn't do a damn thing about it.

Looking at all the laughing families and friends around me, I knew that I didn't want to walk into the ceremony that would give me a new homeland by myself.

I took out my phone and posted to my social media pages that I was about to become a citizen, and I asked my friends to celebrate with me. There was going to be a live stream of the ceremony, and I posted that, too.

Congratulations started coming in right away, and I walked into the hall holding hands, via my phone, with a hundred friends who were rooting for me at once.

As I shuffled through the two-hour registration line, only to be directed to an auditorium seat to wait quietly for another half hour before the ceremony began, I started to understand why children, except for nursing infants, were not invited.

I thought of something Shay had said to me recently: that I'd worked so hard to save my baby for so long that not only had it worked, but there wasn't a baby to save anymore. I had protected him until he turned into a kid. I did not have to hold him every moment; I could trust the world to do some holding, too.

The Minister for Justice came onstage and welcomed us to the ceremony. The man in the seat next to me, who had introduced himself as Howard from Los Angeles, pointed out the automated closed captioning's bizarre attempts at transcribing the Irish language. We snorted with stifled laughter like kids at a school assembly.

The minister told us that the Irish state was making a commitment to us: that we will always have a home here, and we will always be safe.

I remembered the marriage vows I'd made with Tommy, holding hands before a Scottish notary with two strangers for witnesses. I thought of the moment I'd signed the contract for the knitting factory, and touched the key charm on my neck. I clutched the script for the vow I was about to make.

After the minister's speech, the judge who was going to lead us in our pledge came out. He looked like what anyone might wish their Irish grandfather would: tall and stern but with kind eyes, smooth white hair, a dark and dapper suit.

He looked out at us, smiling gently for a long moment before he began, as if he wanted to make eye contact with as many of us as possible.

Somewhere off to one side, a baby started crying.

"Another new Irish citizen!" He laughed. "Wonderful, wonderful."

"Sorry!" the mother's voice called back.

"Not at all, not at all. We welcome him here."

He began by saying that he was honored and proud to stand there with us, grateful that we were here to make Ireland better. He said that Ireland understands the immigrant experience better than most countries. He told us quite sternly that even though his family had been in Ireland for centuries, we were just as Irish as he was, and had just as many rights under the law.

I have as much right to be here as my ex-husband does. As my Irish-born child does. And I have a home of my own now. No one can force me to leave my house or my country, or tear me from my child, ever again.

Raising his hands like an orchestra conductor, he led our chorus of a thousand voices through the oath as we solemnly declared our fidelity to the Irish nation and our loyalty to the state, and undertook to faithfully observe its laws and to respect its democratic values.

"Comghairdeas!" he said—*congratulations*—and we were citizens.

A cheer of heartrending sincerity went up.

As we waited for our turn to leave our seats, I asked Howard if he planned to stay in Ireland long-term.

"I think so," he said. "I just bought a house here."

I smiled. "Me too."

I hurried into the sunshine, eager to find Robin and hug him, knowing now that I would never have to let him go.

As Mindy and I said goodbye, the woman who was about to get into the car next to ours gasped.

"Betsy?" she asked. "Is your name Betsy?"

I laughed a little nervously. "Yes, Betsy Cornwell," I said.

"Oh! I follow you online. I love your work at the knitting factory!"

I was stunned.

She enthusiastically introduced herself and her friend, a brand-new Irish citizen like me. We congratulated each other. I invited them to come for tea at the knitting factory sometime; they seemed slightly starstruck by that, which felt surreal to me.

But mostly, I felt welcomed home.

• • •

On the drive back, I got off the motorway early. It was midsummer, and I wanted elderflowers for our yearly cordial. We'd be driving right past somewhere I knew we'd find a fortune in them: the bungalow's road in east Galway.

I'd avoided the whole eastern half of the county ever since we moved to Connemara, my ring of salt keeping me in, too. Even driving past the east Galway exits made me look over my shoulder for Tommy.

My heart beat faster as we approached the village, as we turned up the hill onto the little road that held the bungalow that had been our first home, Robin's and mine.

There was nothing Tommy could do to us now, I told myself.

There was a car in the bungalow's driveway. I stopped briefly to look at the house, but didn't pull over, remembering my own vigilant days and nights working and looking out the windows, watching for cars on the road.

"Do you remember this house, sweetie?" I asked Robin.

He was quiet for a second. "No." He sounded a little worried that he didn't.

"That's okay. We lived here when you were a baby." Natalia overhearing me cry through singing "Now Westlin Winds" to Robin as he fell asleep, because I thought he'd remember his dad singing it; the constant feeling that I was standing alone, holding Robin on a cliff in a howling wind, and we might fall off, or be pushed over, any minute. The rough sweetness of nursing my baby through the endless nights.

And—all the hundred thousand little things that had made us happy in those days, the dreams and loves that had sustained us: watching Robin play with Irene, and later with Natalia, in the driveway. Walks with him looking for wild garlic and strawberries and elderflowers, blackberries and rosehips and elderberries, walks down little secret sideways paths that made me momentarily sure the world was full of half-hidden gifts it was longing to give us, even when we had nothing but our joy in their sweetness to offer in trade. Making jelly from apples in the yard. I could see the hard little beginnings of apples on that tree even from the road. I wondered if the people who lived there now would eat them.

I missed those days and nights, suddenly, with a longing so fierce it hurt. I would never hold my baby, as a baby, ever again, and I had been so frightened and alone I hadn't had it in me to understand what I held when I held it. What parent of a growing child can help mourning that?

But here we were, three years later. The apple tree was starting to fruit again, just as it had the last time we'd seen it. As the tree told it, it was exactly the same time it had been then, in the circle of the year that it repeated all its life and traced inside itself with every ring.

Part of me would always be there, in those endless nights and days, in this first house that I had made just ours, just Robin's and mine, and that I had first shared. I could reach out for those nights and feel them, still as vivid as the present. I'd thought part of my heart and soul had been lost there, in that exhaustion, but maybe it was not so much lost as held in a crucial slice of time that had made me who I am: a woman strong enough to mother well.

Because I saw that, too, looking at the little house that I had agonized over so much just to barely afford, where I had tortured myself almost every second inside its walls over whether I was giving enough to my child, being enough for him.

I saw a very young woman, even if she was only three years younger than I was now, thrust violently into a situation she did not choose, and making of it everything she could; and protecting a child every second of the way. I did not begrudge her a second of the rest or respite or help she'd sought, that she had often felt ashamed of. I knew she'd needed it. And I knew she had been a good mother, too. The child behind me now, who remembered not a bit of it, was my proof of that.

I remembered driving in a different car with my own mother, twenty-four years earlier, talking about the Selkie Bride and how she could never have left her child for the sake of her own freedom.

I knew now what my mother had known then: neither of us could have done that.

But her answer had been to stay in a place where neither of us were safe or free. When I had been her child, the selkie's child, my answer had been to grow up and run away, to take the sealskin myself and leave her behind in-stead. When I became the Selkie Bride, the mother, I took my child with me.

Neither of us are fairy-tale heroines. We're both more complicated than that. But in the language of story, I know: I protected my child in the way my mother could not protect me. I protected him by leaving.

I reached back to hold Robin's hand as we continued down the road, looking for elders.

Epilogue

What is the difference between a dream you're dreaming, and one that has come true?

Tawasul showed up pulling a suitcase about half her own size, smiling a wide and wise and gentle smile. Short, slim, and elegant, with smooth skin and shining eyes, she was someone who seemed to look at everything with love.

She'd decided to leave her preteen children with a friend and use the childcare stipend toward feeding and minding them while she was gone. So it was just her, Robin, and me in the knitting factory: just her and me, really, during the weekdays, when Robin was at naíonra. He'd be starting big-kid school in a few weeks, and that was one of the first things I talked with Tawasul about, how nervous that made me, how I found myself reliving the shyness of my own first school days.

"Oh, you're not shy," she said, laughing in a way that held nothing but kindness. "You managed to do all of this, didn't you?" She gestured around at the garden. She had come, thank goodness, just as one of our magical summer sunsets began climbing the sky, luxuriously epic Day-Glo pink affairs that make you think of My Little Pony and Barbie Dreamhouses and the wonders of the cosmos all at once.

The first time I saw a sunset at the knitting factory, I thought: I'd live in a tent if it had a view like this.

I remembered all I'd longed for, all I'd offered: not luxury or perfection, but simply rest in a beautiful place. Peace and quiet, water, and a sky that would paint itself miracle colors just for you to look at it for a moment.

Sunset light turned my face, and Tawasul's, and the knitting factory walls, all those miracle pinks, too. The three of us, beautiful.

Tawasul basked in her quiet time, reading a lot and going for walks. We weren't sure, I think, how much space we should give each other, but as the first day or so passed, we slowly offered each other our companionship. One late morning she came into the knitting factory's big, high-ceilinged kitchen, summer sunlight streaming through the windows, and asked if she could make lunch for both of us.

She boiled thick, cardamom-spiced coffee on the stovetop and poured us each a cup, then chopped cucumbers and tomatoes and mixed them into a spicy peanut butter dressing, and we sopped it up with pita while we talked.

Her kids were older than Robin, and she told me a little bit about what to expect as he kept growing. Our exes, we learned, were so alike it was spooky, even though they were from different continents.

"That's one thing I've learned from the survivors' group I'm in," I said. "It's like they give all these guys the same playbook, I swear."

She laughed. "It really is."

We talked about immigration issues, about the particular, strange sadness of watching your children grow up in a different culture than your own. Most of all, we talked about our children.

"You should have another baby," Tawasul said, smiling, telling me about her two. "It's wonderful to give your child a sibling, and you don't want them to be too far apart in age."

Before the knitting factory dream came true, I could never have imagined it: that I'd ever recover from the exhaustion and trauma of my first years as a parent, that I'd ever be in a place where I felt I could offer another child any kind of stability or community. That I'd ever feel rested enough again.

I still wasn't ready. But it wasn't a *never* anymore, either, and it was Tawasul who helped me to see that.

A dream of more than just survival.

Journal: August 22, 2022

Tawasul's time here has been more relaxed than I imagined, more everyday than grand miraculous pinnacle of this project that I've been working toward so hard for so long.

But that is good. I want to stop living in a big dramatic story. I want to live quietly. At least for a while.

I was saying to Shay how this project has turned out to feel like writing does. I always think there will be a big, daring, swooping hero moment when it happens, & I know it is done & it feels right—but instead it is just little everyday steps, one at a time, whenever you can make them happen, & none of them really the end or the beginning. Actually, I said, everything in life feels like that.

Shay laughed & said he thinks it's because of birth that we feel that way, that we expect other events to be as cataclysmic as that first one, & they're just not.

I still worry that it's not special enough, that I'm not giving enough. But in time. I hope.

Tawasul is here. We have held her for this time, given her a little bit of love & she has been happy. That is what I dreamed, what I made real. If it feels quiet & everyday, all the better for the spirit of what I wanted to give her in the first place.

& Robin & I are here. Our lives are better.

I am safe. My child is safe.

• • •

Tawasul left the night before Robin started school.

I put him to bed and walked out into the knitting factory's living room, where the windows cast hazy warm rectangles of evening light across the wooden floor, where Robin's red school uniform jumper, brand-new, was hanging by the door.

I sat down at the kitchen table, still covered in the sea-life-print oilcloth that was one of the first things I'd gotten for the bungalow, the first home we had found. I ticked through my mental mom list of what we needed for tomorrow: Robin's school clothes were ready, his lunch bag prepped and in the fridge, his pristine backpack waiting by the door, neon reflective strips tacked to it for cars to see on the morning walk.

God. Big-kid school. Another world opening up.

I stood up from the table. There was one more thing I wanted to do before tomorrow and Robin's first school year began, something I'd been meaning to do for a long time.

I had thanked the knitting factory's fairy-godmother donor many times, over the phone and by email. I'd been meaning to write her a proper thank-you note, too, and I'd had a card by a local artist-mother and one of my tiny key charms engraved with TOKF ready for months. But I'd struggled, again, to know how to truly thank her.

Finally, I began to write.

Dear Terry,

As I write this to you, the knitting factory's first official single mother rest resident has just completed her stay with us, and tomorrow my son is starting Junior Infants, the Irish version of kindergarten. I am writing to you from the knitting factory's living room, where I cooked dinner with my kid today, where we packed his backpack together and got his new uniform ready for tomorrow. This is the table where I drank coffee and chatted about the challenges and gifts of single motherhood with Tawasul, our rest resident, who came to Ireland from Sudan.

This is the room where a hundred and sixteen years ago, Irish women found knitting work that allowed them to save their own money for the first time in their lives.

I still feel that I don't know what to say to you or how to really thank you. I've been meaning to write this letter for a long time and I haven't until now because I don't have the words, and I'm a writer, so I should, right?

Years ago, before I had Robin, my then-husband took me to see a folk healer (someone people claimed was the seventh son of a seventh son, although no one seemed to know for sure) for the persistent pain in my shoulder. He took the pain away by putting his hand on me. He refused to take any payment. I cannot deny that his treatment worked any more than I can explain it. But what I do know is that I am grateful to live in a universe that contains so many beautiful things that I don't understand.

Something I've heard here a lot is: "If you ask an American a question, they'll give you an answer. If you ask an Irish person a question, they'll tell you a story." I didn't think of the healer until I started trying to tell you how much I don't know how to thank you, so there is the story to answer my own question, I guess.

Since I am still American, too, I will say more directly: what you did for me is a miracle. You have made my life and my son's so much better—permanently better and safer and gentler, and hopefully the lives of the single parents and their children who will come here too—but you have also given me the tremendous gift of remembering that there are so many things in the universe that are beautiful and beyond my understanding.

I have enclosed a very, very small token of my thanks.

Go raibh maith agat. Thank you so much.

From one mother to another,
Betsy

Acknowledgments

If *Ring of Salt* is nothing else, I hope it is an expression of thanks. Each person who helped my child and me find our way home is part of this story. Some of them are mentioned in the book itself, some here, and some in the following list of donors.

COPE Galway's domestic violence services supported me in more ways than I can name. The survivors' group I met there made me more proud to be a single mom than I am of anything else I've done.

The idea to turn a book into a house took shape in Friday Tea, where that group's belief in me helped me believe in myself.

Dara Kaye, the first person to read the castle proposal, has kept the faith and the vision alive ever since—it is because of her, in so many ways, that I could write this book. She is an incredible agent and friend.

Margo Shickmanter, my editor, understood perfectly what this story needed to become, and meticulously and lovingly made it all that and more. Team Magic forever.

Suzannah Ball at WME, and Christina Demosthenous at Renegade/Hachette, made *Ring of Salt* the first of my books to be published on both sides of the Atlantic. The wonderful teams at Avid Reader, including Alison Forner, Sirui Huang, Ruth Lee-Mui, Amy Guay, Hana Handzija, Allison Green, Annalea Manalili, Alicia Brancato, Rhina Garcia, Eva Kerins, Jofie Ferrari-Adler, and Carolyn Levin, and at Renegade, including Eleanor Gaffney, Saida Azizova, Corinna Zifko, and Mia Oakley, have done so much to shepherd this book into being.

Sara Crowe is the agent who believed in my writing first. Lynne Polvino has edited each of my young adult novels with kindness and brilliance. Their work on my behalf is one of the main reasons I was able to survive with my child after leaving my marriage. Tracy Cochran and Jeff Zaleski at *Parabola* also provided me with a wonderful platform for my essays, as well as steady remote work that helped to save my son and me. Part of the first chapter of this book is adapted from my essay "The Search for One Thing," which appeared in *Parabola* vol. 39, no. 2, "Embodiment."

Lisa Chamoff of Indie Untangled also provided an early publication venue for an essay about my work at the knitting factory, as well as bringing the first-ever tour group here.

Marian Schembari came to the Old Knitting Factory to work on her own memoir, and somehow had the generosity and energy to help me hugely with the proposal for mine while she was at it. Her wonderful book *A Little Less Broken* is first on the shelf of books written in our residency space.

Vanessa Fox O'Loughlin, a.k.a. Sam Blake, platformed the knitting factory crowdfund in Ireland and indefatigably cheered it on.

Jackie and Ed Keilthy of JEK Jewellery, who lived here before we did, contributed a beautiful silver-and-gold necklace to offer as a giveaway for crowdfund donors. Bob Quinn, the filmmaker who turned the Old Knitting Factory into an Irish-language cinema, brought us mince pies and shared with us a remarkable documentary about this building's past: *Cinegael Paradiso*, directed by his son, Robert Quinn.

The Irish Writers Centre, together with Varuna, the National Writers' House (Australia) and the Tyrone Guthrie Centre, awarded me a residency in the Blue Mountains of Australia in 2023, where I wrote much of the first draft of *Ring of Salt*. My time there taught me so much through example about what I want the residencies at the knitting factory to be, as well as bringing me the chance to travel with my son for the first time. Varuna gave us the world.

Deirdre Sheridan, in only one of her many forms of staunch support, cat-sat Teapot and took loving care of the knitting factory for that time.

The IWC also connected me with my wonderful mentor Elske Rahill, a breathtaking writer who has also become a dear friend and colleague, and who did so much more for this book, and for me, than I could ever have hoped.

Other early readers and supporters who helped make *Ring of Salt* so much better are Anna Boarini, Kimberly Brubaker Bradley, Christina Dragon, Leah Ingram, Eleanor Lane, Zoë Langsdale, Surnaí Molloy, Abby Palko, Alison Tergis, Diane Walker, Shannon Yarbrough, Natalia Yepez-Frias, and Alex Zaleski.

In 2024 I received a Markievicz Award from the Arts Council of Ireland for my work on this book. The bursary provided crucial time and space for me to complete the manuscript, and the remarkable company I'm in with the other awardees astounds me every time I think about it.

There have been three funded single-parent rest residents at the knitting factory as of this writing: Tawasul Elsheikh, Ann Begay, and Helen Flynn. It has been a gift to know each of you, and a huge honor to give you time at the knitting factory. I will always be grateful for your grace and kindness as the building, and this project, found their feet.

Martha Vail Barker made one of those residencies possible—and in a single week she rescued my broken laptop and gave me both life-changing roast chicken and life-changing advice. What more could a girl ask for?

As this book goes to print, we are circling around to a new beginning: I am preparing for major renovations to the building and grounds. The Old Knitting Factory's monthly subscribers on Patreon, as well as the people who donate to the crowdfunds and spread the word about the project, are the reason we've gotten this far. I cannot thank you enough.

Finally: my child. I have always loved you, and I always will. May we come around again.

The Old Knitting Factory Donors

Joan Sweeney
Susan Molinaro
Charlotte Donlan
Jennifer Rockhill
Belinda Cash
Melinda Smith
Aliza Lesser
Christine Leach
Yulia Smirnova
Evelyn Walsh
Meghan Helms
Annette Skade
Emma Warnock
Lisa Cohen
Claire Kerker
Jacqueline Carroll
Leah Ingram
Charlotte Stanley
Ron Smith
Sylvia Scharf
Bryna Keenan
  Subherwal
Lorna Kavanagh
Emily Gibbons
Deborah Mittelman
Mary Sellers
Meredith Dorner
Alexandra Pratt
Talitha Abramsen
Bridgette Beagen
Emily Cameron
Lise Easter
Sasha Van Katwyk
Mary Swan Summers

Laura Hagg
Lisa Chamoff
Marian Schembari
Lauren Seely
Carissa Barrett
Michaela Gonzalez
Naomi Barry-Perez
Nicola Gunwhy
Dara Kaye
Marilyn Flores
Alexis Suib
Elizabeth Franklin
Stephanie Sirois
Elizabeth Lee
Julie Warren
Michele Olender
Katherine Winick
Abigail Duquette
Jessica Biggs
Janell Doster
Emily Casey
Lindsey Hutchison
Freda Moore
Destiny Barker
Alice Bryson
Christina Firth
Jennifer Guare
Janet Hoffman
Darcy Goddard
Sarah Roberts
Patricia O'Brien
Therese Ahlers
Hannah Quinn
Laura Ehrlich

Samantha Cote
Carly Sturdivant
Lois Buchter
Robin Tate
Destiny Just
Emily Lomax
Sarah Twombly
Laura Goodbody
Emma Bedford-Jack
Anna Boarini
Jackie Keilthy
Jillian Larosa
Shahista Karim
Candace Britton
Kate Carty
Kenneth Arthur
Surnai O Maoildhia
Rosalie Teverow
Elizabeth Bates
Sandra Costanza
Amy Maranville
Vanessa Fox
  O'Loughlin
Charles & Liz-Anne
  Platt
Kiley Roberts
Liz Turner
Eilis Folded Leaf
Kali Lightfoot
Pigsy
Peggy Gillespie
Lara Lugo
Sady Sullivan
Holly Cornwell

Susan Breathnach
Laura Shupeck
Patricia Murray
Kaidi Williams
Allegra Garabedian
Abby Palko
Monica Hynes
Samantha Shannon
Betsy Thrasher
Chloe Horning
Stephanie Mueth
Alexandra Dunne
Lada Soljan
Sarah White
Kimberly Jaussi
Christine Scordato
Ilana Shydlo
Helen Monaghan
Carmen Flores
Marty Maull
Katherine Fleet
Lindsay Roberts
Rhonda Senior
Marta Schaaf
Sana Amini
Alita Edelman
Abbie Chase
Rebecca Rousselle
Jennifer Landrebe
Etta Habegger
Gena Schwam
Mary Helen
  Kennerly
Amy Menkin

Rebecca Badsey
Olivia Mascheroni
Monica Mody
Ruth Spurlock
Amy Trachtenberg
Paige Kimble
Sarah Masi
Laura Thompson
Adrienne Kicza
Nicole Rimedio
April Opoliner
Gina Ko
Jardana Peacock
Karen Sise
Emily Farrell
Melanie Rosen
Elizabeth Olson
Sherie Dodson
Eimile Ni
 Shearraigh
Sonia Brown
Winifred Black
Caitleen Desetti
Katherin Hudkins
Aimie Chapple
Jennifer Casundan-
 Sumi
Catherine Peterson
Abigail Rubin
Andrea Day
Margaret Chilton
Rina Kor
Eva Kowalski-Seile
Katie Lattari
Gretchen Busl
Naomi Dolin-
 Aubertin
Gillian Hemme
Zoe Langsdale
Michele Beasley
Cara Fieseher
Danielle Durkin
Erin McGee
Hilary Kiely
Mary McGraw
Kayleen Duclos
Alex Zaleski
Kathrin Sauter

Lindsay Herko &
 Janet Zienkiewicz
Sophie Green
Sara Crowe
Louise Kennedy
Eilis Fisher
Aoife Light
Kimberly Brubaker
 Bradley
Chris Becker
Liz Krzak
Laura Simeon
Susan Burke & the
 Cox Family
Genevieve Jenner
Susanna Glatz
Melissa Pulis
Kelly Shipman
Kimberly Kahne
Anna Dobbin
Stephanie Aresta-
 Dasilva
Nova Kennelty-
 Cohen
Schuyler Clemente
Michelle Wu
Alison Grady
Amanda Gutowski
Karin Krieger
Lily & Kathleen
 Maynard
Ceire Moylan
Lindsay Eagar Books
Megan Evans
Simone Chess
Kaitlyn Krauskopf
Julia Johnstone
Rachel Balsham
Christie Keeney
Karen Wade
Amber Cushing
Sara Bodinson
Joanna Goldfarb
Evangelia Antonakos
Rosemary Guilliams
Leslie Rosenthal
Annessa Lewis
Alexandra Romer

Rachel Gerstein
Molly Gartrell Earle
Abigail Kellogg
Laurie
 Herboldsheimer
Liza Kessler
Doran Lovell
Karen Lynn Alstadt
Sylvia Altreuter
Ellie Davis
Erin Ostrander
Allison King
Cory Lester
Gillian Brunet
Harrow Disén
Elaine Gormley
Amy Allen
Anne Mooney
Kathleen Waterfall
Erin Northey
Patrick Crowe
Shannon Herber
Tiarra Cooper
Kristin Halloran
Sarah Garner
Tricia McKinney
Brandy King
Carla Lo Coco
Jenna Lovaas
Patricia F.
 Bouteneff
Saar Chittenden
Katharine Robb
Katie Holly
Will Tanner
Elana
Julie Shuman
Louise Hession
Molly
Debbie
Janet Gladden
Su
Betty O'Neill
Sarah Pearson
Caitriona Scully
Chara
Aisling O'Connell
Maura

Ruth Ní Chumhaill
 Maguire
Aisling Hurley
Colleen Jones
Aifric Ni
 Raghallaigh
Heidi Blythe
Nelly Bablumian
Storm Desmond
Alec Stais
Priscilla Nobecourt
Caro
Christina Weese
Erika Loughridge
 Brewer
Claire
Carolyn Hauk
Arielle Derby
Letty Horkan
Deirdre O'Regan
Claire Moss
Ger Halpin
Drury Wellford
Lily Jonsek
Sinead C. Kavanagh
Angela Serratore
Amy Elkins
Julie Richardson
Ganin Lovell
Johnsonable
Katherine E.
 Hoffman
Tammy Arnold
Lev Fein
B. Bixel
Genie Foley
Jenn Ross
Rachel Walwood
Melissa Wakeman
Julie Lambert
Mary Herber
Dia Black
Laura Bang
Dorothée Clinton
Chantelle Leswell
Collette Horkan
Susan Ball
Casey Stanton

Crystal Zimmer
Kelley Buhles
Emily
Mary Clark
Tim Platt
Stacey Kavanagh
Lise Donnelly
Elizabeth Picherit
Megan Lindley
Megan Klose
Rachel
Meg
Liz Johnson
Lorraine Byrne
Megan Maki
Jennifer Rosenthal
Wiebke Henning
Bryna Subherwal
Rachel D
Irene Carracher
  Kistler
Bethany Bond
Jessica Lachewitz
Mary Elizabeth
  Collins
Fin
Laura A Frye-Levine
Martha Vail Barker
Rebecca
Terry McGraw
Naomi O'Brien
Lisa Anchin
Ruth Ford
Sylvia Lara Altreuter
C. Barrett
Natalia Yépez Frías
Laura Carroll
Sara Bailey
Karen O'Connor
Emma Dorsey
Christina Dragon
Elizabeth Walters
Julie
Ana Cristina Perry
Eiren Caffall
Caitríona Ní
  Chadhain
Molly Earle

Andrea D.
Abigail Eckstine
Hannah Bailey
Tracie Mahaffey
Lily Brady
Vinnie Jones
Carina Finn
Andrew
Shannon Yarbrough
Laura Cutter
Alexa
Eleanor Lane
Maggie Slepian
Alison O'Neil
Sarah
James
Lisa Cowley
Cassie A. Stearns
Wendie B
Lisa Wynne
Lisa Beth Kovetz
Sophie Segura
EL Putnam
Magdalena Vinson
Deirdre & Ralph
  Sheridan
Gwen Gethner
Marcy Brinegar
Mary Bruce
Silka Silawulf
Katie Jo Benjamin
Kelly Newton
Janet Marticke
Colleen Byrum
Nancy Franklin
Morgan P
Lisa Patricia
  Burgdoff
Dawn Judd
Angela Chu
Lauren Koslow
Harsha Sheth
Karen Hunt
Hannah Day-
  Woodruff
Jolyne Gollmitzer
Sara Kassa
Amanda Zinoman

Kellye Rowland
Margaret Aisenberg
Jac Cooper
Rebecca Bokoch
Teresa C. Rhodes
Susan Lee
Lara Temperley
Siobhan Farrell
Sue Divin
Emily Carle
Melanie Fedri
Bridget Plante
C. S. Piel
Elizabeth Roy
Meghan Carmody
Whitney McMackin
Pamela Chamberlain
Susan Park Ochsner
Rebecca Pronchick
Ann Jo
Ruth Quiles
Jeanine Raab
Christopher Shaw
Marjorie Rayfield
Ariel Dumas
Kelli Lytle
Delphine Tseng
Carol Curtis
Elizabeth Salamon
Jacqueline Hardisty
Barbara McKenna
L. J. McCoy
Celine Thackston
Angela Florence
Deborah Blankfeld
Alexandra Babalis
Alyssa Becker
Fedelma Ní Raighne
Kimberly Green
Millicent Lang
Sharelle Klaus
Rachel Angus
Kelsey Tardiff
Kendal Mott
Elizabeth Cleary
Helen Hegedus
Molly Vigour
Anna Fletcher

Pat Kaye-Schiess
Doina Olteanu
Irene Lachance
Birgit Kriener
Alison Kreutz
Diana Friend
Diana Page
Heidi Hurst
William Mitchell
Mary Kolar
Joseph Fuchs
Elizabeth Carey
Susan Monsegur
Amy Daniel
Claire Kieffer
Ester Kiely
Kory Stamper
Margaret Kilkelly
Eve Kozina
Shannon Perry
Caroline Norris
Jessica Conger
Annie Xu
Karen Alstadt
Alison McEvoy
Bernadette Jones
Dawn Jonsek
Sharon Dowdell
David Richman
Jennifer Ross
Katherine D'Amato
Reagan Wish
Edith Donnell
Amy Dagley
Rachel Parzivand
Kate Beutner
Rebecka S.
Ben Peirce
Pat Avery Nehls
Emily Yen
Elisabeth Lindsey

A Note on Domestic Violence and Child Abuse

It is not always easy to tell when you're in an abusive relationship. What happens inside a family or an intimate partnership is so private, and it can look very different from typical depictions of abuse in the media. When you're a child, anything you experience can seem normal because it's all you know.

Talking with other survivors, seeing that the things I thought were specific to my own relationships were really patterns, was the most powerful tool for helping me get out and stay out. If you have any questions or doubts about your relationship, even (perhaps especially) if you aren't sure if you're just taking normal things too seriously, please contact your nearest local domestic violence center. Remember, your intuition is the most accurate predictor of how much danger you are in.

Below I've listed a few organizations that help survivors in Ireland, the US, and around the world. You can get excellent information and help from them. However, please also speak with a group local to you if you can—the personal connections they provide, especially with other survivors, are irreplaceable.

COPE Galway: homeless, domestic abuse, and older people services (Ireland): copegalway.ie

Women's Aid: preventing and addressing the impact of domestic abuse (Ireland & UK): womensaid.ie or 1-800-341-900 (Ireland)

One in Four: ending the trauma of childhood sexual abuse (Ireland & UK): oneinfour.ie

FreeFrom: providing cash to survivors of gender-based violence (USA): freefrom.org

RAINN: adult survivors of childhood sexual abuse (USA): rainn.org or 1-800-656-HOPE

National Domestic Violence Hotline (USA): thehotline.org or 1-800-799-SAFE

No More Global Directory: a directory of domestic and sexual violence helplines and services (worldwide): nomoredirectory.org

Further Reading

There are several writers already mentioned in this book, and many more whose ideas I'm deeply indebted to: about Irish culture, language, and history; about storytelling and fairy tales; about domestic violence, child abuse, parenting, and trying to make a better world. I tried to create categories for recommended further reading, but so many of these books lend themselves to all those categories at once that I've decided simply to list them alphabetically by author.

What It Is by Lynda Barry

Pleasure Activism: The Politics of Feeling Good by adrienne maree brown

Belonging: One Woman's Search for Truth and Justice for the Tuam Babies by Catherine Corless

The Handless Maiden by Vicki Feaver

Irish Myths and Legends by Lady Gregory

Undrowned: Black Feminist Lessons from Marine Mammals by Alexis Pauline Gumbs

Twice Upon a Time: Women Writers and the History of the Fairy Tale by Elizabeth Wanning Harries

Gaffs: Why No One Can Get a House, and What We Can Do About It by Rory Hearne

How He Gets Inside Her Head: Inside the Mind of the Male Intimate Abuser by Don Hennessy

Rest Is Resistance: A Manifesto by Tricia Hersey

Courting: Tractor Dates, Macra Babies, and Swiping Right in Rural Ireland by Liadán Hynes

Wild Food by Biddy White Lennon and Evan Doyle

Thirty-Two Words for Field: Lost Words of the Irish Landscape by Manchán Magan

An Aran Reader, ed. Breandán & Ruairí Ó hEithir

The Feminist Architecture of Postmodern Anti-Tales: Space, Time and Bodies by Dr. Kendra Reynolds

The Dynamics of Folklore by Barre Toelken

Beyond Heaving Bosoms: The Smart Bitches' Guide to Romance by Sarah Wendell and Candy Tan

About the Author

BETSY CORNWELL is a *New York Times* bestselling author of fantasy and historical novels for young people. Her writing has appeared in the *New York Times*'s Modern Love, *Fairy Tale Review, Parabola* magazine, and elsewhere. She received the Irish Writers Centre's first Blue Mountains (Australia) residency and a Markievicz Award for her work on this book. She holds an MFA in creative writing from the University of Notre Dame and a BA from Smith College, and teaches at the University of Galway.

Bringing a book from manuscript to what you are reading is a team effort.

Renegade Books would like to thank everyone who helped to publish *Ring of Salt* in the UK.

Editorial
Christina Demosthenous
Kate Hewson
Eleanor Gaffney

Contracts
Stephanie Evans
Sasha Duszynska Lewis
Isabel Camara

Sales
Megan Schaffer
Kyla Dean
Dominic Smith
Sinead White
Georgina Cutler-Ross
Kerri Hood
Jess Harvey
Natasha Weninger-Kong

Rights
Rebecca Folland
Helena Doree
Louise Henderson-Clark
Alexis Alderton

Production
Amanda Jones

Design
Jo Myler
Sara Mahon
Sasha Egonu

Publicity
Corinna Zifzo
Elaine Egan

Operations
Jairiza Rivera

Inventory
Victoria Stephenson
Dan Jones

Finance
Chris Vale
Jonathan Gant

Audio
Ellie Wheeldon

RAISING READERS
Books Build Bright Futures

Dear Reader,

We'd love your attention for one more page to tell you about the crisis in children's reading, and what we can all do.

Studies have shown that reading for fun is the **single biggest predictor of a child's future life chances** – more than family circumstance, parents' educational background or income. It improves academic results, mental health, wealth, communication skills, ambition and happiness.[1]

The number of children reading for fun is in rapid decline. Young people have a lot of competition for their time. In 2024, 1 in 10 children and young people in the UK aged 5 to 18 did not own a single book at home.[2]

Hachette works extensively with schools, libraries and literacy charities, but here are some ways we can all raise more readers:

- Reading to children for just 10 minutes a day makes a difference
- Don't give up if children aren't regular readers – there will be books for them!
- Visit bookshops and libraries to get recommendations
- Encourage them to listen to audiobooks
- Support school libraries
- Give books as gifts

There's a lot more information about how to encourage children to read on our website: **www.RaisingReaders.co.uk**

Thank you for reading.

hachette UK

---

[1] OECD, '21st-Century Readers: Developing Literacy Skills in a Digital World', 2021, https://www.oecd.org/en/publications/21st-century-readers_a83d84cb-en.html

[2] National Literacy Trust, 'Book Ownership in 2024', November 2024, https://literacytrust.org.uk/research-services/research-reports/book-ownership-in-2024